Intersectoral Relationships

in a Developing Economy

THE AUTHOR :

Dr. (Mrs.) R. Thamarajakshi is a distinguished Economist. She belongs to the Indian Economic Service. Presently she is Secretary to Government of India in the Ministry of Planning, Department of Statistics.

(b. 1936, Madras), R. Thamarajakshi was educated at the prestigious universities of Madras and Delhi. Having topped in M.A. Economics, she secured M.Litt. degree in Economics from the University of Madras. She also got a diploma in Statistics. She obtained her Doctorate in Economics from the University of Delhi.

Dr. Thamarajakshi had started her career as a teacher in the universities of Madras and Delhi. She taught economics to post-graduate students in the University of Madras. She was Associate Fellow, Institute of Economic Growth, Delhi. She later moved on to Government of India and held various key posts at senior level. She has been Principal Advisor for Agriculture and Environment, and for Labour, Employment and Manpower in Planning Commission. She was Research Fellow at the International Food Policy Research Institute, Washington, U.S.A. She has functioned as Member Secretary, Agriculture Prices Commission and Economic Advisor, Ministry of Industry, Government of India.

Dr. Thamarajakshi has, to her credit, over fifty research papers/publications/presentations at National/International forums, in various fields, viz., agricultural price policy, employment planning, human resource development, women and development, etc.

An internationally recognised expert, Dr. Thamarajakshi has done consultancy assignments for United Nations' Organisations such as ESCAP, UNIDO, ARTEP (ILO), and also for APDC.

Intersectoral Relationships in a Developing Economy

THE INDIAN EXPERIENCE

R. Thamarajakshi

Academic Foundation

24-A, Sriram Road, Civil Lines, Delhi - 110 054, (India).
Phone : 233730, 232966, 2911852.

First Published in 1994 by
ACADEMIC FOUNDATION
24 - A, Sriram Road, Civil Lines, Delhi - 110 054.
Tel : 232966, 233730, 2911852.

Intersectoral Relationships in a Developing Economy
R. Thamarajakshi
ISBN 81-7188-040-1

Laser-Typeset in 'ITC Garamond' by
COMPRINT INDIA, Delhi

Dedicated to my parents

CONTENTS

Preface

THE subject of intersectoral relationships can be studied in different ways. A conventional input-output table can be prepared by dividing each sector into several industries or subsectors, and the various input-output coefficients analysed. Alternatively, it can be based on an institutional approach wherein institutions like banks and cooperatives in each sector having a bearing on the activity of other sectors can be studied. Still another way is to analyse the aggregate flows of products and factors between sectors and their interrelationships including price changes. It is the last of these approaches which has been adopted in this book.

The book has undertaken the estimation and examination of intersectoral relationships in Indian economy for a period of four decades, against a theoretical statement of the behaviour of these relationships in a changing economy. The doctoral dissertation of the author on "Agriculture-Industry Relationships in India 1948-49 — 1958-59" submitted to the University of Delhi in 1963, which finds place in Part II of the book in an abridged form is the first ever attempt to identify these relationships and empirically examine them on a time series basis, at a time when data needed for this complex exercise was scattered, scanty and limited. The thesis was fulfilled under the guidance of Prof. A.M. Khusro, then Professor of Economics, Institute of Economic Growth, Delhi and was made possible by a Research Fellowship awarded by the Institute. Part I looks at the intersectoral relationships between agriculture and non-agriculture for three decades commencing from 1961-62. In view of the primacy of agriculture in India economy, the book examines the relationships from the point of view of agriculture.

A study of linkages between commodity/service producing sectors in product and factor markets, the resulting terms of exchange among the sectors and the impact of terms of trade on production, consumption, levels of living, capital formation, labour flows and productivity is relevant for formulation of economic policies. This will assume special significance in the current context of globalisation of the economy. It is possible that the relationships may emerge to be of a different type from those perceived so far in the pre-reform period or from the received knowledge based on experience of economic transformation of the already advanced economies. Also, considering the structural differences among different countries going through the economic reform process, it would be difficult to draw generalisations on the expected behaviour of these relationships on the basis of inter-country experiences. Basically, however, the real factor of "production" with the prime movers of technological change and investment and its balanced performance in sectoral as well as world context would come in its own for the sustainability of the economic reform process.

A word on the timelag in the publication of the thesis would not be out of place, specially when almost on the heels of the award of the degree in 1963, assistance was available from the UGC for its publication. Even so, the ambition of updating it and the continual race between time and work kept on deferring it. The 1969 article of the author in this area in the Economic and Political Weekly, Review of Agriculture was only a partial fulfilment in this respect. However, as years passed by, the reproduction in subsequent studies by others, of the author's methodology and conceptualisation prompted the author to publish her thesis for a wider and fuller awareness about her work among her research fraternity. The task became easier specially because of the permanent relevance of the methodological content of the work. It is hoped that the book is of use to development analysts.

— R. Thamarajakshi

New Delhi,
April 1994.

List of Diagrams

(respective page nos. given alongside)

PART — I

PART — II

Chapter 2

Chapter 5

Chapter 8

Part-I

Intersectoral Relationships in India 1961-62 — 1991-92

Intersectoral Relationships in India 1961-62 -- 1991-92

[1]

Introduction

1.1 The subject of intersectoral relationships is an area of enduring interest to development analysts. There are changing and complex relations between the sectors in the process of growth. The linkage between agriculture and other sectors of the economy is primarily a reflection of the crucial role of agriculture in economic development. These interrelationships become more explicit, activised and conspicuous as development proceeds. The relative forces of intersectoral demand and supplies of resources, factors of production and products not only set the pace of development but are also a manifestation of the stage of growth.

1.2 There are links between the two sectors in the product and factor markets. Agriculture supplies the major wage good (food) for the nonagricultural sector and raw materials for industrial expansion. Agriculture can also yield an exportable surplus with which the necessary capital goods can be imported for development. On the demand side, agriculture provides a market for industrial products both for intermediate and final uses. The surplus labour in agriculture is a relatively cheap source of supply of this factor for industrial development. There could also be in-migration of labour into agriculture during periods of downswing. Besides, there are financial flows between the sectors. A part of the private investment in agriculture may be financed by 'external' funds from the other sectors of the economy in addition to a net inflow of resources on Government account for agricultural development.

1.3 In considering the contribution of agriculture or for that matter of any sector to the economic growth of the country, we may first recognise that all sectors function in an interdependent system. What a sector does is therefore not fully attributable to that sector alone but is contingent upon what happens to other sectors (and perhaps also outside the country). Even so, it is important to note three characteristics of agriculture in general; these characteristics influence the actual functioning of intersectoral relations. Firstly, there is a persistent tendency for low per capita income or low value productivity of labour in agriculture. Secondly, the supply of food is either scarce or abundant, the former in underdeveloped countries and the latter in developed countries. The problem is one of supply in both cases – one of accelerating it in the former case where it is largely a problem of consumers and restricting it in the latter case where it is more a problem of producers. Thirdly, in many underdeveloped countries, agriculture is an industry of major dimensions, contributing a significant proportion of Gross Domestic Product (GDP) and accounting for a sizeable share of labourforce. Although large quantities of resources (including land) are committed to agriculture, they yield very low levels of productivity. The linkages between the sectors are such that for sustained development, a rise in agricultural productivity would have to precede or accompany the development of the nonagricultural sector.

1.4 The inelasticity of agricultural output can hinder economic growth by making production plans costly for the economy (i.e. higher cost of production including higher cost of labour). It would therefore help if agricultural production becomes more elastic. In this context, it may be noted that there are possibilities of a substantial increase in agricultural production with a constant or declining labour force. Since in the initial stages, capital for industrial development is scarce, the distinction between inputs with high and low opportunity costs should be borne in mind. This is the context of the two-sector models of development with emphasis on labour contribution. Since in thickly populated agricultural economies, a considerable proportion of the rural labour force may provide an increment to production less than the requirements for subsistence, it has been assumed that there is a surplus manpower in the subsistence (agriculture) sector and that the non-agricultural (capitalist) sector is the dynamic element which absorbs the surplus labour force.

1.5 Three phases could be identified in the structural transformation involving declining proportion of labour in agriculture as development proceeds. The early phase may be called a stationary phase when there is an oversupply of labour with zero marginal physical product in agriculture. The supply curve of labour in the industrial sector is infinitely elastic at the institutional wage rate since the opportunity cost of labour is zero. As development progresses, agricultural workers are withdrawn and added to the industrial sector. If those remaining on the land do not increase their consumption, this transfer of labour amounts to a release of free resources for creation of overhead capital in industry. Generally, the opportunity cost of labour increases to a positive figure and the industrial sector has also to raise its wages to attract additional workers from agriculture. Finally, when the value of marginal product of labour in agriculture is equal to or greater than the institutional wage rate, disguised unemployment disappears, and larger supply of agricultural labour is forthcoming only at higher wages. In this commercial stage, the two sectors get fully integrated. In the context of this transformation, the rate of capital formation in the industrial sector determines the rate at which employment can be expanded in the capitalist, high wage sector of the economy. At the same time, the rate of expansion of employment in the capitalist sector relative to the growth of the total labour force determines how soon the surplus of rural labour will be reduced to a point where wage levels are no longer depressed by the low level of productivity and earnings in the subsistence sector. There is also a demand side to this process of change. With economic development, demand patterns diversify and production patterns adjust to these demand patterns leading to structural changes in work force and gross domestic product. Consequently, the terms of trade between sectors also can be expected to change in the course of development.

1.6 The important question is the nature of impact of barter terms of trade on (i) agricultural output and (ii) marketed surplus of agricultural produce. It may be argued that factors like asset fixity and resource inelasticity in agriculture may, for any given level of technology, result in a rather weak relationship between relative prices and aggregate agricultural output or the 'effective' supply of agriculture i.e. marketed surplus. In so far as higher relative prices for farm products provide an incentive for better and efficient management of inputs, there could be yield increases even under static technology assumption. However, it appears that for a decisive upward shift in the supply function, new technology and modernisation of agricultural production are preconditions for the operation of economic stimuli. When agriculture is passing through a phase of transformation, an increase in its aggregate supply could be basically a technological phenomenon facilitated by a favourable price climate.

1.7 On the other hand, studies on acreage/output response of individual crops to relative crop prices have shown that the allocative rationality of farmers in traditional and transitional societies is comparable with that in developed economies. At the same time, it has been noticed that in respect of foodgrains, price becomes a weaker consideration vis-a-vis weather except and to the extent foodgrains compete with other foodgrains for the area. Also even allocative decisions are based more importantly on a comparison of relative profitabilities of different competing crops. When new technology has been developed for a few crops only, this by itself could be a potent factor in diverting acreage to these crops from the competing crops which have yet to benefit from similar technological improvement.

1.8 In Part I of this book, we shall examine the relative performance of agriculture and non-agriculture in terms of investments and output, changes in the sectoral distribution of work force, 'export' of product surpluses from agriculture to nonagriculture, changes in the intersectoral pattern of demand and behaviour of the intersectoral terms of trade in India in the last three decades. Section 2 will detail the methodological aspects of studying intersectoral relationships. A comparative analysis of sectoral investments and outputs, changes in sectoral distribution of workforce and value added and relative products per worker in agriculture and nonagriculture will be taken up in Section 3. Section 4 will estimate and analyse the nature and quantum of intersectoral exchange of different products and the behaviour of prices of agricultural and nonagricultural products exchanged, and terms of trade in this period. It will further study the impact of intersectoral terms of trade on agricultural output, marketed surplus and incomes. The canvas of changing intersectoral relationships will be drawn and conclusions derived in Section 5. Part II of the book sets out the theoretical framework of changing intersectoral relationships in a developing economy, during transition to a developed state and in an advanced economy. It evolves a methodology for studying these relationships and examines the empirical aspects of the interrelationships in India in the initial stages of development during 1948-49 -- 1958-59.

[2]

METHODOLOGICAL ASPECTS

Earlier Contributions by the Author

2.1 A study of intersectoral commodity flows and terms of trade was pioneered by the author in the early sixties in her doctoral thesis "Agriculture-Industry Relationships in India, 1948-49 to 1958-59" submitted to the University of Delhi in 1963. This thesis, suitably abridged for publication purposes, finds place in Part II of this book; it has focussed on the intersectoral demand for products for intermediate and final uses, flows of labour and capital and terms of trade between agriculture and industry. The thesis developed a methodology for estimating the marketed surplus of agricultural products and terms of trade. It was the first ever attempt in (i) identifying the products exchanged between the two sectors (ii) estimating the value of these exchanged items at current and constant prices (iii) computing the composite indices of prices of these products for different uses (iv) deriving the time series of intersectoral net barter terms of trade and income terms of trade and (v) estimating the marketed surplus of agricultural products.

2.2 This was followed by the author's paper in 1969[2] on "Intersectoral Terms of Trade and Marketed Surplus of Agricultural Produce 1951-52 – 1965-66" which widened the purview to the sectors of agriculture and non-agriculture and updated the work upto 1965-66. The author's subsequent work[3] in 1977, 1985 and 1990 extended the period of the study. In all these studies, the availability at the different points of time of the latest and revised data was taken into account. The aforesaid contributions of the author starting from 1963 provided for the first time the theoretical and methodological framework for a study of intersectoral relationships.[4] We shall now present the salient aspects of the methodology followed by us here[5] in quantifying the product flows, marketed surplus of agricultural produce and terms of trade between agriculture and nonagriculture. The agricultural sector has been defined to include crop and animal husbandry, and all that is not agricultural constitutes the non-agricultural sector.

A. Identification of Traded Items

2.3 Items traded between agriculture and nonagriculture include not only commodities but also services and factors of production and these may be classified depending on whether they are for current consumption or current production or future consumption or future production and whether they are purchased at a price or are made available free. For a comprehensive treatment, the entire gamut of intersectoral flows would have to be taken into account including capital purchases and factor services. This was recognised by the author in her 1969 work which referred only to intersectoral purchases for current consumption and production, and not to capital purchases or factor flows. The problem is the inadequacy of data in this regard.

2.4 Subsequent to the 1969 work, some data on capital expenditure[6] on farm business by rural households became available. This available data from the All India Debt and Investment Survey in 1981-82 on capital expenditure in farm business includes "maintenance expenditure" and "expenditure leading to asset formation." The maintenance expenditure is taken note of by us as a current item of production. As for the latter i.e. expenditure on fixed capital formation, these include imputed value of expenditure in kind, value of owned assets and materials used and value of work done by members of the household and permanent servants. The constituent items in fixed capital formation are (i) reclamation of land (ii) construction of bunds and land improvements (iii) construction of wells and irrigation sources, (iv) purchase of equipment (agricultural implements, machinery, transport equipment etc.) and (v) construction of farm houses, grain golas and cattle sheds. By and large, these are construction items besides implements. However, to estimate the value of materials purchased from nonagricultural sector (like bricks and cement) to be used as 'weights' in compilation of terms of trade, it is necessary to have detailed information on the input structure of each of these items of fixed capital formation and the purchased component thereof. Moreover, in 1981-82, according to this survey, only 23 percent of rural households in the country reported expenditure on fixed capital formation and the average amount spent per household was Rs. 138. The aggregate value of fixed capital formation in farm business was Rs. 167 crores. In the Debt and Investment Survey in 1981-82, even if the implements, machinery and transport equipment were partly used for farm business and partly for nonfarm business for household purposes, the entire expenditure was taken under farm business. Survey information on fixed capital formation in farm business is not on all fours with that on consumer expenditure. Whereas the latter is representative of the households as a whole, the former pertains to those who have undertaken the expenditure in a reference year. The purchases of nonagricultural products going into fixed capital formation in farm business is not, as of now, a significant proportion of total purchases of products by agriculture.[7]

2.5 Similarly in the case of factor services, specially labour, while some idea can be obtained about how much labour is hired by agriculture, this need not be purchased from nonagriculture nor is it identifiable. On the other hand, there is flow of labour from agriculture to nonagricultural sectors. Even here, it will be difficult to evaluate this labour used in nonagriculture, since bulk of this goes into informal activities. In the light of the aforesaid, it is proposed to examine the trends in the exchange of only goods and services between agriculture and nonagriculture for current consumption. Table-1 gives the commodities that are traded between these two sectors for intermediate and final uses.

TABLE - 1

Items of Intersectoral Exchange for Intermediate and Final Consumption

Purchases by Agriculture from Non-agriculture	*Sales by Agriculture to Non-agriculture*
For Intermediate Consumption	
1. Fertiliser	1. Oilseeds
2. For repair and maintenance of fixed capital	2. Cotton
3. Electricity	3. Jute
4. Diesel oil	4. Other fibres including mesta
5. Pesticides and insecticides	5. Tea
6. Oil cakes	6. Coffee
7. Drugs & Medicines and Salt for working animals	7. Rubber
	8. Sugarcane
	9. Tobacco
	10. Hides
	11. Skins
	12. Wool
For Final Consumption	
1. Edible Oil	1. Cereals
2. Sugar	2. Gram
3. Salt	3. Pulses
4. Clothing	4. Milk and Milk products
5. Fuel and Light (i.e. Kerosene, Matches, Coal, Electricity etc.)	5. Meat, Egg and Fish
6. Non-Food (i.e. Beverage & Refreshment, Footwear, Durable Goods and Miscellaneous Goods & Services)	6. Fruits and Vegetables
	7. Other food (i.e. Spices)

B. Terms of Trade

2.6 The various measures of terms of trade usually used in international trade were examined in detail by the author in her doctoral work, with reference to intersectoral trade. The problems in working out gross barter terms of trade, single and double factoral terms of trade were discussed there. It was argued that net barter terms of trade and income terms of trade are fairly adequate as indicators of changing fortunes of agriculture vis-a-vis industry.

2.7 The net barter terms of trade between agriculture and nonagriculture are derived by us as a ratio of prices received by agriculture for its 'exports' to nonagriculture, to prices paid by the former for its 'imports' from the latter. 'Export' prices are represented by a composite index of prices of all agricultural products purchased by the nonagricultural sector for intermediate and final consumption. Similarly, 'import' prices are indicated by a composite index of prices of all nonagricultural products purchased by agriculture for intermediate and final uses. Time series of prices of the identified products are first noted for the period of study and value of the intersectoral purchase of the relevant commodities estimated for the selected base year for use as 'weights' for deriving the composite index of prices of the basket of goods purchased by one sector from the other. For constructing the income terms of trade between the sectors, the time series of the marketed surplus of agriculture to the nonagricultural sector are estimated.

2.8 A distinction may be made between the interpretations to which net barter terms of trade and income terms of trade lend themselves. Whereas changes in net barter terms of trade show the comparative position of one sector vis-a-vis the other, income terms of trade by definition do not show such a comparison. On the other hand, improvement or deterioration of income terms of trade of any particular sector for the products of the other sector is relative to its own position over time. There can, however, be a comparison of movements of income terms of trade of two sectors.

C. Estimates of Marketed Surplus of Agriculture and Purchase of Non-agricultural Products by Agriculture

2.9 Marketed surplus of agricultural produce to nonagriculture comprises of the surplus meant for final consumption and for intermediate use in nonagriculture. It has been assumed here as in the author's earlier studies that the agricultural exports to other countries first come to the domestic nonagricultural sector for processing and are subsequently exported from the nonagricultural sector.

a. for final use

2.10 At any point of time, the actual consumption of agricultural products (net of imports) by the nonagricultural sector can be taken in *'expost'* sense to be the 'effective supply' or the marketed surplus of agriculture. On this basis, the estimates of marketed supply are derived by combining the estimates of private consumer expenditure based on CSO's national income data with the pattern of consumer expenditure reflected by the National Sample Survey.[8] (NSS)

2.11 We are basically using the NSS data[9] on patterns of consumer expenditure because the NSS is the most scientific method and gives results on observed consumer behaviour. There have been some studies comparing the NSS estimates of patterns with the CSO estimates of consumer expenditure. However, it should be remembered that the Central Statistical Organisation's (CSO's) estimates of consumer expenditure are based on the commodity flow method which is an indirect method subject to limitations. CSO itself has referred to these limitations.[10] We have applied the NSS ratios to aggregate consumer expenditure estimates derived from national income estimates because the other parameters being dealt with are national income/production related. Further, estimates of intersectoral intermediate purchases are based on national accounts data. The following are the detailed steps involved in the estimation.

i. CSO provides estimates of personal disposable income. Deducting therefrom the estimates of savings of the household sector, estimates of private consumer expenditure are derived.[11]

ii. The NSS has brought out reports on rounds of survey on consumer expenditure. These rounds are taken to represent the respective financial years (Table-2).

TABLE-2

National Sample Survey of Patterns of Consumer Expenditure Rounds of Survey and Reference Period

Rounds of Survey	*Reference Period*	*Year to which the Information has been taken to correspond*
27th	Oct' 72 - Sep' 73	1972-73
28th	Oct' 73 - June' 74	1973-74
32nd	July' 77 - June' 78	1977-78
38th	1983	1983-84
42nd	July' 86 - June' 87	1986-87
43nd	July' 87 - June' 88	1987-88
44th	July' 88 - June' 89	1988-89
45th	July' 89 - June' 90	1989-90
46th	July' 90 - June' 91	1990-91

iii. The NSS gives the pattern of consumer expenditure in rupees per person for a period of thirty days by different items of consumption separately for rural and urban areas. In our study, agricultural products are taken to include foodgrains, milk and milk products, meat, egg and fish, fruits and vegetables and spices; the remaining items are grouped as nonagricultural.

iv. The NSS pattern of consumer expenditure in rural areas is taken to represent that of the agricultural sector and the less organised subsectors of forestry, fishery, small enterprises and construction and that in urban areas as representative of the rest of the nonagricultural sector (viz. mining and quarrying, factory establishments, services etc.)

v. Based on NSS data, the ratios of the blown up estimates of consumer expenditure on agricultural products by nonagriculture and of those on nonagricultural products by agriculture, to the economy's total consumer expenditure on all products (agricultural and nonagricultural) are first computed. For purposes of this blowing up of the NSS per capita estimates, estimates of population in agriculture, organised and less organised subsectors of nonagriculture have been worked out, using the results of decennial censuses and the distribution of work force by sectors as given by the NSS quinquennial surveys on employment and unemployment.

vi. Applying these ratios to the estimates of private consumer expenditure ((i) above) and netting the derived results for imports of respective consumer items,[12] the time series of estimates at current prices of nonagriculture's expenditure on domestic agricultural products for final use have been derived. These estimates represent the marketed surplus of agricultural produce for final use. Using the same method, estimates of agriculture's expenditure on nonagricultural items for final consumption have been worked out.

b. for intermediate use

2.12 It has been assumed that after certain retentions in the case of some crops, the outturn of agricultural crops meant for intermediate use in nonagriculture are 'exported' to the latter sector for intermediate use in the manufacturing and processing industries.[13] Information on non-agricultural inputs used in agricultural production given in National Accounts Statistics has been used for getting the weights for combining these input prices.

D. Composite Price Indices and Terms of Trade

2.13 Using the estimates of intersectoral purchase of different items in the selected base year as "weights", the composite indices of prices received by agriculture for its products purchased by nonagriculture were separately computed for intermediate and final uses and then combined to get the series for all uses. Similarly, prices paid by agriculture for the nonagricultural products purchased by it were separately computed for intermediate and final uses and then combined to get the series for all uses. On this basis, the net barter terms of trade of agriculture *vis-a-vis* nonagriculture in respect of (i) inputs, (ii) final products and (iii) all products traded have been estimated. The current value estimates of intersectoral purchases of products for different uses have been deflated with the respective composite price index for obtaining the corresponding constant price estimates. The net barter terms of trade have been corrected with the value (at constant prices) of the estimated 'exports' of the agricultural sector to nonagriculture for all uses and the income terms of trade have been derived.

E. Choice of Prices

2.14 While computing the composite indices of prices for deriving the terms of trade, it will be appropriate to consider the farm harvest prices for the prices received by the agricultural sector and the retail prices of nonagricultural products for the prices paid by the agricultural sector. The need for using retail prices was noted by the author even in 1963 in her doctoral work and again in her 1969 paper.[14] However, the time series data on retail prices of individual products are not available on as systematic a basis as wholesale prices. It is relevant to mention that wholesale prices are collected for the wholesale price index whereas there is no retail price index so far. Also retail price data collected by the NSSO, for the Consumer Price Index Numbers for Agricultural Labourers are representative of markets visited by agricultural labourers only. Moreover, for using this data, it is necessary to make averages of the same across the country, and the question of the kind of averaging/weighting arises. Thus, until the retail price data are stabilised and we have a retail price index on par with the wholesale price index, it is better to use the firmer basis of wholesale price indices. Similarly, we do not have a farm harvest price index. Even for valuation of the GDP from agriculture, while it would be appropriate to use farm harvest prices, this is not done in practice. In this connection, the CSO has observed that "farm harvest prices are collected only from a few selected centres. Moreover, a reassessment of the current condition indicates that the bulk of the transactions actually takes place during the peak marketing period rather than the harvest period, there being a time lag of 1 to 2 months between the two periods. Due to these considerations, cropwise average wholesale prices prevailing in primary markets during the peak marketing periods are being used for evaluation of crop outputs at the State level."[15] In fact, the producer disposes off his produce at different stages and at different points of time, and little information is available on such transactions at each stage. Under the circumstances, use of wholesale prices which have a representative coverage is a more firm basis for our purpose than that of farm harvest prices.

F. Type of Index Number and Base Year

2.15 In any exercise involving the construction of index numbers, there can be a discussion on which type of index number should be used. There are three types of index numbers: viz. (i) the Laspeyre's formula using base year weights (ii) the Paasche's formula using current year weights and (iii) the Fisher's Ideal Index Number formula based on geometric average of two index numbers. The theoretical aspects of each of these index numbers are generally known. Basically, the question is whether to go in for fixed weights or current year weights. However in this kind of exercise, where data for weights have to be collected from various sources and several adjustments have to be made to the basic data, the type of index number ultimately chosen will depend on the availability of data. It may be mentioned here that in her different studies[16] on the subject at different points of time, information pertaining to different years has been used as weights. In this sense, there are common periods for which the author's studies have yielded series with different base years. These studies show that even with shifting base years, the broad trends for common subperiods of the studies are not affected. Keeping this in view and even while recognising the technical merits or otherwise of different types of index numbers, the present study continues to adopt the fixed base index. Here we have used the following latest information viz. (i) NSS data on Consumer Expenditure for 1987-88 (43rd Round),[17] (ii) CSO's Revised Series of National Accounts[18], (iii) Economic Adviser's Revised Series of Index Numbers (1981-82 = 100) and (iv) Census results for 1991.

[3]

Investment, Workforce, Output and Productivity : Agriculture and Nonagriculture

Investment in Agriculture and Nonagriculture

3.1 Investments are the starting point of economic growth. It is true that resources for development include both capital and labour. It is also known that in developing economies, capital is scarce and labour is surplus. Even so, investment has to grow for absorbing the labour surplus, for modernising production and for raising productivity levels. It is not immediately relevant whether this investment is of the public sector or the private sector.

3.2 Estimates of gross fixed capital formation in agriculture and nonagriculture at constant (1980-81) prices during 1961-62 -- 1990-91 are given in Table-3.

TABLE - 3

Gross Fixed Capital Formation :
Agriculture and Non-agriculture

Rs. Crores : At Constant (1980-81) Prices

Year	*Agri.*	*Non-agri.*	*Total*	★	☆
1961-62	1665	7907	9572	17.4	-
1962-63	1804	9233	11037	16.3	-
1963-64	1939	10024	11963	16.2	-
1964-65	2103	10557	12660	16.6	-
1965-66	2258	11341	13599	16.6	-
1966-67	2313	10926	13239	17.5	-
1967-68	2580	10692	13272	19.4	-
1968-69	2558	10198	12756	20.0	-
1969-70	2754	10824	13578	20.3	-
1970-71	2625	11137	13762	19.1	-
1971-72	2767	11584	14351	19.3	831
1972-73	2938	13339	16277	18.1	1092
1973-74	2902	12865	15767	18.4	978
1974-75	2709	12806	15515	17.5	871
1975-76	2935	15182	18117	16.2	1001
1976-77	3646	15213	18859	19.3	1384
1977-78	3744	16183	19927	18.8	1512
1978-79	4246	17904	22150	19.2	1634
1979-80	4440	17213	21653	20.5	1720
1980-81	4537	19080	23617	19.2	1817
1981-82	4346	22062	26408	16.5	1730
1982-83	4409	24198	28607	15.4	1716
1983-84	3957	24751	28708	13.8	1709
1984-85	4287	26273	30560	14.0	1618
1985-86	4068	27713	31781	12.8	1458
1986-87	3798	30433	34231	11.1	1373
1987-88	4219	31624	35843	11.8	1448
1988-89	4257	34045	38302	11.1	1371
1989-90	4258	35956	40214	10.6	1192
1990-91	4286	37884	42170	10.2	1287

★ % of investment in agriculture to total investment.
☆ public sector investment in agriculture.

Source : GOI, Ministry of Planning, Department of Statistics, National Accounts Statistics, New Series, Various Issues.

While capital formation in both agriculture and nonagriculture has increased, the rate of growth has not been similar in the two sectors. The average level of gross fixed capital formation in the economy in the successive decades has progressively increased; it rose from Rs. 12544 crores in the decade ending 1970-71 to Rs. 18623 crores in the decade ending 1980-81 (i.e. by 48 percent) and to Rs. 33682 crores in the recent decade upto 1990-91 (i.e. by 81 percent). While the respective levels of investment in the non-agricultural sector in these decades rose in step with total investment, (i.e. by 47 percent and 95 percent), the corresponding increase in investment in agriculture decelerated from 54 percent to 20 percent. Further, as against a distinct growth in investment in agriculture by 47 percent between the triennium ending 1963-64 and that ending 1970-71 and by 54 percent between the triennium ending 1973-74 and that ending 1980-81, it virtually remained unchanged in the following ten years. Whereas around 18 to 20 percent of total investment was undertaken in agriculture during the twenty years upto 1980-81, there was a continuous decline since then from 16.5 percent in 1981-82 to 10.2 percent in 1990-91. It is clear that there has been a certain deceleration in investment in agriculture in the post-eighty period. More importantly, there has been a considerable decline in the level of public sector investment in the eighties. It fell from Rs. 1718 crores in the triennum ending 1983-84 to Rs. 1283 crores in the triennum ending 1990-91 (i.e. by 25 percent); more than 90 percent of public investment in agriculture goes to irrigation. It is, however, encouraging that a large inflow of current resources has taken place in the form of subsidies for fertiliser, irrigation, electricity, credit and other agricultural inputs.

Sectoral Distribution of Workforce : Agriculture and Non-agriculture

3.3 The estimated size of total workforce in the economy and its distribution among different sectors in 1961, 1972-73 and 1989-90 may be seen in Table-4. During 1961-73, there was virtually no change in the structure of workforce;

TABLE - 4

Sectoral Distribution of Employed Workforce

(In Millions)

Particulars	*1961*	*1972-73*	*1989-90*	*Percent Change*	*Share of Sector in Increase (Percent)*
				In 1989-90 over 1972-73	
1. Agriculture	137.8 (73.0)	174.9 (74.0)	211.5 (62.0)	20.9	35.0
2. Non Agriculture	50.9 (27.0)	61.4 (26.0)	129.3 (38.0)	110.6	65.0
i. Secondary	19.6 (10.4)	26.5 (11.2)	55.4 (16.3)	109.1	27.7
ii. Tertiary	31.3 (16.6)	34.9 (14.8)	73.9 (21.7)	111.7	37.3
Total	188.7	236.3	340.8	44.2	100.0

* Figures in the brackets are percent to total workforce in the year.

Notes: 1. Estimates for 1961 are based on Government of India, Census of India, 1961.

2. Estimates for 1972-73 have been taken from Government of India, N.S.S.O., Sarvekshana, Special number, September 1990, pp. 60.

3. Estimates for 1989-90 have been worked out by applying the workforce participation rates from N.S.S. for that year (Sarvekshana, Third Annual Survey on Consumer Expenditure and Employment and unemployment, 45th round 1989-90, Vol XVI, No. 1, July-Sep 1992) to the estimated population based on Census 1991.

4. Estimates based on N.S.S. are on Usual Status Basis (Principal and Subsidiary Status).

5. Definition of sectors correspond to National Industrial Classification (1970).

the share of workforce in agriculture, mining and quarrying and manufacturing, and rest of the economy stayed at around 74 percent, 10 percent and 16 percent. In the subsequent two decades however, significant changes have taken place in the sectoral distribution. Compared to an overall increase of 44 percent in the total workforce in the economy in this latter period, the corresponding increase in the agricultural and nonagricultural sectors was 21 percent and 111 percent respectively; within the nonagricultural sector, the growth was slightly higher in the tertiary sector than in the secondary sector. While agricultural sector contributed 35 percent of the increase in total workforce, nonagricultural sector naturally had a larger share of 65 percent; (tertiary sector had a share of 37 percent in the increment). The share of agriculture in total workforce declined from 74 percent in 1972-73 to 62 percent in 1989-90. An estimated 41 million workers, who would have been in agriculture had the structure of workforce in 1989-90 remained the same as in 1972-73, seem to have diverted themselves to the nonagricultural activities.

Growth of Sectoral Output and Value Added : Agriculture and Nonagriculture

3.4 We may now examine the growth patterns of agricultural and nonagricultural production and incomes. As far as gross output is concerned, whereas information is available both in terms of indices of agricultural production and gross value of output of agriculture, such information is not available for all the subsectors of nonagricultural sector.[19] Hence we propose to use the indices of agricultural production and of industrial production for comparative analysis of growth of gross production of agriculture and industry. For value added comparison, however, we would be examining the same for agricultural and nonagricultural sectors.

3.5 Table-5 gives the indices of agricultural and industrial production for the period 1971-72 – 1991-92. During this period, agricultural production and industrial production recorded respectively a compound growth rate of 3

TABLE - 5

Agricultural Production and Industrial Production

Indices : 1971-72 – 1991-92 (1987-88 = 100)

Year	*Agricultural Production*	*Industrial Production*
1971-72	73.5	41.4
1972-73	67.5	43.1
1973-74	74.3	44.0
1974-75	71.8	45.1
1975-76	82.7	48.1
1976-77	76.9	52.8
1977-78	87.8	54.4
1978-79	91.2	58.8
1979-80	77.3	57.8
1980-81	89.4	60.1
1981-82	94.4	65.7
1982-83	90.9	67.8
1983-84	103.4	72.4
1984-85	102.2	78.5
1985-86	104.7	85.4
1986-87	100.8	93.2
1987-88	100.0	100.0
1988-89	121.1 @	108.7
1989-90	123.6 @	118.0
1990-91	126.9 @	127.8
1991-92	123.3 @	127.7 @

Notes : 1. Index of Agricultural Production : Base Triennium ending 1969-70=100. (Here, this is expressed with 1987-88=100 as base) : Source : GOI, Ministry of Agriculture.

2. General Index of Industrial Production: Base : 1980-81=100. For years prior to 1980-81, the earlier index with 1970-71=100 has been first linked with the revised index with 1980-81=100. (Here, this is expressed with 1987-88 = 100 as base) : Source : GOI, Ministry of Industry.

@ Provisional

percent and 6 percent per annum. Diagram-1 depicts the movements of these indices. It shows the persistence of fluctuations in agricultural production notwithstanding the rising trend, and the accelerated pace of growth since 1982-83 of industrial production. During the earlier period 1960-61 to 1973-74 also, the differential growth of the two sectors was observed; agricultural production showed an annual rise of 2.3 percent compared to 5.5 percent in industrial production.

DIAGRAM - 1

Indices of Agricultural Production (O_a) and Industrial Production (O_i)

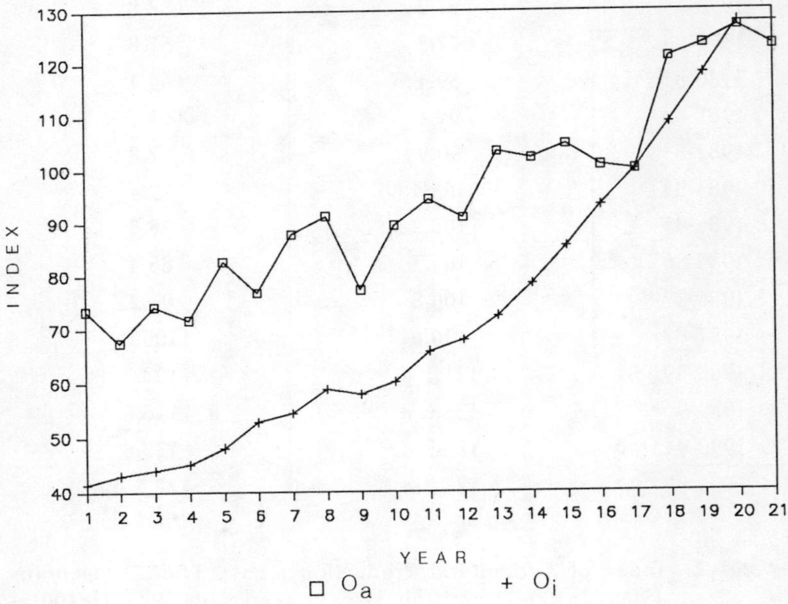

Note :

In all Diagrams in Part-I, the years 1971-72, 1972-73,....... 1990-91, 1991-92 are indicated as 1, 2,....... 20, 21 respectively.

3.6 The pattern of sectoral growth of value added (GDP) in agricultural and nonagricultural sectors during the triennium ending 1962-63, 1973-74 and 1990-91 is given in Table 6. Information pertaining to the secondary and services sectors is separately shown under the nonagricultural sector. During 1960-1974, Gross Domestic Product (GDP) from agriculture grew by only 23 percent compared to 63 percent in the case of non-agriculture; overall GDP rose by 43 percent in this period. Subsequently during 1971-1991, total GDP rose by 115 percent; whereas GDP from agriculture grew only by 65 percent, that from the secondary and tertiary sectors increased by around 150 percent. There was a significant decline in the share of agriculture in GDP through these thirty years matched by an increase in the share of secondary and tertiary sectors. It is noteworthy that the prevailing share of the tertiary sector at around 40 percent is higher than that of the other two sectors.

TABLE - 6

GDP – Agriculture and Nonagriculture : 1960-61 – 1990-91

At Constant (1980-81) Prices • Rs. Crores

Particulars	*Period*			*Overall Change % in 1988-91 over 1971-74*
	Triennium Averages			
	1960-63	*1971-74*	*1988-91*	
1. G.D.P	64663	92526	199272	115.4
2. G.D.P from Agriculture	31800	39039	64262	64.6
3. G.D.P from Non-Agriculture	32863	53487	135010	152.4
i. from Secondary Sector	13531	22689	56757	150.1
ii. from Tertiary Sector	19332	30798	78253	154.1
4. Share of (2) to (1) percent	49.2	42.2	32.2	
5. Share of 3 (i) to (1) percent	20.9	24.5	28.5	
6. Share of 3 (ii) to (1) percent	29.9	33.3	39.3	

Source : GOI, Ministry of Planning, Department of Statistics, National Accounts Statistics, New Series, Various Issues.

Sectoral Levels of Value Added Per Worker

3.7 Let us examine how the differential movements in GDP and workforce in the different sectors have influenced the relative levels of value added per worker in these sectors (Table 7). As is generally expected, per worker value added in agriculture is low and considerably lower than that in nonagriculture. There is not much difference in the levels between the secondary and the tertiary sectors. However, whereas the per worker value added in agriculture had remained almost stagnant during the sixties, the order of increase thereof in the seventies and the eighties was quite impressive. The recent two decades saw an overall increase of 36 percent in per worker value added in agriculture, which is much higher than that in nonagriculture. However, compared to the sixties, the increase in per worker value added in secondary and tertiary sectors was lower; it was considerably lower in the case of tertiary sector. The ratio of per worker value added in nonagriculture to that in agriculture which had widened from 2.8 in the early sixties to 3.9 in the early seventies, declined, though marginally, to 3.4 in the late eighties.

TABLE - 7

Per Worker Value Added : 1960-61 – 1990-91

Rs. at constant (80-81) Prices

Sector	*1960-63*	*1971-74*	*1988-91*	*Percent change in 1988-91 over 1971-74*
Agriculture	2307.7	2232.1	3038.4	36.1
Non Agriculture	6456.4	8711.2	10441.6	19.9
i. Secondary	6903.6	8561.9	10244.9	19.7
ii. Tertiary	6176.4	8824.6	10589.0	20.0
All Sectors	3426.8	3915.6	5847.2	49.3

Note : Derived from Tables 4 and 6.

[4]

Product Movements and Terms of Exchange : Agriculture – Non-Agriculture

Intersectoral Trade in Products for Current Use

4.1 There have been significant changes in the pattern of consumer demand in the rural and urban sectors (Table 8). The percentage of per capita consumer expenditure of the rural sector on non-agricultural products to total consumer expenditure had remained more or less constant at around 37 percent from 1961-62 to 1972-73. Subsequently however, this had considerably increased from 37 percent in 1972-73 to 47 percent in 1990-91. The increase which was substantial in 1977-78 has thereafter been gradual. The percentage of per capita total consumer expenditure in the urban sector on agricultural products did not show much change during 1961-62 to 1972-73. However, it declined in subsequent years from 48 percent in 1972-73 to 41 percent in 1990-91.

4.2 On the basis of household expenditure data[20], substantial variations have also been observed in marginal budget shares and expenditure elasticities for different commodities. The marginal budget share of cereals declines from 0.43 to 0.03 in rural areas and from 0.37 to 0.01 in urban areas when the shift is from the very poor to the non-poor higher groups. With an increase in expenditure level, the expenditure elasticities for food items generally decline and those for other non-food items as a group increase (Table-9).

4.3 While the above gives some idea of changes in patterns of household final consumption expenditure, we need to examine the pattern of intersectoral aggregate consumption for both intermediate and final uses. Such aggregate estimates of intersectoral sales and purchases will throw light on the trends in the volume and pattern

TABLE - 8

Percentage of Per Capita Total Consumer Expenditure on Agricultural and Non-Agricultural Products

Products	*Rural Sector*					*Urban Sector*				
	1972-73	*1977-78*	*1983*	*1987-88*	*1990-91*	*1972-73*	*1977-78*	*1983*	*1987-88*	*1990-91*
Agricultural	62.9	55.5	55.2	51.8	52.7	48.3	46.2	44.5	41.4	41.2
Non-Agricultural	37.1	44.5	44.8	48.2	47.3	51.7	53.8	55.5	58.6	58.8
Total	100.0	100.0	100.0	100.0	100.0	100.0	100.0	100.0	100.0	100.0

Source : Ministry of Planning, Department of Statistics, NSSO, various issues of *Sarvekshana*.

TABLE - 9

Expenditure Elasticities

Commodity Groups	(All India Rural)				(All India Urban)			
	Very Poor	*Moderate Poor*	*Non-Poor Middle*	*Non-Poor Higher*	*Very Poor*	*Moderate Poor*	*Non-Poor Middle*	*Non-Poor Higher*
1. Cereal & Cereal substitutes	0.8107	0.5191	0.2831	0.1694	0.8829	0.3608	0.0704	0.0665
2. Milk and Milk Prod.	2.0440	2.3565	1.8457	0.5599	1.7637	1.8328	1.1660	0.6372
3. Edible Oils	1.2852	1.1525	1.0076	0.5811	1.3059	1.2014	1.1009	0.3776
4. Meat, Egg and Fish	1.1569	1.4673	1.2000	0.6226	1.3205	1.2631	1.0852	0.6755
5. Sugar and Gur	1.5137	1.3998	1.2829	0.5573	1.1963	1.1597	0.7358	0.3847
6. Other Food	1.1126	1.1209	1.0455	0.5393	0.9729	1.0849	1.0850	0.7221
7. Fuel and Light	0.7324	0.7710	0.7548	0.4243	0.8709	0.7967	1.2515	0.4715
8. Clothing	1.7779	2.2513	2.3064	1.1256	1.6730	2.0673	1.6282	1.4821
9. Other Non-Food	1.3321	1.6639	1.8097	1.9625	0.9631	1.4701	1.6987	1.5640

Source : GOI, Planning Commission : Report of the study group on parameters on consumption submodel March 1991, p 14.

of intersectoral trade. For this purpose, we have estimated at constant prices the value of products exchanged between agriculture and non-agriculture. These estimates have been prepared, using the methodology outlined in previous pages for three decadal points viz. 1971-72, 1980-81 and 1989-90 (Table-10). The following inferences emerge :

i. Both sales and purchases by agriculture increased during each of these decades; the percentage increase in both cases has substantially increased during the recent decade compared to the earlier decade. Sales during the first decade increased by a higher percentage (40 percent) than its purchases (31 percent). During the latter period, sales and purchases increased more or less by the same order (around 60 percent).

ii. Whereas the rate of increase in agriculture's purchases for intermediate consumption has been higher than that for final use, the opposite is true of its sales.

iii. The rate of increase in agriculture's purchases of final consumption goods in the recent decade is more than double that in the previous period. Similarly, the rate of increase in nonagriculture's purchases of raw materials from agriculture has almost doubled in the latter period.

iv. The proportion of agriculture's purchases of inputs from nonagriculture to its total purchases for all uses has improved over the years. The proportion of agriculture's sales to nonagriculture for final use to its sales for all uses has somewhat bettered itself in this period.

4.4 We have examined the available information on disposal of output of different sectors between input use and final use for 1983-84 (Table-11). 42.5 percent of primary sector output was used as inputs in different sectors compared to 50 percent in the case of output of secondary sector. However, only 38 percent of tertiary

TABLE - 10

Intersectoral Exchange of Products : 1971-72 – 1989-90

Rs. Crores (At Constant 1987-88 Prices)

	Purchases by Agriculture from Nonagriculture					*Sales by Agriculture to Nonagriculture*				
	1971-72	1980-81	Percent Increase	1989-90	Percent Increase	1971-72	1980-81	Percent Increase	1989-90	Percent Increase
1. For Intermediate Use	3741	6489	73	12119	87	12367	15287	24	22284	46
	(10.4)	(13.7)		(16.0)		(41.0)	(36.2)		(32.5)	
2. For Final Use	32386	40860	26	63823	56	17777	26944	52	46279	72
	(89.6)	(86.3)		(84.0)		(59.0)	(63.8)		(67.5)	
3. All uses (Total)	36127	47349	31	75942	60	30144	42231	40	68563	62

Notes : Derived by using the methodology for estimating intersectoral purchases of different products for different uses, as explained in the text.

sector's output went as inputs in the economy. A larger percentage of output of primary sector (23 percent) went as inputs in secondary sector than in primary sector itself (17 percent). Only 6 percent and 4 percent respectively of outputs of secondary and tertiary sectors were used as inputs in primary sector. As against this, 35 percent of secondary sector's output and 20 percent of tertiary sector's output was used as inputs in secondary sector.

TABLE - 11

Disposal of Sectoral Output 1983-84

Sector	*Primary*	*Secon-dary*	*Tertiary*	*Total Input Use*	*Total Final Uses*	*Total Output*
Primary	16.7	23.3	2.5	42.5	57.5	100.0
Secondary	5.5	35.0	9.2	49.7	50.3	100.0
Tertiary	4.0	20.4	13.1	37.5	62.5	100.0

Source : Derived from G.O.I., Ministry of Planning, Department of Statistics, Input-Output Transactions Tables 1983-84 P 35; Table 3.3.

4.5 Taking the structure of inputs in each sector, it is observed that (Table-12) the percentage of own inputs to total inputs has significantly declined in the primary sector from 74.5 percent in 1968-69 to 57.8 percent in 1983-84. Correspondingly, the percentage of total inputs purchased by the primary sector from the secondary and tertiary sectors has risen from 17.1 percent to 27.7 percent and from 8.4 percent to 14.5 percent respectively in this period. Although the primary sector is using a larger order of inputs from the secondary sector than from the tertiary sector, the overall increase in this period in the percentage of inputs bought from the tertiary sector (73 percent) is higher than that in inputs bought from the secondary sector (62 percent). The input structure has remained more or less unchanged over time in the secondary sector. Bulk of the secondary sector's inputs are own inputs as in the

TABLE - 12

Percentage Distribution of Inputs in Primary, Secondary and Other Sectors

Sector	*Year*	*Primary*	*Secondary*	*Transport Commu-nication & Trade*	*Other Services*
Primary	1968-69	74.5	25.4	12.4	1.2
	1973-74	71.4	31.5	26.4	0.8
	1978-79	60.7	22.8	10.8	1.9
	1983-84	57.8	24.2	10.7	2.3
Secondary	1968-69	17.1	51.5	43.8	69.3
	1973-74	20.8	48.0	33.5	71.3
	1978-79	25.8	54.6	33.9	56.3
	1983-84	27.7	53.3	38.8	63.4
Tertiary	1968-69	8.4	23.1	43.8	29.5
	1973-74	7.8	20.5	40.1	27.9
	1978-79	13.5	22.6	55.3	41.8
	1983-84	14.5	22.5	50.5	34.3
Total Inputs	1968-69	100.0	100.0	100.0	100.0
	1973-74	100.0	100.0	100.0	100.0
	1978-79	100.0	100.0	100.0	100.0
	1983-84	100.0	100.0	100.0	100.0
Percentage of Total Inputs to Total Output	1968-69	23.9	60.6	28.3	26.1
	1973-74	23.1	61.5	30.7	24.7
	1978-79	27.5	62.4	37.8	21.5
	1983-84	28.9	63.6	39.2	17.5

Source : Derived from G.O.I. Ministry of Planning, Department of Statistics Input-Output Transactions Table 1983-84, p. 37. Table 3.5.

case of the primary sector while the inputs purchased from the primary and the tertiary sectors are more or less equal. In the case of the transport, communication and trade sector, the percentage of their inputs from tertiary sectors has risen while that from the secondary sector has fallen. It would thus be seen that primary sector's dependence on the rest of the economy for its inputs has relatively increased. No such change has occurred in the secondary sector. Own input consumption vis-a-vis use of inputs from other sectors has increased for the tertiary sector. On the whole, the input intensity (i.e. percentage of inputs in a sector to total output of that sector) has increased in all the sectors with the exception of other services.

Behaviour of Intersectoral Terms of Trade

4.6 We have seen that the volume of trade between the sectors has considerably expanded. It would be worthwhile examining the terms of exchange of the goods between the sectors. In this connection, the following tables and diagrams are presented. Table-13 furnishes the composite indices of prices of all agricultural products purchased by nonagriculture and of prices of all nonagricultural products purchased by agriculture (Diagram 2). Diagrams 3 and 4 show the movements of the composite price indices of these products separately for final consumption products and inputs in each case. Table 14 contains the computed estimates of net barter terms of trade between agriculture and nonagriculture for (a) final consumption products, (b) intermediate products and (c) all products and (ii) foodgrains terms of trade[21] for 1971-72 -- 1991-92 (Diagrams 5 and 6). It also presents indices of income terms of trade. All these indices have been calculated by using the methodology already outlined and the latest available information on consumer expenditure patterns and disaggregated national accounts statistics for weights. Table 15 contains these net barter terms of trade with 1987-88 weights expressed with 1978-79 as 100 and also our earlier series[22] of terms of trade with 1978-79 weights (Diagram 7). Table 16 presents these earlier series for the back period of 1951-52 to 1970-71. The estimates of marketed surplus of agriculture to non-agriculture at constant prices as also those of the percentage of the same to agricultural output are given in Table 17.[23]

TABLE - 13

Composite Indices of Prices Received and Prices Paid by Agriculture

Year	*Index number of prices of all agricultural products purchased by nonagriculture*	*Index no. of prices of all nonagricultural products purchased by agriculture*
1971-72	28.1	28.1
1972-73	30.9	30.4
1973-74	38.5	35.4
1974-75	47.6	45.3
1975-76	44.1	45.4
1976-77	43.6	46.2
1977-78	47.5	48.1
1978-79	46.7	48.6
1979-80	50.8	55.0
1980-81	57.0	65.2
1981-82	64.0	71.8
1982-83	68.1	74.5
1983-84	76.1	78.3
1984-85	80.7	82.6
1985-86	81.0	87.0
1986-87	88.3	92.3
1987-88	100.0	100.0
1988-89	107.2	106.7
1989-90	110.4	116.1
1990-91	123.3	129.2
1991-92	148.0	146.6

Note : These composite indices are made up with the individual price indices from EA's Revised Index of wholesale prices (1981-82 = 100) expressed with 1987-88 as base. For years prior to 1981-82, the individual price indices from the earlier series of EA with 1970-71=100 have been linked with the Revised Index.

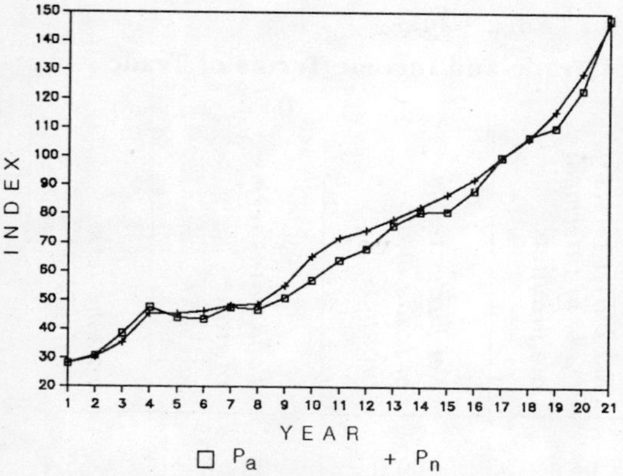

DIAGRAM - 2

Composite Indices of Prices Received (P_a) for Products sold by Agriculture to Nonagriculture and Prices Paid (P_n) by Agriculture for Products Purchased from Nonagriculture

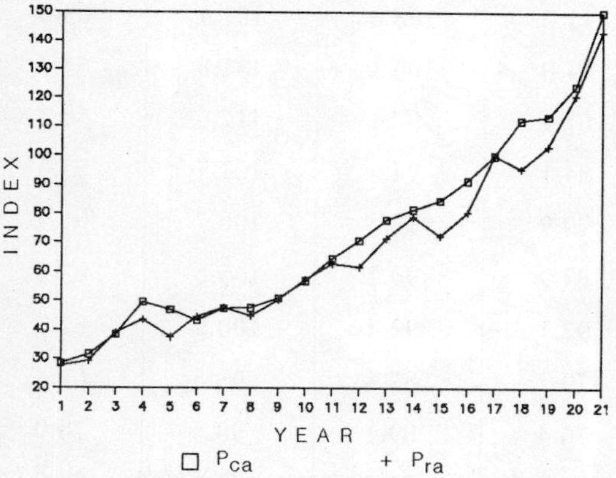

DIAGRAM - 3

Composite Indices of Prices Received by Agriculture (P_{ca}) for Agricultural Consumption Goods and for Agricultural Raw Materials (P_{ra}) Sold to Nonagriculture

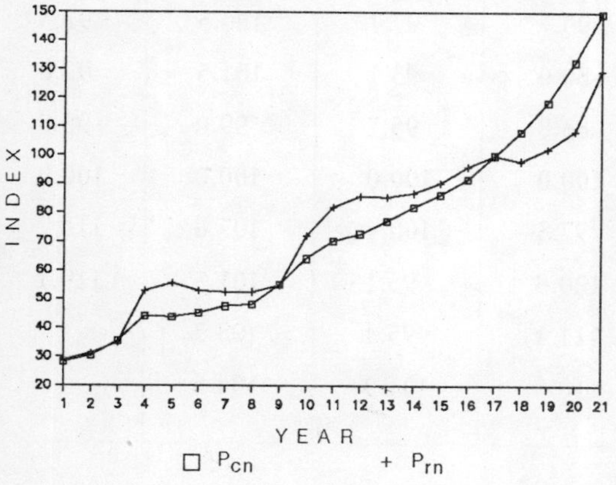

DIAGRAM - 4

Composite Indices of Prices Paid by Agriculture for Non-Agricultural Consumption Goods (P_{cn}) and Nonagricultural Inputs (P_{rn})

TABLE - 14

Net Barter Terms of Trade and Income Terms of Trade

Year	*Net barter terms of trade of consumption products*	*Net barter terms of trade of intermediate products*	*Net barter terms of trade of all products*	*Foodgrains terms of trade*	*Income terms of trade*
1971-72	101.1	96.1	100.0	112.5	55.1
1972-73	104.0	94.5	101.6	119.4	57.1
1973-74	108.2	111.5	108.8	121.1	63.0
1974-75	112.3	81.8	105.1	131.8	53.7
1975-76	106.8	67.4	97.1	117.6	50.3
1976-77	95.8	84.1	94.4	101.7	53.6
1977-78	100.0	90.9	98.8	106.7	61.9
1978-79	98.9	84.9	96.1	105.6	62.5
1979-80	92.4	92.1	92.4	100.9	62.9
1980-81	88.8	79.7	87.4	98.5	67.4
1981-82	91.9	76.4	89.1	98.5	70.9
1982-83	97.2	71.8	91.4	103.1	74.9
1983-84	101.2	83.5	97.2	107.4	84.6
1984-85	99.5	90.7	97.7	100.5	92.5
1985-86	97.8	80.0	93.1	101.5	92.0
1986-87	99.7	83.8	95.7	99.0	98.8
1987-88	100.0	100.0	100.0	100.0	100.0
1988-89	103.5	97.3	100.4	107.8	114.2
1989-90	95.8	100.8	95.1	101.5	119.1
1990-91	93.7	111.4	95.4	98.7	
1991-92	100.3	110.6	101.0	104.6	

DIAGRAM - 5

Indices of Net Barter Terms of Trade : For Products for Final Use (T_c), for Products for Intermediate Use (T_i) and for Products for All Uses (T)

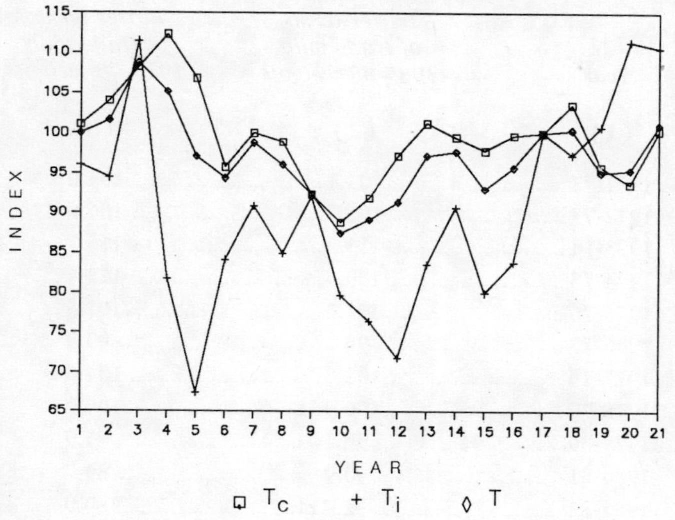

DIAGRAM - 6

Indices of Foodgrains Terms of Trade (T_f)

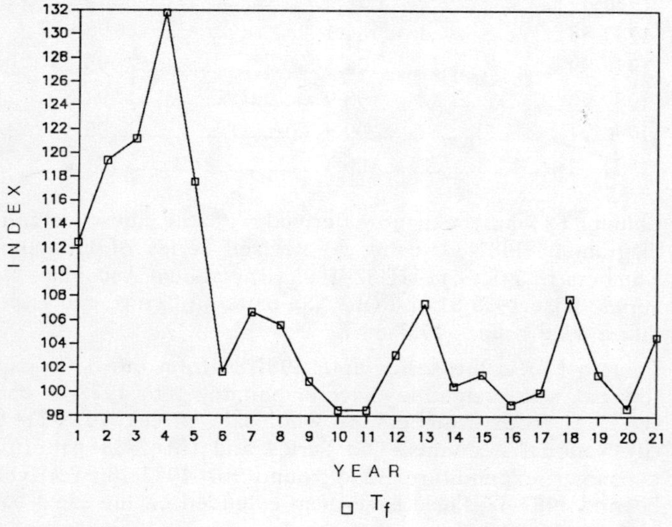

TABLE - 15

Net Barter Terms of Trade with Alternative Weighting Diagrams

Year	*Barter terms of trade with 1987-88 weights*	*Barter terms of trade with 1978-79 weights*
(1)	(2)	(3)
1971-72	104.1	104.0
1972-73	105.7	106.8
1973-74	113.2	115.7
1974-75	109.4	112.4
1975-76	101.0	101.5
1976-77	98.2	99.9
1977-78	102.8	104.5
1978-79	100.0	100.0
1979-80	96.1	95.9
1980-81	90.9	89.7
1981-82	92.7	89.9
1982-83	95.1	91.7
1983-84	101.1	97.0
1984-85	101.7	97.0
1985-86	96.9	91.6
1986-87	99.6	91.1
1987-88	104.1	98.5
1988-89	104.5	98.2
1989-90	98.9	94.6
1990-91	99.3	95.3
1991-92	105.1	101.2

Notes : Column (2) has been now derived with the latest weighting diagram in 1987-88, using (i) Revised Series of EA's Index Numbers of Prices (1981-82=100) (ii) National Accounts, New Series, Base 1980-81 and (iii) NSS pattern of consumer expenditure 43rd round, 1987-88.

Column (3) is the series upto 1987-88 from our 1990 paper (op cit) with weighting diagram pertaining to 1978-79 using (i) EA's Index Numbers of wholesale prices 1970-71=100 (ii) National Accounts, Old Series and (iii) NSS pattern of consumer expenditure 32nd round for 1977-78. For years beyond 1987-88, these have been extended on the same basis as in the 1990 paper.

DIAGRAM - 7

Indices of Net Barter Terms of Trade with 1978-79 Weighting Diagram (S) and 1987-88 Weighting Diagram (R)

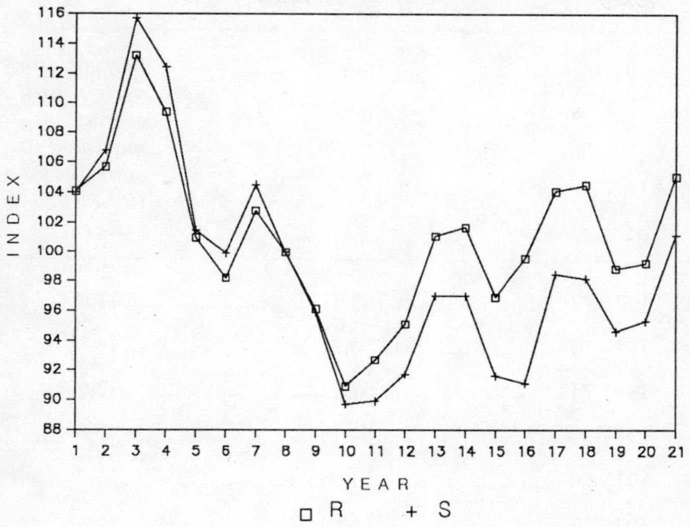

TABLE - 16

Net Barter Terms of Trade : 1951-52 – 1970-71

(Base 1978-79 = 100)

Year	*Index*	*Year*	*Index*
1951-52	86.9	1961-62	86.9
1952-53	85.6	1962-63	85.5
1953-54	89.5	1963-64	84.1
1954-55	83.7	1964-65	93.8
1955-56	81.8	1965-66	98.8
1956-57	88.4	1966-67	106.2
1957-58	85.0	1967-68	107.9
1958-59	87.8	1968-69	100.4
1959-60	87.8	1969-70	108.5
1960-61	86.3	1970-71	109.9

Source : Thamarajakshi, R., Op. Cit. 1990.

TABLE-17

Indices of Marketed Surplus

(1987-88 = 100)

Year	*Index*	*Percent of agricultural output marketed at constant (87-88) prices*
1971-72	55.1	41.0
1972-73	56.2	43.8
1973-74	57.9	42.0
1974-75	51.1	37.6
1975-76	51.8	34.2
1976-77	56.8	39.3
1977-78	62.7	39.2
1978-79	65.0	39.6
1979-80	68.1	45.8
1980-81	77.1	44.8
1981-82	79.6	43.7
1982-83	81.9	45.3
1983-84	87.0	44.0
1984-85	94.7	47.5
1985-86	98.8	49.2
1986-87	103.2	51.7
1987-88	100.0	50.3
1988-89	113.7	49.3
1989-90	125.2	53.0

4.7 The following inferences emerge from a study of the tables / diagrams, pertaining to prices and terms of trade :

i. The composite indices of prices of all agricultural products purchased by nonagriculture and of nonagricultural products purchased by agriculture have shown more or less similar annual rates of growth (viz 7.6 percent and 7.8 percent). Whereas the composite indices of agricultural consumption products as well as agricultural raw materials used by nonagriculture rose by around 7.5 percent per annum, indices of prices of nonagricultural consumption products used by agriculture rose by 8 percent per annum and of nonagricultural inputs used by agriculture by nearly 7 percent per annum.

ii. Net barter terms of trade of final goods, inputs and all products have all fluctuated, the fluctuation being quite large in the case of those for inputs.

iii. In the overall, net barter terms of trade have not shown any distinct trend taking the long period 1971-72 -- 1991-92.

iv. However, on a close scrutiny, we find three sub periods in terms of trade for all products viz. from 1971-72 to 1973-74 when they were looking up, from 1973-74 to 1980-81 when they were inclined downward and from 1980-81 to 1991-92 when they have shown a tendency to recover. On the basis of our earlier series with 1978-79 as base, it is seen that terms of trade did not show much of a trend during 1951-52 to 1963-64, but had generally increased during 1963-64 -- 1970-71.

v. Our earlier series with 1978-79 weights and the present series with 1987-88 as weights show similar trends in the common period of their coverage viz. 1971-72 to 1991-92.

vi. Foodgrains terms of trade rose upto 1974-75, dipped in the next two years and subsequently fluctuated showing no distinct trend. During the earlier decade 1961-62 – 1971-72, they had shown a rising trend.[24]

Terms of Trade, Agricultural Output and Marketed Surplus

4.8 Notwithstanding the fluctuations in barter terms of trade, agricultural output has grown at 2.99 percent per annum during this period. Similarly, despite fluctuations in foodgrains terms of trade, foodgrain production has shown an impressive growth rate. During 1967-68 -- 1990-91, foodgrain production increased at an annual rate of 2.8 percent, with an equally sizeable growth rate of 2.3 percent in yield levels. The relative movements of agricultural output and terms of trade are graphed in Diagram 8. A log-linear function with the index of agricultural production (O_{at}) as the dependent variable, and terms of trade (T_{t-1}) (lagged by a year), and time factor (t) as the independent variables was fitted to the data on the relevant variables for this period. The equation worked out to :

$$\log O_{at} = 0.502 + \underset{(1.613)}{0.601^{@}} \log T_{t-1} + \underset{(9.607)}{0.282^{*}} \log t$$

$\bar{R}^2 = 0.842$

D.W. Statistic = 1.619

@ Not significant

* Highly significant

(Figures in brackets indicate 't' values)

4.9 The coefficient of terms of trade in the equation is statistically not significant. It follows that agricultural output is solely influenced by "time factor" which represents changes in real factors such as irrigation, progress of high yielding varieties and use of modern inputs. In fact, some real factors have been at work in promoting agricultural growth. Table 18 shows the growth of modern inputs and gross irrigated area. At constant (80-81) prices, the value of modern inputs[25] rose from Rs. 1631 crores in the triennium ending 1973-74 to Rs. 6375 crores in the triennium ending 1989-90. As percentage of gross output of agriculture, this represented an increase from 4.5 percent to 11.1 percent in this period, while the percentage of these inputs to total inputs in agriculture doubled (i.e. from 16.8 percent to 33.2 percent). Similarly, gross irrigated area increased by 54 percent from 38.4 million hectares in 1971-72 to 59.3 million hectares[26] in 1988-89. As percentage of gross sown area, this meant a step up from 23.3 percent to 32.9 percent. Consumption of fertilisers per hectare of gross cropped area has risen from 13 kgs. in 1970-71 to 64 kgs. in 1989-90.[27] The proportion of cropped area under high yielding varieties of paddy, wheat, jowar, bajra and maize increased from 16.7 percent in 1970-71 to 64 percent in 1990-91.[28]

DIAGRAM - 8

Indices of Net Barter Terms of Trade (T) and Agricultural Production (O_a)

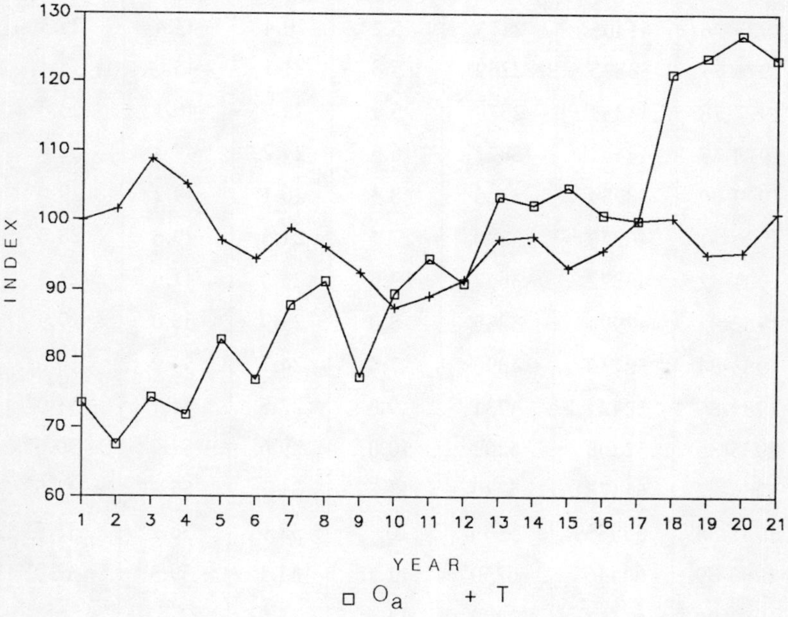

TABLE - 18

Output and Modern Inputs : Agriculture

(at 80-81 prices)

Year	Value of Gross Output in Rs. Crores	Value of Modern Input in Rs. Crores	% of Value of Modern Input to Gross Output	% of Modern Input to Total Inputs	Gross Irrigated Area in million hectares	% of Gross Irrigated Area to Gross Sowr. Area
(1)	(2)	(3)	(4)	(5)	(6)	(7)
1971-72	36901	1519	4.1	15.8	38.4	23.3
1972-73	34596	1674	4.8	17.5	39.1	24.1
1973-74	37609	1699	4.5	17.1	40.3	23.7
1974-75	36776	2033	5.5	19.5	41.7	39.4
1975-76	41465	2173	5.2	20.4	43.4	25.3
1976-77	38875	2269	5.8	21.1	43.6	38.4
1977-78	43331	2570	5.9	22.7	46.1	26.8
1978-79	44441	2872	6.5	24.2	48.3	27.6
1979-80	38754	3220	8.3	26.1	49.2	29.0
1980-81	46278	3280	7.1	21.5	49.8	28.8
1981-82	48872	3697	7.6	23.3	41.6	23.5
1982-83	47999	3855	8.0	23.9	52.0	29.9
1983-84	52730	4096	7.8	24.7	54.2	30.0
1984-85	52421	4731	9.0	27.5	54.7	31.0
1985-86	52208	5202	10.0	29.6	54.7@	30.6@
1986-87	51175	5720	11.2	31.7	55.7@	31.5@
1987-88	50555	5385	10.7	30.6	56.2@	32.7@
1988-89	60446	6730	11.1	34.1	59.3@	32.9@
1989-90	61318	7009	11.4	35.0		

@ Provisional

Source : GOI, Ministry of Agriculture; Agricultural Statistics at a glance 1992. "GOI, CSO, Various Issues of National Accounts."

4.10 Public policies have been directed to output price support, better input and credit deliveries and extension system. The procurement/minimum support prices for selected crops from 1980-81 to 1993-94 are given in Table 19. The increase in the period has been nearly 150 percent for wheat, coarse cereals and gram, 195 percent for paddy, 288 percent for groundnut-in-shell and 108 percent for sugarcane. The increase was 100 to 125 percent for cotton during 1983-84 — 1993-94 and 52 percent for jute between 1989-90 and 1993-94. It may be noted that the elasticities of current market prices of rice and wheat with respect to their corresponding procurement prices have been found to be more than unity.[29] The flow of institutional credit for agriculture has risen from Rs. 885 crores in 1970-71 to Rs. 11,199 crores in 1991-92. Fertiliser subsidies increased from Rs. 495 crores in the triennium ending 1982-83 to nearly Rs. 5000 crores in the triennium ending 1992-93.

4.11 Thus technology, irrigation and modern inputs have been the prime movers for agricultural growth. As Dantwala had observed "In many developing economies, agricultural productivity is very low. The greatest disincentive in farming is low income. And at the root of low income are the scanty resource base of the cultivator and its low productivity.... The relationship between prices of farm products and prices of purchaseable inputs is no doubt important. But more important is the output response to the inputs, which can be greatly increased by technical research and better farm management."[30]

4.12 We have also examined the responsiveness of marketed surplus (M) to terms of trade (Diagram 9). A log-linear equation explaining marketed surplus in terms of agricultural output and terms of trade was fitted to the data for the period 1971-72 – 1989-90. The resulting equation is as follows:

$$\log M_t = -0.724 + \underset{(9.353)}{1.504^{*}} \log O_{at} - \underset{(0.329)}{0.170^{@}} \log T_t$$

* Highly significant; @ Not significant

(Figures in brackets indicate 't' values)

$\bar{R}^2 = 0.843$ D.W Statistic = 1.495

TABLE - 19

Procurement Prices

	Paddy (common) (P)	Coarse Cereals FAQ@ (P)	Wheat FAQ (P)	Gram FAQ (M)	Cotton F414/ H777 (M)	Cotton H4 (M)	Jute W5 (Assam) (S)	Jute TD5 (Assam) (S)	Groundnut in Shell FAQ (M)	Sugar-cane FAQ@@ (S)
1980-81	105	105	130	NA			160		206	13.00
1981-82	115	116	142	NA			175		270	13.00
1982-83	122	118	151	235			175		295	13.00
1983-84	132	124	152	240	400	527	185		315	13.50
1984-85	137	130	157	NA	410	535	195		340	14.00
1985-86	142	130	162	260	425	535	215		350	16.50
1986-87	146	132	166	280	430	540	225		370	17.00
1987-88	150	135	173	290	440	550	240		390	18.50
1988-89	160	145	183	325	500	600	250		430	19.50
1989-90	185	165	215	421	570	690		295	500	22.00
1990-91	205	180	225	450	620	750		320	580	23.00
1991-92	230	205	*275	500	695	840		375	645	26.00
1992-93	270	240	*330	600	800	950		400	750	27.00
1993-94	310	260			900	1050		450	800	

NA : Not Announced; (P) : Procurement Price; (M) : Minimum Support price; (S) : Statutory Minimum Price

@ Jowar
Bajra
Ragi

* including Central bonus of Rs. 25/- per quintal

@@ Linked to a basic recovery 8.5% with a proportionate premium for every 0.1% increase above that level.

DIAGRAM - 9

Indices of Agricultural Output (O_a) and Marketed Surplus of Agriculture (M)

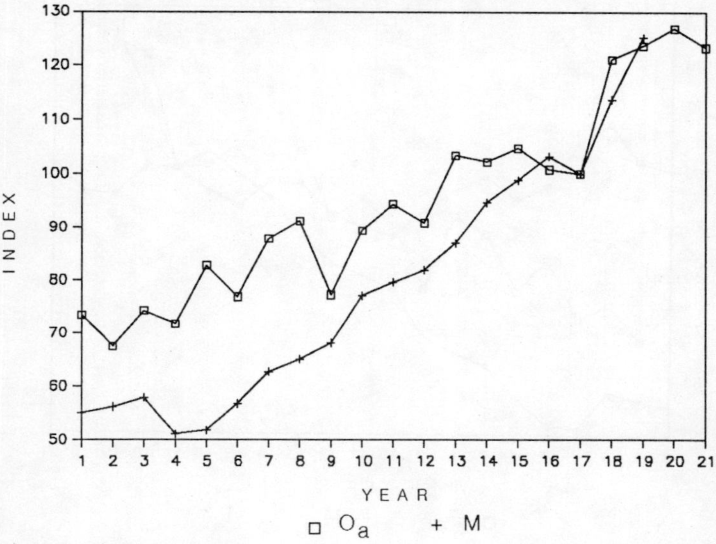

4.13 In line with the increase in agricultural output, marketed surplus has increased at an annual rate of 5 percent. The percentage of agricultural output that was marketed to nonagriculture rose from 42 percent in the triennium ending 1973-74 to 44.8 percent in the triennium ending 1981-82 and then to 50.9 percent in the triennium ending 1989-90.

4.14 Marketed surplus is significantly and positively related to agricultural output. The elasticity of marketed surplus with respect to agricultural output is 1.5. On the other hand, there is no statistically significant impact of terms of trade on marketed surplus. This is evident from Diagram 10 depicting the movements of output, marketed surplus and terms of trade. This impressive growth of agricultural output and marketed surplus had had its influence on the income terms of trade. Income terms of trade although fluctuated and looked somewhat downwards in the early seventies upto 1975-76, had shown a continuous uptrend since then (Diagram 11).

DIAGRAM - 10

Indices of Net Barter Terms of Trade (T), Agricultural Output (O_a) and Marketed Surplus of Agriculture (M)

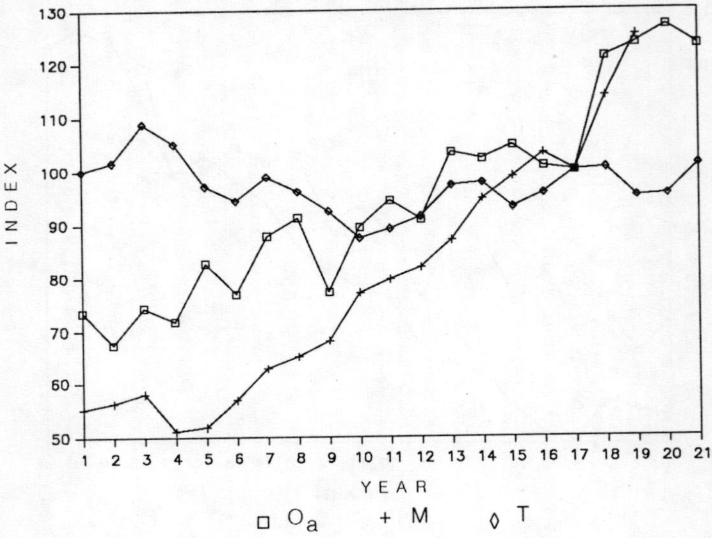

DIAGRAM - 11

Indices of Income Terms of Trade (I)

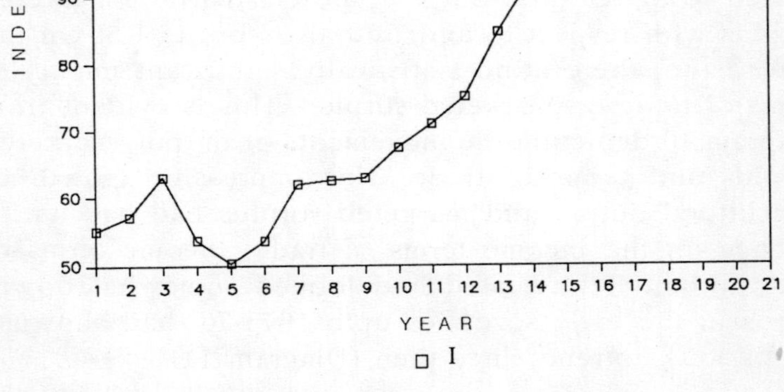

4.15 That growth of agricultural output is the dominant factor also comes out from an analysis by Jose (1990)[31] of real wages in agriculture during the seventies and the eighties. His study has noted that during the mid seventies, there was a reversal of an earlier trend towards stagnancy or even decline of real wage rates, and that this uptrend in 1974-75 continued through the eighties. Further, real wages in agriculture registered larger increases during the decade of the eighties compared to the seventies. Explaining this distinct improvement in the eighties, Jose points out that (1) growth of agricultural output was an important factor that provided the growth in real wages in agriculture and (ii) this factor of agricultural growth was more pervasively present among the Indian States during the latter half of the 1990's. In consonance with the growth of real wages in agriculture, there was a continual decline in the percentage of rural population below the poverty line. It declined from 54 percent in 1972-73 to 51 percent in 1977-78, 40 percent in 1983-84 and 33 percent in 1987-88. As we have said elsewhere,[32] a combination of factors affect the conditions of rural poor (who are mainly rural/agricultural labour households). These are (i) employment (ii) wages and (iii) food prices. Given the short term stickiness of nominal wages to food price changes, it is the wage earners specially in rural areas who need to be protected against inflation in food prices. In the period of our study, certain positive developments in crop production in general and food production in particular have helped to create more employment for the rural poor. At the same time, food rate of wages (real wages) have improved. The process has been also helped by the accelerated wage employment programmes of the Government in the post eighties. As a result, rural poverty has declined.

[5]

CONCLUSIONS

5.1 We have observed the behaviour of intersectoral relationships in the Indian economy for a long period of three decades since 1961-62. Part II of this book has presented a theoretical scheme of intersectoral behaviour at different stages of economic development and the methodology for studying the same.

5.2 During this period, real investments in the economy have increased manifold. Investment in agriculture had generally kept pace with the overall investment in the economy upto the eighties. Subsequently however, there has been a deceleration in the investment rate in agriculture. It is disconcerting that public sector investment in agriculture of which bulk is constituted by investment in irrigation has decelerated. At the same time, there has been a sizeable inflow of current resources in the form of subsidies on irrigation, electricity, and fertilisers. This has been accompanied by substantial increases in procurement prices and institutional credit for agriculture.

5.3 The sectoral distribution of workforce which had remained more or less unchanged upto 1971 has since undergone a change. The share of workforce in agriculture to total workforce has declined in the last two decades and an estimated 40 million workers who would have been in agriculture, had the structure in 1989-90 remained the same as in 1972-73, seem to have taken to nonagricultural activities.

5.4 All through the period, industrial production registered a faster rate of growth than agricultural production. Agricultural production has fluctuated, although it has maintained its uptrend of 2.5 to 3 percent depending upon the base year taken. The share of agriculture in GDP continually declined from 55 percent in the triennium ending 1952-53 and was only 32 percent in the triennium ending 1990-91. Compared to this, the share of the secondary and tertiary sectors improved respectively from 16 percent and 19 percent in the former period to 28 percent and 39 percent now. As a result of these changes in sectoral distribution of workforce and GDP, the per worker value added in agriculture which had shown a decline in the first two decades, i.e. 1951-71, improved during the subsequent two decades ending 1991. Even so, the ratio of per worker value added in agriculture to that in nonagriculture continued to be unfavourable to agriculture.

5.5 The percentage of percapita consumer expenditure of the rural sector on nonagricultural products which had remained more or less constant till 1972-73 considerably increased thereafter while that of the urban sector on agricultural products showed a decline in the same period. Moreover, the expenditure elasticities for food items generally declined with an increase in expenditure levels and those for other non-food items as a group increased.

5.6 There has been a diversification of consumer demand of the agricultural sector for nonagricultural products and a significant modernisation of agriculture through induction of purchased inputs, besides expansion of the area under high yielding varieties. There has also been a satisfying pick up in real wages in agriculture which is consistent with the relative reduction in workforce in agriculture.

5.7 In these recent decades when structural changes have occurred in consumption patterns, GDP, and workforce, there has been a significant expansion of intersectoral trade. During 1971-90, both sales and purchases by agriculture increased, the former by a somewhat higher order. Marketed surplus of agriculture to nonagriculture has risen in absolute terms and as a proportion of agricultural output. Whereas the rate of increase in agriculture's purchases for intermediate consumption has been higher than that for final consumption, the opposite in true of its sales. The proportion of agriculture's purchase of inputs from nonagriculture to its total purchases for all uses has improved. Purchased inputs in agriculture from secondary as well as tertiary sectors both as a percentage of all inputs and as a percentage of gross value of agricultural output have significantly risen. The overall increase in inputs bought from the tertiary sector is higher than that in inputs bought from the secondary sector. In all sectors, whether agriculture or secondary or tertiary sectors, the input intensity has increased.

5.8 Alongside the more or less similar order of expansion in intersectoral trade, the long term trends in the composite prices of agricultural products purchased by nonagriculture for intermediate or final use and in those of nonagricultural products purchased by agriculture for intermediate or final use have also been similar. Consequently, a distinct trend is not visible in the long term movements of net barter terms of trade for inputs or final goods or all products although they have all fluctuated. Foodgrains terms of trade have also not exhibited a visible trend from mid seventies, while they had risen during 1961-62 – 1974-75. Notwithstanding the absence of a long term trend in barter terms of trade, there was a general increase in income terms of trade for agriculture, since sales of agriculture to nonagriculture expanded.

5.9 Although net barter terms of trade during the last few decades taken as a whole do not exhibit a clear trend, the period is seen to consist of four subperiods characterised by differential movements in the barter terms of trade. These are (i) 1951-52 to 1963-64 when there was not much of a change (ii) 1963-64 to 1973-74 when they improved (iii) 1973-74 to 1980-81 when they were inclined downward and (iv) 1980-81 to 1991-92 when they seem to have a tendency to recover. We may examine the behaviour of some crucial variables viz. production, share of agriculture in GDP, percentage of workforce in agriculture, value added per worker in agriculture, ratio of value added per worker in nonagriculture to that in agriculture, capital formation in agriculture, agriculture's demand for inputs from non-agriculture, percentage of percapita consumer expenditure on nonagricultural commodities and rural poverty in the three subperiods from the sixties onwards (Table 20).

TABLE - 20

Terms of Trade and Crucial Economic Variables

PERIOD	Behaviour of terms of trade	Growth of agricul. productn. (percent per annum)	Growth of industrl. productn. (percent per annum)	Share of agri. in G.D.P. (percent)	Share of agri. in workforce (percent)	Value added per worker in agri. at const. 1980-81 prices (Rs.)	Value added per worker in non-agri to that in agri.	Gross fixed capital formation in agri. at const. 1980-81 prices* (Rs. crores)	% of purchased inputs to total inputs in agri.	% of per capita consumer expenditure on non-agri. commodities in rural sector	Rural poverty (% of population below poverty line)
1963-64 to 1973-74	Increase	2.31 (1960-61 to '73-74)	5.46 (1960-61 to '73-74)	49.2 (1960-63)	73 (1961)	2308 (1960-63)	2.8 (1960-63)	2260 (1961-71) (18.0%)@	17.1 (1973-74)	34.6 (1967-68)	54 (1972-73)
1973-74 to 1980-81	Decline	2.89 (1973-74 to '83-84)	5.0 (1973-74 to '83-84)	42.2 (1971-74)	74 (1972-73)	2232 (1971-74)	3.9 (1971-74)	3486 (1971-81) (18.7%)@	21.5 (1980-81)	44.5 (1977-78)	51 (1977-78)
1980-81 to 1991-92	Tendency for Recovery	2.99 (1971-72 to '91-92)	6.0 (1971-72 to '91-92)	32.2 (1988-91)	62 (1989-90)	3038 (1988-91)	3.4 (1988-91)	4189 (1981-91) (12.7%)@	35.0 (1989-90)	48.2 (1987-88)	40 (1983-84) 33 (1987-88)

Note : i. See Thamarajakshi, R., 1990 Op. Cit. Table 3.
ii. *Average for the decade indicated.
iii. @ refers to percentage of gross fixed capital formation in agriculture to total gross fixed capital formation.

5.10 The different movements in barter terms of trade do not seem to have particularly affected the growth impulses in agriculture and industry. The level of real investment in agriculture improved through the decades, while the percentage of investment for nonagriculture rose. The percent of per capita consumer expenditure in the rural sector on nonagricultural commodities as also the percent of purchased inputs to total inputs in agriculture increased. The share of agriculture in GDP and in total workforce each declined. Value added per worker in agriculture in real terms showed an improvement; in relation to nonagriculture, the deterioration in early seventies compared to the early sixties, was somewhat reversed in the late eighties. There was a continual decline in the percentage of the rural population below poverty line, through these three subperiods. Thus, despite different trends in barter terms of trade, the real factors of technological change and modernisation have helped promote growth and have brought about a closer integration of the sectors in factor adjustments and trade flows.

Future Scenario for Intersectoral Relationships

5.11 The important question is whether the aforesaid experience in the last few decades would be as such valid for the period ahead which would be qualitatively different from the period so far. The coming years may be expected to place increasing challenges on both agricultural and nonagricultural sectors in the context of the economic reforms. There would be growing domestic requirements for foodgrains, livestock products and fruits and vegetables due to increasing population and incomes, and also for providing effective food security to the poor. More importantly, the ongoing economic reforms depend on an acceleration in the growth of exports. A considerable part of exports is to be contributed by increases in those of agricultural and allied products. For farm surpluses to emerge on an increasing scale to cope with both the rising requirements of domestic population and exports, there is need for diversifying and expanding the agricultural production base. This would call for investments, technological change and modern inputs on a much larger scale, on a wider basis and at a faster pace than in the past.

5.12 Economic reforms have begun to take off in the industrial sector and with the flow of economic benefits from liberalisation measures, real investments in nonagriculture are likely to grow faster in absolute and relative terms. There is an inevitable time lag in the process of globalisation to catch up in agriculture. Given the overall resource constraints and since no new forces may immediately operate to substantially enhance the profitability in agriculture, the already observed deceleration in investment in agriculture/irrigation may continue. At the same time, with the increasing integration with the world economy, there could be some constraints in the availability of industrial commodities for domestic agriculture. The faster pace of investment and technological change in industrial sector in response to economic liberalisation may improve the profitabilities in industry and lead to a widening of real income gaps between agriculture and nonagriculture. Imbalances in the pace of globalisation of different sectors may set out new trends in intersectoral relations in product market, labour market and of prices. These trends may fall outside the purview of the observed trends and hypotheses. For carrying forward the process of economic reforms in a sustained and smooth manner, it is necessary for the domestic sectors to get increasingly integrated with one another in a global context.

NOTES & REFERENCES

1. Thamarajakshi R : Agriculture – Industry Relationships in India, 1948-49 – 1958-59, Doctoral Thesis submitted to University of Delhi, 1963.

2. Thamarajakshi R: Intersectoral Terms of Trade and Marketed Surplus of Agricultural Produce, 1951-52 – 1965-66, Economic and Political Weekly. Vol IX, No. 26, Review of Agriculture, June 28, 1969.

3. Thamarajakshi R. "Role of Price Incentives in Stimulating Agricultural Production in a Developing Economy" in Ensminger, Doughlas (Ed), Food Enough or Starvation for millions. Tata-McGraw Hill, 1977. Thamarajakshi R. "Interrelation between Agriculture and Industry in India" 68th Conference Volume

of Indian Economic Association, 1985. Thamarajakshi R: "Intersectoral Terms of Trade Revisited" Economic and Political Weekly, March 31, 1990.

4. Also see subsequent work by Bardhan, Kalpana (1969), Venkataramanan LS (1979), Kahlon A. and D.S. Tyagi (1980) and Mundle, Sudipto (1981). The author's 1969 article drew comments from Kahlon and Tyagi in 1980 who had made some adjustments based on suggestions already made by the author in her studies in matters such as coverage and nature of prices to be included. A substantial critique of Kahlon/Tyagi was provided by Vittal, Nalini (1986, 1988). Later, Tyagi (1987) appears to have reversed in some respects his earlier position of 1980. The author has handled the observations of Kahlon/ Tyagi in her 1990 work.

5. This is the same as followed by the author from 1963 onwards. There has been, however, a difference in the method adopted in the thesis (Part II of this book) for estimating the value of intersectoral consumption of products and that in her subsequent writings.

6. Reserve Bank of India, Department of Statistical Analysis and Computer Services, All India Debt and Investment Survey, 1981-82, Statistical Tables Relating to Capital expenditure and capital formation of households during the year ended 30th June, 1982.

7. That the exclusion of capital items does not affect the final trend in the barter terms of trade even in a period where prices of goods going into capital formation had exhibited sharper increases has been corroborated. It has also been recognised elsewhere that "as regards purchases made for capital purposes, there are severe data gaps and therefore it is very difficult to generate precise estimates" Tyagi, DS, (1987).

8. In her thesis, the author had used as such the blown up estimates based on the National Sample Survey (NSS) without combining the same with the consumer expenditure data based on National Accounts Statistics (NAS) of the Central Statistical Organisation (CSO).

9. GOI, Department of Statistics, N.S.S on Pattern of Consumer Expenditure, Different Rounds.

10. G.O.I., C.S.O., N.A.S., Sources and Methods, April 1980, p. 86. The CSO observes, "The basic data on output and prices are mostly the same as those utilised for the preparation of domestic product estimates and as such any shortcomings in these estimates would be inherent in the measurement of private consumption as well. The weakness of the estimates also lies in the fact that the estimate of inputs of agricultural commodities in agriculture and livestock industry and marketable surplus in respect of agricultural produce are based on outdated marketing reports often referring to one point of time only. The disaggregation of group level expenditure on government account to individual items is based on DGS&D data on 'orders placed'. Besides the fact that the coverage of the DGS&D data (particularly for the State Governments) is quite inadequate and incomplete, basic information does not relate to actual transations but the 'order placed'. The data for allocation of partly capital goods to private consumption expenditure and capital formation also need improvement. Trade and transport margins used for making up estimates of value of output at factor cost are based on extensive price data in the case of agricultural items only. For manufactured articles, these margins are calculated for broad industry groups on the basis of wholesale and retail price data for a few representative items only. Data on change in stocks are also not always complete, thus limiting the reliability of the estimates of private final consumption expenditure".

11. GOI, Department of Statistics, C.S.O., N.A.S., Various issues: It may be clarified that the estimates of private consumer expenditure thus derived from national income estimates are not the same as the estimates of private consumer expenditure through product flow method.

12. In the author's thesis, the imports were distributed between different sectors in the same proportion as the sectoral value of consumer expenditure gross of imports. In the subsequent papers of the author, however, it was assumed that imports of agricultural products go entirely to the nonagricultural sector and hence were netted from the gross consumption estimates of these products in that sector only.

13. In the author's thesis, a slightly different method was used. The global method was applied for some crops like tobacco, tea, coffee, rubber, oilseeds, hides and skins; in the case of others, the value of inputs bought by industries from agriculture were noted for the respective industries from Reports of Census of Manufacturing Industries (CMI) (with due corrections: Vide Part II of the Book).

14. Vide Part II of the Book. Also see Thamarajakshi. R. Op cit, 1969, item 18 under notes.

15. G.O.I., C.S.O., Sources and Methods, NAS, 1989, p. 42.

16. In the author's thesis, the base year was 1951-52 and information on consumer expenditure from NSS Fourth Round and on intermediate products from the CSO's Proposals for a Revised Series of National Income Estimates for 1955-56-1959-60 was used. In her 1969 work, the base information for 1951-52 continued for consumer expenditure but for intermediate products used in agricultural sector, information from the then released Brochure of the CSO on Revised Series on National Product, 1961 was used. The information base of 1969 remained in the 1977 work. However, while earlier, the census estimates of population for 1951 and 1961 (preliminary/final) were used, the 1971 census results were used in the 1977 paper. In her 1985 work, the base year for "weights" was (i) the 32nd Round of NSS on consumer expenditure for 1977-78 applied to 1978-79 population and (ii) the relevant statistics from NAS for 1978-79 for intermediate products; the base year remained unchanged in 1990 work. The 1981 census results were used in the 1985 and 1990 paper. It may be also mentioned that whereas for her work upto 1977, the Economic Adviser's (EA) Index Number of wholesale Prices with 1952=100 were used, in her 1985 and 1990 papers, the EA's Index Numbers with 1970-71 = 100 were used for computing the composite prices and terms of trade.

17. Although consumer expenditure data are available for subsequent Rounds of NSS, these are based on a thin sample. The 43rd round being a quinquennial survey has a larger sample size, and hence these data are considered more firm.

18. CSO have released revised series of national income and disaggregated estimates from 1980-81 onwards, and also comparable series from 1951-52, G.O.I., C.S.O.

19. In the NAS, the estimates of value added in small enterprises, construction etc. is based on "income approach" and the accounts of these sectors in terms of gross output, costs and net output are not available for all years.

20. GOI, Planning Commission, Report of the Study group on Parameters on Consumption Sub-Model, March 1991, pp - 9-10. This study is based on a time series of cross-section data for the rounds 24th (1969-70) through 28th (1973-74), 32nd (1977-78) and 38th (1983).

21. This is derived as a ratio of foodgrain prices to the prices of all products purchased by agriculture from nonagriculture.

22. Thamarajakshi Op cit, 1990; the base of the index was 1978-79.

23. Availability of NAS disaggregated input and output data for sectors on revised basis are available only upto 1989-90. As a result, the series of

marketed surplus and income terms of trade could be worked out only upto that year.

24. Thamarajakshi Op cit, 1977.
25. Includes chemical fertilisers, electricity, diesel oil, pesticides and insecticides.
26. GOI, Ministry of Agriculture, Directorate of Economics and Statistics, Agricultural Statistics in India at a glance, May 1992.
27. Ibid. and Thamarajakshi Op cit 1990. Figure for 1989-90 is estimated.
28. GOI, Ministry of Finance, Economic Survey, 1992-93 and Thamarajakshi, Ibid.
29. Gulati, Ashok and Pradeep K. Sharma, "Prices, Procurement and Production: An Analysis of wheat and rice" Economic and Political Weekly, March 31, 1990.
30. Dantwala, M.L. "Incentives and Disincentives in Indian Agriculture". Indian Journal of Agricultural Economics, Vol. 22 No.2 P.19.
31. Jose A.V.: "Agricultural Wages in India", Economic and Political Weekly, Review of Agriculture, June 25, 1988 and his subsequent paper for GOI, National Rural Labour Commission.
32. Thamarajakshi R : "Food Policy and Rural Poverty Alleviation in India" Asia-Pacific Journal of Rural Development, DHAKA, Vol I, July 1991, No.1.

Part-II

Agriculture-Industry Relationships in India 1948-49 — 1958-59

1

Theoretical Scheme of Intersectorial Relations

THE close interdependence of agriculture and industry in any economy, be it underdeveloped, developing or developed, is an axiomatic truth. There are links between the two sectors in every economic field. Agriculture is the main source of food supply, though some amount of processing may be conducted in the industrial sector. Secondly, agriculture supplies raw materials to many of the industries. On the other hand, the agricultural sector provides a market for industrial products. It demands intermediate products like fertilisers and farm machinery produced by the industrial sector and also buys some of the industrial products for final use.

The intersectoral movement of the products produced by this or that sector is itself a function of the rate of growth of the economy. The demand for food, as we shall see presently, is, after a point of time, a declining proportion of increasing incomes. The demand for raw materials produced by the agricultural sector devolves on two variables : (a) the demand for manufactured goods, which is determined by the level of incomes in the community and (b) the input-output ratios in the industries using these raw materials, which in turn depend on the degree of technical progress attained in the economy. Similarly, the capacity of the agricultural sector to buy the consumer and producer goods produced by the industrial sector would depend, in the first instance, on the incomes of the agriculturists and on the proportion of agricultural output marketed to the industrial sector. Whether it is intensive or extensive cultivation, the use of large fixed and working capital (say in the form of fertilisers and farm machinery) per worker or per acre as the case may be, is at the same time the cause and the result of higher efficiency and better economic conditions of the farmers. Much in the same way, the size of the market which the agricultural sector provides for industrial consumer goods depends on the stage of economic growth, which is reflected in the extent of diversity and flexibility of the pattern of consumer demand of the agricultural sector.

Apart from the links in the product market, there is mutual dependence between the two sectors in the factor market as well. Thus intersectoral movements of labour occur. The agricultural sector serves as the "shock-absorber" for the economy when the latter is subject to a downswing. The unemployed industrial labour falls back on land with an apparent feeling of security which is more psychological than real. On the other hand, during times of rapid industrial growth, it is possible, at least in the long run, to recruit labour from the agricultural sector. Again, despite some amount of internal financing in the agricultural sector, much of the capital needed, flows from the industrial sector. The migrated labour in the towns send money to its kith and kin on the land. As against these industrial-agricultural flow of funds, there are the current payments of interest, taxes and other fees by the agricultural sector to the industrial sector. This considerable complementarity between agriculture and industry ought, in itself, to promote the belief that the economic growth of the one is inextricably bound in a definite way, with that of the other.

More specifically, and to give a sharper focus to this proposition, we may consider the role of agriculture in a developing economy and then contrast it with that in an advanced economy. The take-off of an economy is not a phenomenon confined to the industrial sector nor indeed the responsibility of that sector alone. On the contrary, there is evidence to the effect that every important sector of the economy gets closely geared to developmental activity during the take-off period. The economic development of densely populated agrarian economies depends to a great extent on the mopping up of the human and other real surpluses in agriculture for effective investment. Three classical examples exist in economic history where the industrialisation of the country was made to depend, in a major way, on the "fund of real working capital"[1] of the agricultural sector. Thus, what is known as the Scissors' Crisis in Russian economic history was overcome by the setting up of large state farms and the collectivisation of agriculture. As a result, marketable surplus of grain is said to have gone up by about 250% in 1938 compared to 1928. Japan, when faced with a similar situation during the period of her rapid economic development (1887-1914), resorted to heavy land taxes to siphon off agricultural surpluses. Chinese agriculture was organised into cooperative farms, and agricultural tax accounting for about 10% of total revenue was collected in kind.[2] Thus in one way or the other, farm surpluses were generated and were actively utilised in economic development. We are not at present, interested in the methods by which these farm surpluses were effectively used. But the point to be noted is that the strategy of industrialisation has been to increase agricultural productivity, and then ensure that the benefits of increased productivity flow to the other sectors in the form of larger marketed surpluses. This surplus may consist of either direct sales to the industrial sector in the economy or an export surplus for the economy as a whole which may be subsequently used to import the capital base needed for industrialisation.

When we speak of the role of agriculture in the growth of an economy, we refer to the contribution of agriculture to economic activity (howsoever we may define economic activity)[3] and not to the question of whether agriculture can be a leading sector. It has been observed that "The take-off into industrialisation fails to occur in agriculture mainly because the comparative advantage of exploiting productive land and other natural resources delays the time when self-reinforcing industrial growth can profitably get underway."[4] A similar view has been expressed by Schultz; according to him "(1) economic development occurs in a specific locational matrix; there may be one or more such matrices in a particular economy. This means that the process of economic growth does not necessarily occur in the same way, at the same time or at the same rate in different locations. (2) These locational matrices are primarily industrial – urban in composition; as centres in which economic development occurs, they are not mainly cut in rural or farming areas although some farming areas are situated more favourably than are others in relation to such centres. (3) The existing economic organisation works best at or near the centre of a particular matrix of economic development and it also works best in those parts of agriculture which are situated favourably in relation to such a centre; and it works less satisfactorily in those parts of agriculture which are situated in the periphery of such a matrix."[5]

It is implied in the above statements that industrial development is the prime mover in economic growth and that agricultural growth is a dependent, though, an important, variable in the overall pattern of industrial – urban growth. This has been clearly stated by Arthur Lewis.[6] He observes that of the three broad alternative patterns of development involving agriculture, viz. (i) development beginning outside agriculture (ii) development beginning with agricultural exports and (iii) development beginning with greater productivity in food for the home market, the first pattern alone is self-sustaining. The second is not commendable, as it may retard industrial growth in the economy. The third is considered to be self destructive for the following two reasons: Firstly, the demand for food being inelastic, an increase in home production of food, when the other sectors of the economy are stationary, is sure to make the farmers poorer. Secondly, while it is true that the sectors other than agriculture shall benefit from the lowering of agricultural prices, since it would, however, mean selling less to the farmers, the effect might be to increase urban unemployment rather than stimulate industrial production. If development began outside agriculture, it will generate an increase in the demand for agricultural products and thus enable development to spread from sector to sector. However, this depends on an elastic supply of agriculture, which is not quite possible specially in developing economies.

Further it would be difficult to always define agriculture as 'purely agriculture'. Agriculture contains within itself many with dual occupations capable of diversifying and developing the non-farm aspect as the demand for its products expands. In fact, growth of industry can be a process of hiving-off from agriculture the occupations which can form independent crafts, guilds for factories. Thus, industry might as well grow from the fringes of agriculture. It is, therefore, not a question of whether this or that sector is a leading sector. What is noteworthy is that there are complementary contributions and adjustments of different sectors in the course of development. Speaking of the process of development in countries like Great Britain, Sweden, Denmark and the South of United States, Youngson summarises that "...there went on not only the continual reallocations of resources within agriculture and the rise and decline of competing systems of land tenure, but also the shifting of persons into and out of the agricultural sector, to the advantage of both agricultural efficiency and the developments of other sectors in the economy, and so in these cases, agriculture was an integral part of the economy, advancing along with other activities..."[7] Schultz himself makes this point when he says "agriculture can make, as it has in some countries, important contributions to economic development. Agriculture also finds it necessary to make major adjustments as a consequence of economic development. These particular contributions and adjustments do not come easily, quickly or automatically. Whether the contributions are large and whether the adjustments are made satisfactorily is dependent in large measure upon economic development."[8] It would be appropriate to say that for successful development, a rise in agricultural productivity should either precede or accompany industrial development. At the same time, a definite position cannot be taken that development should be launched in this or that sector. It is important to recognise that there are changing, complex and close relationships between agriculture and rest of the economy in the process of development.

Having stated the nature of the part played by the agricultural sector in the development of an economy, it is proposed to state in terms of a series of connected hypotheses, the economic relationships between agriculture and industry in a developing economy as well as in an advanced economy. This would also give an idea as to the direction of change in these relationships, as an economy passes from a state of under-development to development.

Before proceeding further, it seems necessary to clarify certain definitions used in the present work. 1. The economy has been broadly classified into three sectors (i) the agricultural sector consisting of agriculture proper (crop production) and animal husbandry; (ii) the industrial sector comprising of the sub-sectors of fishery, forestry, mining and quarrying, small enterprises and construction and factory establishments; and (iii) rest of the economy consisting of all other subsectors of the economy not included in (i) or (ii) above. In the present work, the economic relationships between agriculture and industry have been studied in detail while the flows between agriculture or industry on the one hand and rest of the economy on the other have been taken into consideration only to a limited extent when the total domestic demand for the products of agriculture or industry has been analysed. The sectors have been defined on the basis of the type of activity or occupation they undertake i.e. on lines similar to those used by the National Income Committee for purposes of computing national income in India. 2. The value of output of a sector is the value of its gross output expressed either at current or constant prices. The money income of a sector is the value of its net output (net of all costs of production and depreciation) at current prices. The real income of a sector refers to the value of its net output at constant prices. With these definitions, the hypotheses regarding the relationships between agriculture and industry in (a) under-developed but developing economies, (b) advanced economies and (c) the transition period when an underdeveloped economy transforms itself into a full-fledged advanced economy may be postulated.

Hypotheses Regarding Intersectoral Relations[9]

Developing Economies

The following hypotheses are evolved to explain the general behaviour of intersectoral flows and relative prices, in thickly populated, developing economies like India.

We may assume that in an underdeveloped economy which begins to develop, investments are undertaken in both the sectors, viz., agriculture and industry and that these investments lead to a primary increase in money incomes. We may then have the following set of hypotheses:

i. In the initial stages of development, the economy may have very low levels of living and some sections of it may be on the margin of subsistence or even starvation. Hence a very large proportion or conceivably even the whole of the increment in incomes may be spent on food. It is true, as the well known Engel's law points out, that as nations become rich, they are likely to spend a smaller and smaller proportion of their additional income on food. But this is only in the long run. As Khusro has argued, "this stage is reached only after the basic requirements of food have been met and the back-logs of hunger, malnutrition and unbalanced diet, which arise out of low incomes, unemployment and underemployment have been substantially liquidated."[10] Until then, the demand for food will keep on rising rapidly in quantitative terms. This would be further accentuated by the substitution of superior foodgrains for inferior ones thus leading to a qualitative shift in the demand for food.

ii. The phenomenon of rapidly rising demand in the face of growing incomes also holds good for non-food crops like oilseeds, cotton, jute, sugarcane, tea and tobacco in so far as the consumption levels of the corresponding manufactured products of edible oils, cloth, sugar etc. are low in a developing country. As a matter of fact, the income elasticity of demand for these products works out quite often to be much higher than that of foodgrains.[11] It is, therefore, possible to generalise that when incomes rise in a developing economy, most or all of the increased incomes are spent on food and other agricultural products so that the income elasticity of demand of the economy for the products supplied by the agricultural sector may be presumed to be at least equal to unity, if not more.

iii. This means that in the early stages of economic development, the contribution of agriculture to economic activity (or welfare) relative to that of industry may be expected to increase, if economic activity (or welfare) is defined as "the flow of goods to ultimate consumers at market prices."[12]

iv. As against this, the supply side of the picture usually presents many rigidities. It should be mentioned here that we are thinking in terms of thickly populated, agrarian economies like India, which are on the threshold of economic development. In such economies, in response to the increase in demand owing to increase in incomes, the supply of agricultural products may rise very slowly or may not rise. This may be due to the use of traditional techniques of cultivation or the adverse land-man ratio or both, not to speak of the natural, structural, institutional and organisational handicaps of agriculture in over-populated, backward economies. The small responsiveness of supply relative to demand would result in increased prices for agricultural products.

v. Even if agricultural supplies do increase, they may not increase at a rate consistent with that of industrial production. When development takes place and demand for manufactured products also increases, industrial production may rise only with a time-lag so that industrial prices too are bound to rise. But if agricultural production in relation to a rapidly rising demand rises at a lesser rate than industrial production in relation to a less intense demand, agricultural prices would rise faster than industrial prices. Thus the ratio of all agricultural prices to all industrial prices would become favourable to the agricultural sector.

vi. The price elasticity of demand for most agricultural products being relatively small, rising agricultural prices do not dampen the demand to a considerable extent.

vii. On the other hand, rising agricultural prices do not have a large effect on the supply side in terms of bringing forth significant increases in output. Though it is difficult to generalise on the backward sloping nature of the agricultural supply or marketed supply curves, the relative inelasticity of these curves (positive or negative) appears much less to be a matter of doubt.[13] We may assume on the basis of a good deal of available evidence[14] that the price-responsiveness of agricultural supply and of marketed surplus is weak, though positive. The curve of marketed surplus is highly inelastic in subsistence economies like India, mainly due to the phenomenon of underdevelopment. The nonmonetised nature of the agrarian sector, the rigid consumption pattern of the agriculturists, the very small number of fixed items of cash expenditures are all at the same time symptoms of a thickly populated, agrarian, backward economy and also the factors which make the curve of marketed surplus inelastic.

viii. While on all these grounds, the ratio of agricultural to industrial prices may become favourable to the agricultural sector for some time, the per capita money income in agriculture, however, would be very much lower than that in industry. This state of affairs may be explained as follows: Output per head in a sector in relation to that in another sector is determined by three factors viz; (a) Number of persons engaged in the activities of the two sectors (b) Output per person in these sectors and (c) the average price of the products in each of the sectors. That such a large proportion of the population (and hence of labour force) in over populated countries is engaged in agriculture so as to depress the average productivity of labour to very low figures and consequently make its marginal productivity near zero, zero or even negative has been stressed by many writers on this subject. In these economies, agricultural output may either not increase at all or increase at a pace slower than industrial production. Since in the very early stages of economic development, the cost structure of either of the sectors may not change to any considerable extent, net output of agriculture too would be increasing at a rate slower than that of industry. While this is so, the proportion of population dependent on agriculture is high and that population is growing at fairly fast pace. Thus net output per person in agriculture in relation that in industry may decline and may even decline at a faster rate than the rate at which agricultural prices are rising; consequently, the per capita money income level, already unfavourable to agriculture, would tend to become more unfavourable relative to the industrial sector.

ix. While the inelasticity of output of agriculture may cause the agricultural prices to rise both absolutely and relatively, the same inelasticity may also depress the per head productivity and hence the per capita money income in agriculture both absolutely and in relation to industry. This inelasticity is partly caused by the perfectly elastic supply of labour i.e. by the excessive pressure on land. It seems that persons engaged in agriculture do not leave agriculture for industry at a rate required for making the average output in agriculture comparable with that in industry. While industrial output may increase at a faster rate than agricultural output, it may, however, not progress at the rate needed for absorbing not only the backlog of unemployed and the new hands thrown up by the natural growth of population in that sector but also the surplus labour on land. Or alternatively it may be stated that economic organisation of agricultural production is not yet developed so well as to effectively use the surplus hands in agriculture for improving agricultural production i.e. for shifting upwards the supply curve of agriculture, say, by increasing capital construction works within agriculture or by developing irrigation projects etc.

An altogether different set of hypotheses seem to define the relationships in an advanced economy.

Advanced Economies

i. Though incomes are high, the income elasticity of demand for food in particular, and for all agricultural products in general, is generally less than unity. This is because of the physiological and psychological phenomenon that "as its income rises, the family's expenditure on food represents a diminishing proportion of its total outgo."[15] Beyond a minimum, rising income is devoted increasingly to the satisfaction of wants associated with the desire for comfort and distinction which however seems to have no "certain boundary."[16] Though the income elasticity of demand for manufactures exceeds unity and hence the income elasticity of the derived demand for raw materials might also be greater than unity, this may not very much influence the income elasticity of demand for all agricultural products because of a continuous tendency towards economy in the use of raw materials in these countries. A given volume of output is produced with an ever-decreasing quantum of raw materials and more and more substitutes for raw materials are being developed in the form of synthetic products. It may be deduced from this that the demand for all agricultural products, including raw materials, grows only slowly, if at all, relatively to rising income levels.

ii. Hence, the relative contribution of agriculture to economic activity (or welfare) shrinks continuously.

iii. As against this relatively stagnant demand, agricultural output, however, rises thereby depressing the agricultural prices.

iv. Agricultural output in relation to an almost stagnant or very slowly rising demand rises at a faster rate than does industrial production in relation to a more rapidly rising demand. Hence agricultural prices in advanced economies seem to have an inexorable tendency to fall relative to industrial prices; that is to say, the ratio of agricultural prices to industrial prices tends to turn unfavourable to the agricultural sector.

v. The price elasticity of demand for agricultural products being less than unity, the lower agricultural prices may not boost demand to any considerable extent.

vi. Nor do low agricultural prices bring about a contraction of supply. It has frequently happened that low agricultural prices have only stimulated greater efforts on the part of farmers with a view to compensate lower valuation by increasing the volume of output to be valued. The difficulty involved in realising capital invested in farming, the high proportion of fixed costs to total costs and the postponement of voluntary liquidation through persistence of the conviction that fortunes will change, also make agricultural supplies inflexible during times of falling prices.[17]

vii. Further, relative money income per head in agriculture tends to be lower than that in industry. We said that in advanced economies, agricultural output may rise faster than industrial output. Since the very basis of this rise is increase in productive efficiency, net output in agriculture would also rise faster than that in industry. But the population dependent on agriculture does not perhaps contract at a rate consistent with the rate of increase in net output in agriculture. Real income per head in agriculture relative to industry would therefore not rise faster than the fall in agricultural prices relative to industrial prices. Though technological advance and the greater use of capital per man or per acre might have helped to shift upwards the output curve in agriculture, the fast depression in agricultural prices keeps the money income per head in agriculture at levels lower than that in industry.

We may now summarise the theoretical issues in the developing and the developed countries. The problem for the underdeveloped economies seems to be one of non-response of marketed supply, not to speak of supply itself, of agricultural produce in relation to an increasing demand. In advanced countries, the issue appears to be one of excess of agricultural output over a relatively stagnant demand. As a result, absolute agricultural prices may be rising in the first case and falling in the second.

Secondly, in developing economies, agricultural output in relation to an increasing demand may not rise at all, or rise at a slower rate than industrial output in relation to a lesser increase in demand. Hence agricultural prices may generally rise faster than industrial prices and the ratio of the former to the latter would become favourable to the agricultural sector. On the other hand, in developed countries, agricultural output in the face of a relatively steady demand, may rise faster than industrial production in relation to a more intense demand. In these economies, one expects agricultural prices to be depressed compared to industrial prices and the ratio of the former to the latter to be generally unfavourable to the agricultural sector.[18]

Thirdly, despite favourable agricultural prices vis-a-vis industrial prices in developing economies, the ratio of money income per head in agriculture to that in industry may be less than unity. The almost stagnant or relatively slowly rising agricultural output has to be distributed among a relatively large proportion of population dependent on land. Consequently, productivity per head in agriculture compared to industry falls and may quite plausibly, under certain circumstances, fall faster than the rate at which agricultural prices may rise relative to industrial prices. In advanced economies, not only the ratio of agricultural to industrial prices may tend to be unfavourable to the agricultural sector, but also the relative money income per head in agriculture may be depressed. For, as already explained, the numbers dependent on agriculture may not be leaving agriculture at a fast enough rate. In that case, the rate at which per head productivity in agriculture rises in relation to industry would be slower than that at which agricultural prices fall relative to industrial prices.

Though in the case of both the developing and the advanced economies, the ratio of money income per head in agriculture to that in industry is low[19], the absolute income per head in agriculture in the advanced economies may actually rise due to rising agricultural productivity. This has been very well expressed by Ojala "The agriculturists in the advanced countries have gained infinitely more in real standards of economic welfare by raising productivity and thus increasing the productive labour force in industry and provision of services than they could possibly have gained by combining to secure high agricultural prices under conditions of static agricultural productivity. The relative income position of agriculturists has deteriorated on the whole, but their absolute income position has improved immensely, thanks to rising agricultural productivity."[20] In the developing economies, not only the relative money income per head in agriculture is low, but the absolute money income per head is also very low. And during the early years of development, if the absolute money income per head in agriculture rises, it is not due to any significant rise in agricultural productivity, but largely due to the rising agricultural prices.

The Transition

With these differences between developing and developed economies thus stated (though imperfectly and at a level of broad generalisations), it seems pertinent to raise the question : What changes may be expected to occur in the long run, when an underdeveloped economy transforms itself into a full-fledged advanced economy? It is possible to state the following :

i. The relative contribution of agriculture to economic activity (or welfare) may increase for some time due to backlogs of unsatisfied demand for food etc. (until the basic requirements of food are substantially covered) and then start declining (with the working of Engel's law).

ii. Agricultural output in relation to demand may not rise at all in the beginning (due to inelasticity of supply) and then rise slowly and finally rise even faster than demand (owing to technological change and inflexibility of agricultural supply in the direction of contraction).

iii. Agricultural output in relation industrial production may not rise at all in the early stages, then rise at a slower rate and finally may even outstrip the rate of rise of industrial output.

iv. The ratio of agricultural to industrial prices may be expected at first to move in favour of the agricultural sector; but as development proceeds, it would become unfavourable.

v. The proportion of population dependent on agriculture is generally large in the initial stages of development. It would start declining, as development gets on its way.

vi. At the threshold of development, the absolute money income per head in agriculture is very low. As economic development proceeds, however, it begins to rise, first owing to increases in agricultural prices and then due to rise in agricultural productivity.

vii. Relative income (both money income and real income) per head in agriculture is always less than unity, whether a country is developed or not. But as development takes place, the ratio may tend to become less unfavourable to the agricultural sector than earlier and closer to unity.

We have seen how the general trend of relationships between agriculture and industry may be expected to behave in the long run as a country develops and transforms itself into an advanced economy.[21]

OBJECTIVES OF THE PRESENT STUDY

Our purpose in the present work shall be to examine for India in the context of her developmental efforts, the relationships between the two major sectors of her economy viz. agriculture and industry, for the decade 1948-49 -- 1958-59. Since India is still in the very early stages of economic growth and since her experience of planned economic development is only slightly longer than a decade, our endeavour will be to see if the set of hypotheses stated here which purport to define the relationships between the two sectors in a developing economy during the initial period of development, holds true for

India and if there are indications of some alternative hypotheses.

To be able to do this, we should know for the entire period of our study, the following in quantitative terms for the two sectors, agriculture and industry. (i) Value (at constant prices) of investments (ii) Value (at current and at constant prices) of gross and net outputs (iii) (a) Value (at current and at constant prices) of intermediate products produced by agriculture/industry and demanded by industry/agriculture.[22] (b) Value (at current and at constant prices) of final products produced by agriculture/industry and demanded by industry/agriculture. (iv) (a) The ratios of value (at constant prices) of intermediate products produced by agriculture/industry and used by industry/agriculture to the value (at constant prices) of gross output of industry/agriculture. (b) Income elasticity of demand of each sector for the final products produced by either of the two sectors. (v) Composite price indices of (a) agricultural products, (b) industrial products, (c) intermediate products produced by agriculture/industry and used by industry/agriculture, (d) final products produced by agriculture/industry and used by industry/agriculture and (e) all products (intermediate and final) produced by agriculture/industry and used by industry/agriculture. (vi) Quantum of labour demanded by industry to examine if there was any net movement of labour from agriculture to industry. The time-series of estimates of the aforementioned variables have been estimated and analysed in this work.

The main sources of data for the work are only secondary and will be specified in the following pages at appropriate places. Primary data derived from field work by a single individual (working within fairly rigid time limits) could not be expected to overcome the basic difficulties of obtaining representative and unbiased estimates. Nevertheless, we have had the advantage of commencing this work at the end of nearly a whole decade of planned development. The upsurge of statistical and other information about the Indian economy, though often rudimentary, made the plea of non-availability of statistics unreal and prompted a desire to estimate and study intersectoral flows and relationships.

The present work thus represents, however partially and imperfectly, the fulfilment of a desire to quantify and study the behaviour of some basic variables and their inter-relationships "without which we can hardly rise above the statement that everything affects anything else."

NOTES & REFERENCES

1. Dobb, Maurice; Soviet Economic Development since 1917 (1957) p. 24.
2. Bansil, P.C.: "Problems of Marketable Surplus in Indian Agriculture" *Indian Journal of Agricultural Economics,* January-March, 1961, Conference Number, p. 31.
3. Different definitions of economic activity (or welfare) have been dealt with by Professor E.M. Ojala in his book *Agriculture and Economic Progress* (1952) Ch. II, p.6.
4. Rostow, W.W.: "The take-off into self-sustained growth", *Economic Journal,* March, 1956, Vol. IXVI, p. 28.
5. Schultz, T.W. *Economic Organisation of Agriculture* (1953), p. 147.
6. Lewis, W. Arthur: "The shifting fortunes of agriculture; the general setting", Tenth International Conference of Agricultural Economists, Mysore-India, 25-8-1958, pp. 1-4.
7. Youngson A.J.: Possibilities of Economic Progress (1959), p. 231.
8. Schultz T.W. op. cit., p (vii).
9. The term "intersectoral" is used in this work in a restricted sense to mean the relationship between agriculture and industry.
10. Khusro, A.M. "General and Sectoral Price Instability" Occasional paper, Institute of Economic Growth, Delhi, p.15.
11. National Council of Applied Economic Research "Long term projections of demand for and supply of selected agricultural commodities 1960-61 to 1975-76," Table 19, p.85.
12. Ojala, E.M., *op.cit.* p.9.
13. See Khusro, A.M. "General and Sectoral Price Instability", pp. 22-23. He shows how empirical evidence for India supports the hypothesis of forward sloping agricultural supply and also marketed surplus curves. He concludes "... that the backward sloping nature of the supply curve of agricultural output as a whole is not an established fact, and that the existing evidence leans more heavily towards the forward sloping curve... The price elasticity of supply, all things considered, seems to be small but positive." Similarly, he maintains that on the aggregate, the marketed supply curve is quite inelastic although perhaps positive.

14. John, P.V.: 'Some Aspects of the Structure of Indian Agricultural Economy 1947-48 -- 1957-58' Ph.D. thesis, Delhi University, (unpublished).
Dharm Narain: "Impact of price movements on areas under crops in India – Cotton – A case study" *Indian Economic Review, August,* 1960.
Raj Krishna : "Farm Supply Response in the Punjab (India-Pakistan) A Case Study of Cotton" Ph.D. Thesis, Chicago University (unpublished).
Khusro, A.M.: *Op. cit.*

15. Ojala, E.M.: *op.cit.* p.6.
This law relating income and food consumption was first enunciated by Ernst Engel. On the basis of a study of expenditures of a group of German families, he found a relationship between income and certain classes of expenditures, which he stated as follows: "The poorer a family is, the greater is the proportion of the total outgo which must be used for food".

16. Smith, Adam Wealth of Nations Book I Ch. XI Part II: Quoted by Ojala, E.M., *op.cit.* pp. 6-7.

17. To the question "why in the face of falling farm prices and declining gross incomes do farmers persist in adopting new techniques and thus expand output?" W. Cochrane replied that the answer has to be found in the market organisation of agriculture i.e. in the perfectly competitive nature of agricultural market. The farmer is just a price-taker. When new technology is adopted, total output is increased; this lowers the gross returns. Thus the average farmer is on a tread mill with respect to technological advance. In the quest for increased returns or the minimisation of losses, which the average farmer hopes to achieve through the adoption of some new technology, he runs faster and faster on the tread mill. But by running faster, he does not reach the goal of increased returns -- the tread mill simply turns over faster and as the tread mill speeds up -- it grinds out more and more farm products for consumers (Cochrane, W. *Farm prices: Myth and Reality,* pp. 94-96).

18. What we are sketching here is a brief, generalised model. However, it may actually happen that even in the advanced economies, agricultural output though increasing at a fast rate, is not rising faster than industrial output. This has been Ojala's finding from his study of the countries U.K., U.S.A., and Sweden during their long period of economic progress. He notes that "the actual movement in the purchasing power of agricultural products under conditions of economic progress will result from the interaction of demand with the complex of forces affecting supply, a major factor being the relative rise of productivity in agriculture and in other production; and the extent to which the benefits of rising productivity are passed on to consumers" (Ojala, E.M. *Op.cit.* p. 161).

19. Though the ratio is low in both the developing and the advanced economies, it is lower in the former than in the latter. As a matter of fact, Prof. J.R. Bellerby in his study on *"Agriculture and Industry -- Relative Income"* 1951, has ranked the countries he has studied according to the estimated ratio, for the year 1938. It is found from this ranking (Table 61, p.260, *op.cit.*) that there are wide variations as between countries, when they are compared on the basis of this ratio.

20. Ojala, E.M.: *Op.cit.* pp.167-168.

21. Apart from these long run phenomena, there may be short period movements in the ratio of agricultural to industrial prices. These may be in the nature of cycles around the long-run curve of relative prices and may be the result of seasonal, cyclical and random fluctuations in agricultural supplies.

22. The value (at current and at constant prices, of products (intermediate and final) produced by agriculture/industry and demanded by the rest of the

economy (i.e. other than agriculture and industry) has been computed only partially.

23. Fox, Karl, A: "The Study of Interactions between agriculture and the non-farm economy, Local, Regional and National", *Journal of Farm Economics,* Vol. XLIV, February, 1962, No.1, p.1).

2

Sectoral Outputs and Investments

THIS chapter estimates for the period 1948-49 — 1958-59 the time-series of value, at current and at constant prices of (i) gross and net outputs of agriculture and industry and (ii) net investment in agriculture and non-agriculture and analyses the growth of these variables, both independently and in relation to one another.

Estimates

Gross and Net Output of Agriculture and Industry

It may be expected that the official estimates of net national income at factor cost as published by the Central Statistical Organisation (CSO) Government of India, based on the methods adopted by the National Committee in their First (1951) and Final (1954) Reports on National Income[1] would provide a convenient starting point for our purpose. However, "since 1954 the basic data used by the National Income Committee have become outdated and they hardly provide an adequate basis for preparing the level estimates not to speak of their providing indicators for sensitive changes in the aggregate national income or its components. The use of the decennial rate of growth in the working force based on the 1941 (2% sample) and 1951 census economic data for the post 1951-period serves as an illustration, particularly in the context of economic planning in India in which purposive efforts are being made to effect structural changes in the economy."[2]

The aforesaid position puts a student of intersectoral relations in the country in a dilemma as to the choice of the data on national income. The weaknesses of the official income statistics are of course statistical rather than methodological.[3] However, if it is true that the official estimates leave much to be desired in providing "a firm, empirical basis for measuring sensitively sectorwise growth of national income"[4], then it is important to improve these estimates, in order that the intersectoral flows and relations may be measured and interpreted accurately and in a dependable manner.

In fact, the CSO has realised the need for this improvement and has published a Revised Series of National Income Estimates on the basis of wider and more recent data.[5] However, these revised and improved estimates are available only for the period 1955-56 to 1959-60. While this forms a good basis for our study, we are still left with the task of computing, on a comparable basis, estimates of gross value, costs and net value of output of each of the sectors for each of the years 1948-49 to 1954-55 (both years inclusive).

Further, the CSO adopts the "product method" in estimating the incomes of the sectors agriculture, forestry, fishery and mining. With respect to the sectors small enterprises and construction, however, the "income method" has been used. As regards the factory establishments, the estimates (with a few adjustments), from the Annual Reports of the Sample Survey of Manufacturing industries, have been used. The above methodology holds true for both the Official estimates and the Revised estimates. Now, we are interested in the estimates of gross value of output, costs and net value of output of each sector. From the aforementioned, it is obvious that such an analysis of the components of the value of the gross output, even on the basis of the Revised estimates, is possible only for the sectors agriculture, forestry, fishery and mining. In the case of small enterprises and construction, we have been able to derive the ratio of gross to net output of this sector from other sources of information[6] and this ratio has been applied to the 'Revised Estimates' of income from this sector, in order to estimate the value of gross output. But the factory establishments subsector forms a big chunk of the industrial sector and includes the industries which buy raw materials from agriculture in substantial quantities. It, therefore, becomes necessary to have a detailed analysis of the costs of inputs of this subsector.

Thus, while for agriculture and for all subsectors of industry excepting factory establishments, the value of gross output and costs (and therefore the value of net output) for the years 1948-49 to 1954-55 have been estimated by projecting backwards the respective 'Revised estimates' for 1955-56, an entirely original estimation of the relevant magnitudes for factory establishments has been resorted to by us. It is intended here to outline only broadly the methods of estimation in the case of agriculture and all sub-sectors of industry other than factory establishments, relegating to the Appendix,[7] the details of projection. The methods of computation adopted by us for the factory establishments would, however, be detailed in the current chapter itself.

METHOD OF ESTIMATION

Agriculture

The method of estimation of the gross value of output of agricultural sector (i.e. agriculture proper and ancillary activities) for the years 1948-49 to 1954-55 has been generally to project backwards, the 'Revised estimates'[8] of physical production of each crop for 1955-56 with the help of a suitable and comparable annual index of production[9] of that crop and then superimpose upon it the price factor. This factor has been arrived at by extrapolating backwards the 1955-56 price of each crop implied[10] in the 'Revised estimates,' with the Economic Adviser's Revised Series of Index Numbers of wholesale prices.[11]

From this value, necessary adjustments have been made for (i) the difference between the market value and the actual value at which foodgrains have been procured by the Government[12] and (ii) the value added by organised rice-milling industry.[13] Further, deductions have to be made on account of the following items of costs, in order to estimate the value of net output of this sector : (i) seed, (ii) manure, consisting of (a) chemical fertilisers and (b) organic manure, (iii) current repairs and maintenance of implements and various operational costs, (iv) irrigation charges (payable to government), (v) cost of feed of livestock required on farm, (vi) market charges and (vii) depreciation of implements and other fixed assets (e.g. farm buildings, wells, tanks etc.). Of these inputs, data on the cost of chemical fertilisers and irrigation charges are available in government and other publications.[14] With regard to the rest of the items, we have again made the "Revised estimates" for 1955-56 as the base and projected the same for earlier years with suitable indicators.

The estimates of the value of net output thus computed have been subjected to an upward adjustment of 2%[15] to allow for the coverage of non-reporting areas. This 2% inflation in the value of net output has subsequently been effected with respect to each of the cost items also (excepting the cost of chemical fertilisers and irrigation charges); the implicit assumption being that the value of these cost items has been affected in the same proportion as the value of net output.

Animal Husbandry

Here again, the year 1955-56 has been taken as the bench-mark year. Firstly, the 1945, 1951 and 1956 All India Livestock Censuses[16] have been made use of to linearly interpolate the numbers of each category of the livestock and poultry population. The values of the various livestock products for 1948-49 to 1954-55 have been estimated by correcting the "Revised estimate" of the respective livestock product in 1955-56 for changes in the numbers of animals relevant for the category of livestock product and also for changes in prices. For the years 1955-56 to 1958-59, the "Revised estimates" have been taken as such. The value of net output has been computed for 1948-49 to 1954-55, by deducting from the estimated gross value, the cost of upkeep of non-service animals and materials and depreciation. These costs have been evaluated on comparable terms with the "Revised estimates" for the subsequent years. Table 2.1 presents the estimates at current prices of gross output, costs and net output of agriculture and animal husbandry.

Industry

Forestry

Data on physical production of this sub-sector for earlier years have been taken from the Indian Forest Statistics[17], with certain adjustments for unrecorded production, and also for minor forest produce. The estimates of physical production have been valued at prices which were derived by moving the 1955-56 implicit price in the "Revised estimates" with the Index Number of prices of logs and timber. As in the "Proposals", we have assumed that 5% of the value of gross output of this sub-sector constitutes its costs.

Fishery

In the "Proposals", estimates of production of fish in India[18] are given for 1948-49 to 58-59. We have adopted these estimates of production for the years 1948-49 to 1954-55 and evaluated them at the respective prices estimated by projecting the 1955-56 implicit price of the relevant category of fish with the index numbers of wholesale prices of fish. Further, 5% of the value of gross output of commercial fishing and 1% of the value of subsistence fishing have been assumed to form the costs of this sub-sector.[19]

Mining and Quarrying

The difference between the "Revised estimates" and the official estimates of income from this sector lies in the netting proportion adopted. Instead of a 5% deduction for mining expenses and nearly another 5% deduc-

TABLE - 2.1

Gross Output, Costs and Net Output of Agriculture

1948-49 - 1958-59 (at Current Prices - In Rs. Crores)

ITEMS (1)	1948-49 (2)	1949-50 (3)	1950-51 (4)	1951-52 (5)	1952-53 (6)	1953-54 (7)	1954-55 (8)	1955-56 (9)	1956-57 (10)	1957-58 (11)	1958-59 (12)
Agriculture											
1. Gross Output	4280	4410	4716	5065	4811	5379	4532	4278	5459	5097	6185
2. (a) Seed	232	240	256	275	261	293	246	232	289	280	320
(b) Market Charges	16	17	18	19	19	21	17	16	20	19	24
(c) Depreciation	127	127	125	125	128	132	133	136	138	136	143
(d) Organic Manure	141	142	139	139	142	147	148	151	154	150	154
(e) Current Repairs	56	59	52	52	55	57	58	60	61	61	64
(f) Chemical Fertiliser	8	11	17	8	13	16	20	20	22	30	37
(g) Irrigation Charge	13	15	16	18	17	20	19	18	20	20	23
(h) Cost of Feed of Livestock Required on Farms	220	204	170	224	237	213	161	172	206	200	223
3. Net Output	3467	3595	3923	4205	3940	4481	3730	3473	4549	4201	5196
Animal Husbandry											
4. Gross Output	1071.7	1110.4	1146.5	1135.4	1099.4	1108.2	1064.1	1066.1	1104.7	1143.7	1174.7
5. Net Output	755.8	816.6	900.4	816.2	762.8	806.1	832.5	813.2	803.0	852.3	846.5

tion for coal consumed in collieries made in the official estimates, the "Revised estimates" make a 17% allowance for mining expenses. Assuming that the avarage ratio of the revised estimates of gross value of output to the official estimates for 1955-56 to 1958-59 holds good for the earlier years of the study, estimates of gross output on comparable terms with the revised estimates have been worked out. Subsequently, the 17% deduction for costs has been made. Further, depreciation has been allowed at the rate of 5% for coal mines and 3% for non-coal mines.

Small Enterprises

The method adopted for deriving the 'Revised estimates" of income from this sector is broadly to build up estimates of the total value added for a bench mark year, viz. 1955-56 for each of 7 industrial groups: (i) Textiles and Tailoring (ii) Leather and leather products (iii) Wood, glass, stone and ceramics (iv) Metal manufacturing and engineering, (v) Chemicals (vi) Food, drink and tobacco industries, and (vii) Other industries. This bench mark estimate of total value added has been projected for later years on the basis of physical production of relevant commodities[20] and adjusted for changes in prices. A similar procedure has been adopted in extrapolating the 'Revised estimates' for 1955-56 to earlier years. The gross value of output has been derived by applying the available information[21] on the average ratio of net value to gross value to the net income estimates of the respective group of industries.

Construction

The 'Revised estimates' of net income from this subsector have been prepared in the "Proposals" by correcting the bench-mark estimate (1955-56) for changes in the average value added per person and in the number of persons engaged in this activity. We have followed the same procedure for estimating the net income for earlier years. Further, assuming that the rates of net value added to gross value of output in the case of "all other industries"[22] in the small enterprises subsector holds good for the "construction" subsector too, the estimates of gross value of output of "construction" have been obtained.

The estimates of gross and net outputs at current prices of forestry, fishery, mining and quarrying, small enterprices and construction subsectors are given in Table 2.2.

Factory Establishments

The relevant estimates for factory establishments for the period of study have been computed by us from basic data as detailed below.

There are two annual surveys of factory establisments in India : the Census of manufacturing Industries (CMI) and the Sample Survey of Manufacturing Industries (SSMI)[23]. The SSMI has a wider coverage; it covers all the 63 industries into which the factory establishments subsector falls and covers industries employing 20 or more workers and using power as also industries employing 20 or more workers and not using power. It does not however furnish detailed information on inputs used by various industries, which is our requirement for the study. Even value added of industries is available only for some years.[24] The CMI covers only the first 29 of the 63 industries (the rest of the 63 industries not covered by the CMI shall be referred to by us as "30-63" industries). It covers only industries employing 20 or more workers and using power. Its geographical coverage has not been uniform. There is also the problem of non-response. However, it furnishes information on gross output, value as well as quantity of inputs, depreciation and value added for each industry. It is such a detailed data on costs of atleast those industries which buy basic materials from agriculture that we are interested in. Almost all the industries which have input relations with agriculture are covered by the census.

Table 2.3 gives the names of industries that buy inputs from agriculture, the inputs bought as also their census industry classification number. Of the 17 indus-

TABLE - 2.2

Gross Output and Net Output of Forestry, Fishing, Mining & Quarrying, Small Enterprises and Construction

1948-49 - 1958-59 (At Current Prices - In Rs. Crores)

ITEMS (1)	1948-49 (2)	1949-50 (3)	1950-51 (4)	1951-52 (5)	1952-53 (6)	1953-54 (7)	1954-55 (8)	1955-56 (9)	1956-57 (10)	1957-58 (11)	1958-59 (12)
Forestry											
1. Gross Output	120.0	114.8	128.3	133.5	112.3	112.6	133.8	140.9	152.8	167.5	176.8
2. Net Output	114.0	109.1	121.9	126.9	106.7	107.0	127.2	133.8	145.2	159.1	167.9
Fishery											
3. Gross Output	43.5	46.8	49.8	50.8	53.2	48.2	51.9	55.7	63.8	73.1	73.0
4. Net Output	41.8	44.9	47.8	48.6	51.0	46.3	49.8	53.4	61.1	70.1	70.0
Mining & Quarrying											
5. Gross Output	57.9	57.9	67.8	87.5	87.4	97.4	87.4	98.5	115.0	135.3	141.9
6. Net Output	45.4	45.4	53.4	69.0	68.8	76.9	68.8	77.7	90.7	106.6	111.7
Small Enterprises											
7. Gross Output	1204.0	1185.0	1164.0	1134.0	1083.0	1184.0	1175.0	1175.0	1298.0	1312.0	1405.0
8. Net Output	631.0	616.0	609.0	603.0	581.0	633.0	629.0	635.0	697.0	707.0	757.0
Construction											
9. Gross Output	255.7	280.8	258.7	269.0	291.2	317.8	348.8	397.6	413.8	483.3	530.6
10. Net Output	173.0	190.0	175.0	182.0	197.0	215.0	236.0	269.0	280.0	327.0	359.0

TABLE - 2.3

Industries which Buy Inputs from Agriculture

Name of the Industry	*CMI Classn.*	*Inputs bought from Agriculture*
1. Wheat Flour	1	Wheat, Rice, Barley, Gram, Maize, Bajra, Other grains.
2. Rice Milling	2	Paddy, Half milled rice, Underpolished rice, Dhals, Oilseeds, Other grains.
3. Biscuit making	3	Milk, Butter and Margarine, and eggs.
4. Fruits & Vegetables	4	Fruits; Vegetables.
5. Sugar	5	Sugarcane.
6. Distilleries & Breweries	6	Barley, Hops and Mahua.
7. Starch	7	Maize, Wheat; and other grains.
8. Vegetable oils including edible oils	8A & 8B	All oilseeds and grains.
9. Tanning	11	Hides and skins.
10. Paper and Paper Board	16	Grass, Begasse and Straw.
11. Cotton	18	Raw Cotton.
12. Wool	19	Raw wool (including scoured wool & wool hops).
13. Jute	20	Raw Jute.
14. Tobacco		Raw Tabacco.
15. Tea		Tea.
16. Coffee		Coffee.
17. Rubber		Rubber (crude).

tries purchasing intermediate products from agriculture, the first 13 are covered by the Census. As for tobacco, tea, coffee and rubber, it may be assumed that their entire production less exports constitutes the purchases by the domestic industrial sector. Thus it appears that for these 13 industries, the CMI should suit our requirement after due corrections for geographical, industrial and size coverage. However, a comparison (after correction) of CMI estimates of value added for each of these 13 industries with the respective SSMI estimates available for some years showed that the CMI estimates were understimates for five industries viz. Rice-Milling, Biscuit making, Distilleries and Breweries, Vegetable oils and Tanning. It was therefore decided not to use the CMI data for these industries. Of these five industries, the estimates of value added according to SSMI are available[25] for rice-milling industry for all the years from 1948-49 to 1958-59 except for 1954-55. For 1954-55, the CMI estimate of value added has been adjusted with the ratio of number of workers in the industry according to SSMI to that according to CMI. With regard to the remaining four industries, estimates of value added for selected years are avilable in SSMI Reports[26]. For the other years, corresponding estimates have been derived by relating to the growth of value added according to CMI. For these industries, the estimates of gross output and depreciation have been worked out by applying the respective ratios to value added from the CMI data. For the other eight industries (using inputs from agriculture) and for the rest of the industries covered by the CMI, we shall use the value added estimates according to the CMI. For all other industries not covered by the CMI viz. '30-63' industries and the non power using industries, use will be made of the SSMI data.[27] The estimates of gross output and value added of the aforesaid 8 industries have been adjusted for geographical and size coverage at the all-industry rate and for industrial coverage in the respective industry. The estimates of the remaining sixteen industries for which CMI data are used, have been similarly adjusted for geographical, industrial and size coverages[28]. Allowance has been for minor operational costs (i.e. printing, advertisement, postage etc.) at half of one percent of the value added in the years where CMI data were used and upto 1954 where SSMI data were used[29], and also for bank charges and insurance premia on the basis of available information.[30]

Estimates of gross output and value added at current prices of factory establishments derived on the above lines are given in Table 2.4.

Gross and Net Outputs of Agriculture and Industry (at current prices)

As already mentioned, agriculture in this study includes agriculture and animal husbandry while Industry covers factory establishments, forestry, fishery, mining and quarrying, small enterprises and construction. Estimates at current prices of gross and net outputs of agriculture and industry are presented in Table 2.5. The table also presents estimates at current prices of (i) percentage of agricultural net output to the total net outputs of agriculture and industry (ii) per head money income in agriculture and (iii) per head money income in industry. For purpose of (ii) and (iii), we have used the estimates of population in agriculture and industry, which are calculated in chapter 3 of this work.

Gross and Net Outputs of Agriculture and Industry (at constant prices)

For a study of trends and movements, estimates at constant prices are required. "The importance of real output series which seeks to present estimates of net output at constant prices lies in the fact that it isolates the year to year change in the net volume of production of the country from the price fluctuations and thus helps to assess the economic growth over a period of time. In other words, it serves to measure the real levels of the country's economic performance and to indicate the rate of growth undisturbed by any change in prices."[31] For deriving the estimates at constant (51-52) prices[32], the double deflation method has been adopted to some

TABLE - 2.4

Gross Output and Net Value Added : Factory Establishments

1948-49 - 1958-59 (At Current Prices - In Rs. Crores)

ITEMS (1)	1948-49 (2)	1949-50 (3)	1950-51 (4)	1951-52 (5)	1952-53 (6)	1953-54 (7)	1954-55 (8)	1955-56 (9)	1956-57 (10)	1957-58 (11)	1958-59 (12)
Gross Output	1595.7	1633.6	1820.9	2526.5	2136.7	2174.1	2303.6	2484.2	2896.4	3222.9	3402.4
Net Value	530.8	482.0	508.7	559.8	562.6	619.0	631.0	691.7	780.9	842.0	913.7

extent. Current values of both outputs and inputs have been adjusted for changes in prices. In this connection, use has been made of some results given in Chapter 4. In that Chapter, we have worked out for agriculture and industry the time series of values at current prices of (i) inputs purchased from the other sector and (ii) inputs produced and retained by either of them or purchased from the rest of the economy. In both cases, the imports of respective category of inputs have been separately estimated. In chapter IV has also been worked out the composite price indices of all products produced by agriculture/industry and used as inputs by industry/agriculture. Thus the gross value of agricultural output in current prices has been first deflated with the index of prices of agricultural[33] products to derive the series at constant prices. Then the following cost deductions at constant prices have been made:

i. The first deduction is in respect of the value of inputs bought by agriculture from industry (domestic as well as the foreign industrial sector). (chapter 4) We have used the index of prices of inputs bought by agriculture from industry to deflate the value in current prices of not only the inputs bought by agriculture from the domestic industrial sector but also those imported from foreign countries. An import price index would

TABLE - 2.5

Gross Output and Net Outputs : Agriculture and Industry

Some Simple Relationships : 1948-49 - 1958-59 (At Current Prices - In Rs. Crores)

ITEMS (1)	1948-49 (2)	1949-50 (3)	1950-51 (4)	1951-52 (5)	1952-53 (6)	1953-54 (7)	1954-55 (8)	1955-56 (9)	1956-57 (10)	1957-58 (11)	1958-59 (12)
1. Gross Output											
a. Agriculture	5352	5520	5863	6200	5910	6487	5596	5344	6564	6241	7360
b. Industry	3277	3319	3489	4201	3763	3934	4101	4352	4940	5394	5730
2. Net Output											
a. Agriculture	4223	4412	4823	5021	4703	5287	4563	4286	5352	5053	6044
b. Industry	1536	1487	1516	1589	1567	1697	1742	1861	2055	2212	2379
3. Percentage of Agricultural Net Output to Total Net Outputs of Agriculture and Industry	73.3	74.8	76.1	75.9	75.0	75.7	72.4	69.7	72.3	69.6	71.8
4. Per Head Money Income in Agriculture per Year (in Rs.)	175.6	180.3	193.3	197.5	180.9	199.6	169.2	156.0	191.3	177.3	208.2
5. Per Head Money Income in Industry per Year (in Rs.)	432.7	410.9	409.7	421.6	407.0	431.9	435.4	454.9	492.8	520.4	548.2

have been a more precise deflator in the case of the imported inputs. An index of import prices is available but this is quite different from index of prices of imports used in agriculture, which is not available. Hence, we have assumed that import prices and domestic prices have moved closely with each other.

ii. The second deduction is of the value of inputs which might have been produced and retained by agriculture itself or which might have been bought from the rest of the economy:(chapter 4) Due to paucity of information, we have used the general agricultural price index to deflate the series to constant prices.[34]

Netting the gross value (at constant prices) of agricultural output for (i) and (ii) above, the value of net output of agriculture at constant (51-52) prices has been estimated. A similar procedure has been followed for deriving the estimates of gross and net outputs in industry, at constant prices. Results are given in Table 2.6. In this table are also presented some simple relations viz. (i) ratio of gross agricultural output to net agricultural output, (ii) ratio of gross industrial output to net industrial output, (iii) per head net output in agriculture, (iv) per head net output in industry, (v) percentage of per head net output in agriculture to that in industry and (vi) percentage of agricultural net output to total of agricultural and industrial net outputs.

Value of Net investments in Agriculture and Industry

Outputs are the result of investments. Investment undertaken in a sector, in conjunction with the capital-output ratio of that sector, generates capacity and output, after a certain time-lag. Thus investment is the prime mover of output generation. It therefore seems necessary to note the time-series of value of net (or new) investment undertaken in each of the sectors of our study. For this purpose, use has been made of the data contained in the Reserve Bank of India (RBI) estimates of savings in India[35] and the CSO's estimates of gross capital formation

TABLE - 2.6

Gross and Net Outputs : Agriculture and Industry

Some Simple Relationships : 1948-49 - 1958-59 (At Constant (51-52) Prices – In Rs. Crores)

ITEMS (1)	1948-49 (2)	1949-50 (3)	1950-51 (4)	1951-52 (5)	1952-53 (6)	1953-54 (7)	1954-55 (8)	1955-56 (9)	1956-57 (10)	1957-58 (11)	1958-59 (12)
1. *Gross Output*											
a. Agriculture	6557	6312	6202	6200	6923	7245	6947	7065	7438	6838	7648
b. Industry	3594	3738	3769	4201	4483	4494	4825	5322	5439	5825	6031
2. *Net Output*											
a. Agriculture	5193	5052	5088	5021	5555	5937	5743	5744	6113	4981	6321
b. Industry	1505	1607	1678	1592	1711	1941	1931	2107	2219	2332	2448
3. Ratio of Gross Agricultural Output to Net Agricultural Output	1.26	1.25	1.22	1.23	1.25	1.22	1.21	1.23	1.22	1.37	1.21
4. Ratio of Gross Industrial Output to Net Industrial Output	2.39	2.33	2.25	2.64	2.62	2.32	2.49	2.53	2.45	2.49	2.46
5. Percentage of Agricultural Net Output to the Total of Agricultural and Industrial Net Output	77.6	75.9	75.2	75.9	76.5	75.4	74.8	73.2	73.4	68.1	72.1
6. Per Head Net Output in Agriculture per Year (in Rs.)	215.9	206.2	203.8	197.5	213.7	224.2	212.9	209.1	218.5	174.8	217.7
7. Per Head Net Output in Industry per Year (in Rs.)	423.8	443.9	453.6	421.6	444.5	493.8	482.7	515.3	532.2	548.7	564.0
8. Percentage of per Head Net Output in Agriculture to that in Industry	50.9	46.5	44.9	46.8	48.1	45.4	44.1	40.6	41.1	31.9	38.6

in India[36]. The CSO presents figures of net fixed capital formation at current prices for the years 1948-49 to 1958-59. These estimates are based on recent data and are quite comprehensive. Hence we have decided to use them for our enquiry. However, the CSO does not give a sectorwise break-down of total investment. Such a sectorwise apportionment of total investment estimates at current prices has been attempted by the RBI study under the heads of (i) farm investment, (ii) non-farm investment, (iii) rural construction, (iv) urban construction and (v) others for each of the years 1950-51 to 1957-58. We have applied this pattern of investment to the respective annual total net investment estimates from CSO[37]. It has been further assumed that the entire farm investment, 50 per cent of non-farm investment, and 90 per cent of rural construction constitute the net fixed investment undertaken in the agricultural sector[38]. Since further refinement seems difficult to undertake with the current availability of sectoral investment data, it has been assumed here that the trends of investment in the non-agricultural sector represent those of the industrial sector.

Value of Net Investment in Agriculture and Industry (at constant '51-52 prices)

The estimates of total net investment have been deflated with a weighted index of prices of "construction" and "machinery and equipment[39]. Thereafter the same assumptions as for current price estimates regarding the pattern of investment as also for deriving the estimate of agricultural and non-agricultural investments have been made. The estimates of net investments at constant prices in agriculture and non-agriculture are shown in Table 2.7. In this table are also given the percentages of investment in agriculture to total net investment in different years.

TABLE - 2.7

Value of Net Investments in Agriculture and Non-Agriculture

1948-49 - 1958-59 (At Constant '51-52 Prices — In Rs. Crores)

ITEMS (1)	1948-49 (2)	1949-50 (3)	1950-51 (4)	1951-52 (5)	1952-53 (6)	1953-54 (7)	1954-55 (8)	1955-56 (9)	1956-57 (10)	1957-58 (11)	1958-59 (12)
1. Value of Net Investments in Agriculture	195.1	248.6	240.1	346.5	237.2	314.6	345.5	492.4	494.5	648.8	591.6
2. Value of Net Investments in Non-Agriculture	130.9	166.8	161.1	153.6	231.6	176.3	294.4	398.8	662.6	600.2	547.3
3. Total Value of Net Investments in the Economy	326.0	415.4	401.2	500.1	468.8	490.9	639.9	891.2	1157.1	1249.0	1138.9
4. Percentage of Net Investments in Agriculture to Total Net Investments in the Economy	60.0	59.8	59.8	69.3	50.5	64.1	54.0	55.3	42.8	51.9	51.9

ANALYSIS

The percentage of total investment in agriculture has shown a declining tendency during the period of our study. As against this, we shall examine the value of gross and net outputs of agriculture and industry. It must be clarified that while investment is related to output through the capital-output ratio and to money incomes through the multiplier, yet the propagation of income and the creation of capacity through investment involves time-lags. Hence a neat correspondence cannot be expected between net investments of a given year and outputs and incomes of the same year. Nevertheless, the time-series of values of investments and outputs will have some broad indications. Investments in both the agricultural and the non-agricultural sectors have been increasing steadily and the gross and net outputs of agriculture and industry have also been showing a rising trend. However, while industrial output has recorded a gentle, persistent rise, agricultural output has been fluctuating. This is perhaps due to seasonal and random influences on agricultural production. Also gross and net outputs of agriculture have been exhibiting similar flutuations. This is not so in the case of industry. The ratio of gross to net output of agriculture has fluctuated between 1.21 and 1.37 through these years (Table 2.5). In other words, the costs of raw-materials (or inputs) in agriculture as a proportion of net output of agriculture have varied between 21 to 37%. On an average, costs of raw-materials form 25% of the net output of agriculture. The ratio of gross to net output of industry has been ranging between 2.25 to 2.64. Thus costs of raw materials in industry are 1.25 to 1.64 times the net output of industry. On an average, costs of raw materials of industry are 1.45 times as high as its net output. The input-net output ratio in industry is nearly 5 times that in agriculture. Despite this unfavourable cost difference, the relative performance of the industrial sector has been good.

The percentage of agricultural output to total net output (both at current and at constant prices) are inclined in a downward direction (Diagram). From 1953-54 onwards,

DIAGRAM

Ratio of Agricultural Net Output to Total Net Outputs of Agriculture and Industry

At Constant and At Current Prices (Percentage)

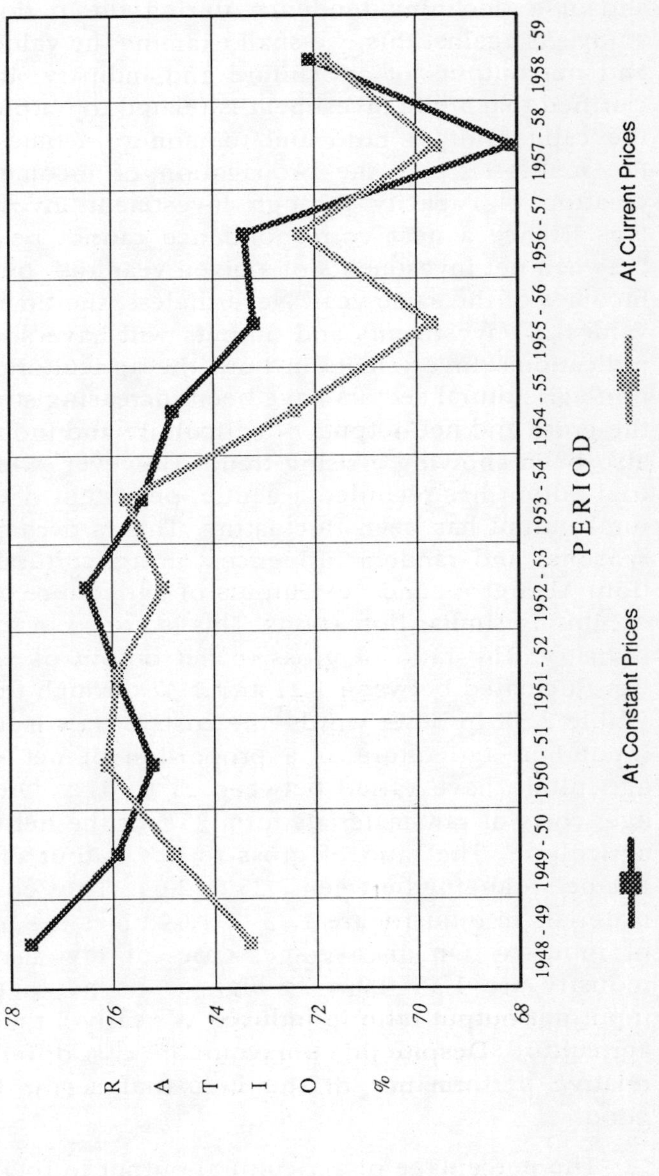

the movements of percentages at current prices have been more or less similar to those at constant prices. It is expected that agriculture would tend to become less important in terms of its relative contribution, as years of development go by.

We may also see the movements in per head net output in current prices (i.e. per head money income) and in constant prices in agriculture and industry. Per head money income and per head net output in industry are higher than the respective values in agriculture. Per head net output in agriculture which was nearly 51% of that in industry in 1948-49 has fallen to 38% in 1958-59. On an average, per head net output in agriculture has been 43.5% of that in industry. While per head net output as well as income in industry have been steadily rising, per head net output as well as income in agriculture have been fluctuating.

From what has been said so far, it seems that industrial output, gross or net, total or per capita, at constant or at current prices has been exhibiting a steady growth, while agricultural output though growing much more slowly, has been passing through fluctuations. The structural inelasticity of agriculture is a well-established phenomenon. The fact that despite a larger proportion of net investment being devoted to the agricultural sector, the relative performance of this sector has been weak is the consequence of the inflexibility of agricultural production in general, the relative price insensitiveness of the Indian subsistence farmer, the mode of production for self-consumption, the low degree of monetisation, and last but not the least, the seasonal and random factors. The present work does not have a pretence to any detailed or satisfactory analysis of this aspect of Indian agriculture and is concerned with inter-sector relations rather than with intra-sector explanations of inflexibilities and other allied phenomena.

While we have compared the broad trends of gross and net outputs of agriculture and industry as also those of the net investments in agriculture and non-agriculture, it would be fruitful to examine and analyse the magnitudes of flows of these outputs between these two sectors. This is attempted in the following chapters.

NOTES & REFERENCES

1. First report of the National Income Committee, April, 1951 and Final Report of the National Income Committee 1954, Department of Economic Affairs, Ministry of Finance, Government of India. Government of India appointed a Committee in 1949 under the chairmanship of Prof. P.C. Mahalanobis to make recommendations regarding estimation of national income in India. This Committee presented their first report in 1951 and final report in 1954. These will hereafter be referred to as 'First Report' and 'Final Report' in this thesis. The official National Income Estimates that are prepared and published by the Central Statistical Organisation (CSO) are broadly on the lines indicated by the above Committee in their Report.
2. Government of India, CSO: National Income Statistics - Proposals for a Revised Series of National Income Estimates for 1955-56 to 1959-60, 1961 p.(vii). Hereafter, this will be referred to as "Proposals" and the estimates therein as "Revised Estimates".
3. The "Revised estimates" are still based on the methodology outlined in the 'Final Report', "Proposals", Ch.XVI.p.173.
4. "Proposals", p.(vii).
5. Ibid, p.(vii).
6. National Sample Survey. Tables with notes on small-scale manufacturing enterprises (Household enterprises smaller than registered factories) — 9th to 10th Round — May 1955-May 1956 : No. 43.
7. The procedures adopted to obtain comparable time-series of estimates are given in Appendix.
8. "Proposals", p.28.
9. For most of the crops, the Index Number of Agricultural production published by the Ministry of Food & Agriculture, Government of India in "Area and Production of Principal Crops in India, Pre-war Average to 1960, Summary Tables" has been used as the projector.
10. The implied price has been derived by dividing the 'Revised estimate' of the value of a crop with the 'Revised estimate' of physical production of that crop.
11. Index Number of Wholesale Prices — Revised Series (Weekly) : Office of the Economic Adviser, Ministry of Commerce & Industry. The Revised Series of Index numbers of wholesale prices of all commodities by groups and subgroups (1952=100) have been published only from 1951-52. But in a separate compilation by the Economic Adviser's Office, the revised index numbers of prices of almost all the individual articles are available from 1950-51. For years prior to 1950-51, use has been made of the Economic Advisor's Index Number of wholesale prices (old series 1939=100) for some commodities, and the implied prices as in the 'Final Report' for some other commodities.
12. Government may procure grain at less than market prices and in fact have often done so.
13. The price at which rice has been valued is that of cleaned rice. Therefore, the net value added by rice-mills (as estimated in factory establishments

sector) should be deducted from the value of rice in agriculture sector. However, hand pounding of rice etc., is defined as an ancillary activity to agriculture and hence is included in this sector.

14. The author is thankful to the Central Statistical authorities for making available to her data on the value of fertilisers and irrigation charges, as computed for the Official National Income Series. The CSO computes these data from (1) Fertiliser Statistics (Annual) issued by the Fertiliser Association of India (ii) Monthly Statistics of Foreign Trade of India issued by the Director-General of Commercial Intelligence and Statistics and (iii) State Budget Documents.

15. "*Proposals*", pp.44-45.

16. *Indian Livestock Statistics*, Directorate of Economics and Statistics: Ministry of Agriculture, Government of India.

17. *Indian Forest Statistics*, Directorate of Economics and Statistics, Ministry of Agriculture, Government of India.

18. "Proposals", Table 5.2, p.83.

19. "Proposals", p.87.

20. Thus, production of cloth has been used for extrapolating production of textiles, availability of cloth for tailoring, supply of oilseeds for oil crushing and so on.

21. It has been assumed that the ratio computed from data relating to 1955-56 (National Sample Survey — Report No. 43. Tables with notes on Small Scale Manufacturing Enterprises — May 1955 - May 1956) has been constant for the entire period of our study.

22. This category includes wood, glass and ceramics, metal manufacturing and engineering, chemicals and others.

23. a. Central Statistical Organisation: *Census of Manufacturing Industries* (Annual) (CMI).

    b. National Sample Survey: *Sample Survey of Manufacturing Industries* (SSMI).

24. This is available for 1951, 1952 and 1953. For 1957, the SSMI report is a draft report.

25. 'Final report' p 45 and 'Proposals' p 45.

26. 1951, 1952, 1953 and 1957.

27. For the years 1949 and 1950, the SSMI covered only 2j factories. Adjustment has been made for coverage of 2m (i) factories. Also nonpower using industries are covered only from 1951; estimates for 1951 have been taken for earlier years. Depreciation has been estimated by using the all industry ratio of depreciation to value added as per CMI results.

28. The adjustments on account of different factors have been carried out as follows. In regard to geographical coverage, adjustment has been mainly made for the inclusion of Cochin State upto 1951 and its noninclusion upto 1954 and the inclusion of Cochin, Travancore and Mysore since 1954. This has been made using the information for all industries of value added for these areas separately for 1954 and that for Cochin prior to 1951. On this basis, the likely estimates of the increase in value added for years prior to 1954 had all the areas been included were estimated for deriving the inflation factor. For nonresponse, the correction factor has been based on the industrywise information on number of factories sending returns to the number of registered factories. A mark up has also been made on account of factories using power and employing 10-19 workers on the basis of estimates given in "Proposals" P 104.

29. 'Proposals', P. 106. These costs are included in the CMI/SSMI data on value added for the said periods.

30. The CMI and the SSMI have not allowed for these charges: 'Final Report': P 67 and 'Proposals' PP 123-124. There has not been much change in the methodology or statistical data used for the 'Revised estimates' of the incomes of banks, though there has been some change in the case of non-banking companies. Hence we have used the estimates of bank charges and insurance premia as in the 'Final Report' and the 'Proposals' without any adjustment.

31. Proposals, p. 178.

32. The year 1951-52 has been taken as the 'base' year, for two reasons: it marks the beginning of the I Plan period and hence would serve as a good reference year for evaluating progress since planning started; some of the important weights needed for constructing composite price indices were available for this year (Ch.3).

33. For deflating the gross outputs of agriculture and industry, it was necessary to form composite price indices of (a) all agricultural products and (b) all industrial products. Taking the Economic Adviser's Series of Wholesale Prices of cereals, pulses, fruits and vegetables, milk and ghee, eggs, meat, tea, coffee, spices, betulnuts, raw tobacco, fibres, oilseeds, hides and skins, sugarcane and rubber, and using the weights adopted therein, the index of prices for deflating the value of agricultural production was formed. Further, the All commodities price index as published by the Economic Adviser's office was taken and by a process of subtraction and division, the index number of all other products (other than agricultural) was formed and this was used to deflate the gross value of output in industry.

34. Precisely speaking, the retentions of each sector should be deflated with the help of the index of prices of the products of that sector while the purchases by that sector from the rest of the economy should be deflated with a relevant price index. However, since we have not computed separately the value for a sector of its retentions and of its purchases from the rest of the economy, this has not been possible; for the same reason again, a composite index of prices of a sector's retentions and its purchases from the rest of the economy has not been feasible. Hence we have used the index of prices of the products of a sector to deflate the entire value of its retentions and its purchases from the rest of economy.

35. Bhatt, V.V. 'Estimates of savings and Investment in Indian Economy, 1950-51 — 1958-59" ; *Reserve Bank of India Bulletin*, August, 1961.

36. CSO "Estimates of Gross Capital Formation in India for 1948-49 to 1960-61," 1961.

37. The pattern as in 1950-51 has been taken for the two earlier years and that in 1957-58 for 1958-59.

38. A similar assumption has been made by Khusro in estimating the net investment in the non-agricultural sector: "Economic Development with no population transfers" Occasional paper, Institute of Economic Growth, Delhi, P. 13.

39. The indices of prices of "Construction" and "Machinery and Equipment" are separately given for the period 1948-49 to 1958-59 in the CSO study. We have converted the above indices to 1951-52 base and then taking their proportions in 1951-52 in total gross capital formation at current prices as weights, constructed the weighted index of prices. The implicit assumption is that the proportions with regard to gross capital formation are also true of net fixed capital formation.

3

Intersectoral Demand For Products : For Final Use

IN the previous chapter, we had estimated the values of gross and net outputs of agriculture and industry as also those of net investments undertaken in the economy. We had further analysed the movements of these variables. It was found that the relative share of agriculture in the total net outputs of agriculture and industry was declining during the period of our study. As against this, it would be fruitful to examine the behaviour of the ratio of expenditure of the economy on final products produced by agricultural sector to the economy's total expenditure on final products produced by agricultural sector and industrial sector.

In his well-known book "Agriculture and Economic Progress", Ojala has gone into the question of what measures economic welfare. He examines the query "Is economic welfare best indicated by the quantity of goods and services produced , or the quantity consumed over a given period." And concludes with Pigou that "if we are interested in the comparative amounts of economic welfare which a community obtains over a long period of years, and are looking forward for an objective index with which the series of amounts can be suitably correlated", then the conception of economic welfare in terms of the flow of goods into the hands of ultimate consumers during the year is the appropriate one. Hicks also is of the opinion that it is only consumption that contributes to economic welfare. Thus "consumption income" or "the value at market prices, of all finished goods produced during the year less net capital formation during that year"[1] may be regarded as an index of economic welfare; more appropriately, the above at constant prices would be taken to indicate real economic welfare.

In the present thesis, however, we cannot measure economic welfare in the aforementioned sense since we shall not be evolving estimates of the demand of the economy for all finished goods. Our estimates shall indicate only the consumption expenditure on finished goods produced by agriculture and industry but exclude the expenditures on finished goods produced by the rest of the economy. While it is true that the total value of the economy's consumption expenditure on agricultural and industrial finished goods alone cannot be taken to be the index of economic welfare, yet it can as well serve as an indicator. In so far as we confine ourselves to the consumption expenditures of the economy on finished goods produced by agriculture and industry, the relative contribution of agriculture to this total value of 'consumption expenditure' shall be indicated in this work by the ratio of the consumption expenditure of the economy on agricultural finished goods to the economy's total consumption expenditure (i.e. on both agricultural and industrial finished goods). Thus we are not using the term 'agriculture's contribution to economic welfare' in exactly the same sense as Ojala has used it. For Ojala, agriculture's contribution to economic welfare is given by the 'consumption income' in the hands of the agriculturists as a proportion to 'consumption income' in the hands of the people of the entire economy. Probably, this can be better termed as 'agriculture's participation in economic welfare'. We have on the other hand considered the ratio of the value of goods 'contributed' by agriculture for the consumption of the economy to the 'total' (agricultural and industrial goods only) value of 'consumption income' or 'consumption expenditure' of the economy.

For the above purpose, it is necessary to estimate the demand of the economy for final consumption products by the different sectors of the economy, namely, agriculture, industry and the rest of the economy and by the categories of agricultural and industrial goods. We shall present the time series of these estimates of intersectoral demand for final products both at current and at constant prices .

Definition of Products

Intermediate and Final Products

At the outset, it is necessary to distinguish between 'intermediate' and 'final' products. While it is not easy to devise a categorical definition of a product as intermediate or final, it is still possible to classify products consumed by a sector as 'intermediate' or 'final'. A product is 'intermediate' for a sector, if it is used as an input in the production of that sector's output. A product which is 'intermediate' for a sector may in fact, be the finished product of the same or of another sector. Thus fertilisers which are the finished products of the industrial sector are used as intermediate products in the agricultural sector. It is also possible that the same product may be both an 'intermediate' product and a 'final' product. Thus no generalisation can be made as regards the nature of a product, i.e. if it is 'intermediate' or 'final'. Still, from the point of view of a sector, we can use the terms 'intermediate' or 'final' with respect to the use-value of that product for that particular sector. And it is in this sense that we shall be using these terms in this thesis.

The present chapter estimates for agriculture and industry, at current and at constant prices, the values of not only the final products demanded by a sector and produced by that sector itself but also those of the final products it purchases from the other sector. Thereafter, it examines the relative contribution of agriculture to economic welfare, as defined by us. A comprehensive discussion of the fluctuations in intersectoral demand for final products is given in chapter 5 along with that of intersectoral demand for intermediate products.

Estimates

Our main sources of data for this purpose have been (i) National Sample Survey (NSS) of Pattern of Consumer Expenditure -Rounds 3 to 13 (ii) Economic Adviser's Series of Index Numbers of wholesale prices, (iii) Census of India, 1951, Volume IIB — Economic Tables, (iv) Census of India 1961 — Provisional Tables; (v) Annual Statement of Foreign Trade of India and (vi) Monthly Statistics of Foreign Trade of India. Of these, the first source of information, viz., National Sample Survey of Pattern of Consumer expenditure, deserves special consideration, since that has formed the basis of our estimates.

National Sample Survey of Family Budgets

The NSS has so far conducted 13 rounds of survey covering the period 1951-52 to 1957-58. But at the time when this thesis was finalised, the NSS had published reports upto the 10th round only. We had however access to the unpublished reports in the draft form for the 12th and 13th rounds of the survey. We may re-combine[2] these rounds of survey to represent the financial years 1951-52 to 1958-59. This has been done in Table 3.1. The NSS covers the whole of India with the exception of Jammu and Kashmir, Andaman and Nicobar Islands. Except for the 3rd round, all the other rounds have a month as the reference period. The NSS gives the pattern of consumer expenditure in Rs. per person for a period of 30 days by items of consumption and by monthly per capita expenditure classes, separately for rural and urban areas.

In all rounds except the 3rd and the 4th, the items of consumption have been grouped into 12 major categories, viz., foodgrains; milk and milk products; edible oil; meat, egg and fish; sugar; salt; other food items; clothing; fuel and light; rent; taxes; and miscellaneous. Of these, foodgrains, milk and milk products, meat and eggs belong to the agricultural sector. But fish is included in the meat, egg and fish group, and in not a single round is the estimate of per capita expenditure on these items given sepa-

TABLE - 3.1

National Sample Survey of Patterns of Consumer Expenditure

Period of Survey and Reference Period

Rounds of Survey	Reference Period	Period of Survey	Year to which the information has been taken to correspond in this study
3rd	Week	August-November 1951	1948-49, 1949-50, 1950-51
4th	Month	April-September 1952	1951-52
5th	Month	Dec. 1952-March 1953	1952-53
7th	Month	Oct. 1953-March 1954	1953-54
8th	Month	July 1954-April 1955	1954-55
10th	Month	Dec. 1955-May 1956	1955-56
12th	Month	March 1957-August 1957	1956-57
13th	Month	Sept. 1957-May 1958	1957-58, 1958-59.

rately. Since there is very little that can be done about it, we allow 'fish' to be included in agricultural finished consumption products. Edible oil, sugar, salt, clothing and fuel and light are industrial products. There are two broad groups, "other food items" which include refreshments that actually have to be included in the industrial products group and "miscellaneous" which includes 'pan' that should be put in the agricultural products group. This 'miscellaneous' item includes a number of service items like education, medicine, services, conveyance and ceremonials which have to be omitted along with rent and taxes. Fortunately, the values of per capita expenditure by individual items which make up these twelve groups are given in the 3rd and 4th rounds and the 4th round being a more recent one, we have taken from it, the percentage of expenditures on pan, refreshments and other service items in rural and urban areas, and applied to the total expenses in these areas respectively in each of the other rounds and grouped them in the relevant categories or removed them from either of the agricultural or industrial products as the case may be. The per capita consumption expenditures on agricultural and industrial products in rural and urban areas in various rounds have been presented in Table 3.2.

TABLE - 3.2

Per Capita Expenditure on Agricultural and Industrial Finished Products — Rural and Urban Areas by the Various Rounds of the National Sample Survey (Rs Per Month)

Items (1)	3rd Round (2)	4th Round (3)	5th Round (4)	7th Round (5)	8th Round (6)	10th Round (7)	12th Round (8)	13th Round (9)
Rural								
1. Agricultural Products	14.59	12.55	11.34	10.52	9.01	10.75	11.08	11.59
2. Industrial Products	6.11	5.51	4.80	4.11	3.64	4.21	3.66	4.25
Urban								
1. Agricultural Products	15.12	12.55	12.61	12.32	11.71	12.49	13.14	13.19
2. Industrial Products	11.80	9.00	9.11	5.79	7.08	6.67	7.14	6.40

Assumptions

We now assume the following in order to transform the NSS data for rural and urban areas into similar data for agricultural and industrial sectors[3] :

i. tastes of the agricultural sector are similar to those of rural sector so that the per head expenditure on individual items in rural areas can be taken to represent the per head expenditure on the respective items in agricultural sector. For, agricultural sector is a very large part of the rural sector and the overlap between the two is quite enormous;

ii. tastes of the people in sub-sectors, forestry, fishery and small enterprises, which are again mostly rural in character are similar to those of people of rural sector, so that once again the per head expenditure on individual items of consumption in the rural sector may be taken to be representative of per head expenditure on these items in these sub-sectors and

iii. tastes of people in the sub-sectors, mining and quarrying and factory establishments and also of people in the rest of the economy are similar to those of the people in the urban sector so that the per head expenses on individual items of consumption in the urban sector may be taken to hold good for persons in the factory establishments and mining sectors.

Estimates of Population in Agriculture and Industry

With these assumptions, we proceed to classify the population into agricultural and industrial. For this, resort had to be made to the census reports. Firstly, the geometric rates of growth of the entire population,[4] urban population, and rural population were worked out separately with the 1951 census data and the 1961 census provisional figures (after necessary adjustments for net undercount).[5] The Census of India 1951, does not give an economic classification of all population according to the occupation pursued. It, however, gives the economic classification of self-supporting persons by the following categories:

1. Primary industries not elsewhere specified :
   a. Stock raising
   b. Rearing of animals
   c. Plantation industry
   d. Forestry
   e. Hunting
   f. Fishing
2. Mining and Quarrying
3. Food industries, textiles, leather etc.
4. Processing and manufacturing of metals, chemicals and products thereof
5. Processing and manufacturing of products not elsewhere specified
   and
6. Construction and utilities[6], etc.

As against this economic classification of self-supporting persons, the entire population has been given under the categories of agriculture proper, production other than cultivation, commerce, transport and other services and miscellaneous. Making use of these two sets of information, the time series of estimates of population in agriculture and industry have been calculated.[7] These estimates are given in Table 3.3.

Value of Consumption Expenditure of Agriculture, Industry and Rest of the Economy on Agricultural Products and Industrial products

The rural pattern of per head expenditure has been applied to the agricultural sector and estimates made of value of consumption expenditure incurred by agriculture at current prices on agricultural and industrial finished products. Applying the rural pattern to the population of "unorganised" subsector of the industrial sector and the urban pattern to the population of "organised" sub-sector and adding them up, the estimates of value of current consumption expenditure of industry on agricultural and industrial products have been derived. The urban pattern has been applied to the population in the 'rest of the

TABLE - 3.3

Estimates of Population in Agriculture, Industry and the Rest of the Economy

1948-49 — 1958-59

(In Millions)

ITEMS (1)	1948-49 (2)	1949-50 (3)	1950-51 (4)	1951-52 (5)	1952-53 (6)	1953-54 (7)	1954-55 (8)	1955-56 (9)	1956-57 (10)	1957-58 (11)	1958-59 (12)
1. Population in											
(a) Agriculture Proper	235.49	239.87	244.33	248.87	253.50	258.22	263.02	267.91	272.89	277.97	283.14
(b) Animal Husbandry	5.04	5.13	5.23	5.33	6.45	6.57	6.69	6.81	6.94	7.07	7.20
Total in Agriculture (a)+(b)	240.53	245.00	249.56	254.20	259.95	264.79	269.71	274.72	279.83	285.04	290.34
2. Population in											
(a) Forestry, Fishery etc.	1.99	2.03	2.07	2.11	2.15	2.19	2.23	2.27	2.31	2.35	2.39
(b) Small Enterprises	19.50	19.86	20.23	20.61	20.99	21.38	21.78	22.19	22.60	23.02	23.45
(c) Construction & Utilities	5.11	5.21	5.31	5.41	5.51	5.61	5.71	5.82	5.93	6.04	6.15
(d) Factory Estabs.	8.90	9.12	9.35	9.58	9.82	10.07	10.32	10.58	10.84	11.11	11.39
Total in Industry (a)+(b)+(c)+(d)	35.50	36.22	36.96	37.71	38.47	39.25	40.04	40.86	41.68	42.52	43.38
3. Population in the Rest of the Economy	59.97	61.43	62.91	64.44	64.99	66.57	68.20	69.85	71.55	73.28	75.06
4. Total Population in the Economy (1)+(2)+(3)	336.00	342.65	349.43	356.35	363.41	370.61	377.95	385.43	393.06	400.84	408.78

economy' to obtain estimates of its consumption expenditure on agricultural and industrial products.

However, these include indirect taxes paid and imports. The Taxation Enquiry Commission (1954) had estimated[8] that the per capita payment of indirect taxes in rural and urban areas is Rs. 0.62 and 1.69 respectively. We have assumed again that the rural incidence estimate is true of agriculture and of the "unorganised" sub-sectors of industry, while the urban estimate is true of the "organised" sub-sector of industry and the rest of the economy. It has been further assumed that these incidence estimates have been constant over time.[9] Applying these incidence estimates to the respective population estimates, the estimates of indirect taxes paid by agriculture, industry and rest of the economy have been derived. Since indirect taxes are levied mostly, if not entirely on manufactured goods (except for sales tax in a few states on food items), the present work has assumed the bulk of indirect taxes paid by each sector as being paid on the respective sector's consumption expenditure on manufactured goods.

Imports of finished products have been broadly classified as imports of agricultural products (milk and milk products, grain, pulse and flour, fruits and vegetables and spices) and industrial products (textile manufactures, sugar and sugar preparation, beverages, coffee, tea, cocoa, manufactured tobacco, edible oils, kerosene, gasoline etc., drugs and medicines, glassware and earthware, electric lamps, fans etc., sewing machines, typewriters, rubber manufactures, writing paper, automobiles and miscellaneous). Assuming that imports of each category of products were consumed by the different sectors in the same ratio in which they consumed the total value of these products inclusive of imports, the value of imports consumed of these products by the different sectors has been estimated. The values at current prices of consumption expenditure of agriculture, industry and rest of the economy of agricultural and industrial finished products, net of indirect taxes and imports, are given in Table 3.4.

TABLE - 3.4

Value of Consumption Expenditure of Agriculture, Industry and the Rest of the Economy

Net of Imports and Indirect Taxes — 1948-49 - 1958-59 (In Rs. Crores)

ITEMS (1)	1948-49 (2)	1949-50 (3)	1950-51 (4)	1951-52 (5)	1952-53 (6)	1953-54 (7)	1954-55 (8)	1955-56 (9)	1956-57 (10)	1957-58 (11)	1958-59 (12)
Consumption Expenditure of Agriculture on											
1. Agricultural Finished Products	4129.54	4184.86	4285.46	3650.85	3417.10	3284.21	2856.79	3514.06	3695.43	3898.87	3909.67
2. Industrial Finished Products	1511.27	1536.74	1285.43	1392.09	1233.86	1014.15	879.46	1108.31	935.50	1113.12	1173.45
Consumption Expenditure of Industry on											
1. Agricultural Finished Products	615.03	624.34	640.52	541.50	520.16	508.19	456.86	544.56	577.05	602.58	605.32
2. Industrial Finished Products	269.86	275.07	284.59	231.96	218.40	156.23	156.37	180.80	168.07	177.93	188.27
Consumption Expenditure of Rest of Economy on											
1. Agricultural Finished Products	1065.73	1086.86	1119.36	924.89	950.13	967.38	938.86	1037.35	1121.35	1141.03	1150.91
2. Industrial Finished Products	691.38	707.45	734.53	523.70	545.52	294.11	392.93	386.84	425.64	364.54	388.94

Value (at constant prices) of Consumption Expenditure of Agriculture, Industry and Rest of the Economy on Agricultural Products and Industrial Products

In order to represent these at constant prices, four independent price indices have been formed.The Economic Adviser's index numbers of foodgrains, pulses, vegetables, fruits, milk and milk products, meat, egg and butter and fish, spices and pan, have been combined with the weights of value of expenditure of the agricultural sector on these items in 1951-52[10]. That was taken to be the index of cost of expenditure of agricultural sector on agricultural goods and was used to deflate its expenses on its own products while the composite index of the same indices with the values of industry's expenditure in 1951-52 on these items as weights was used to deflate its expenses on agricultural finished products. A similar procedure was adopted for computing the price deflator for the expenses of the rest of the economy on agricultural products. In the same way, the wholesale price indices of edible oil, salt, sugar, tobacco, drugs and intoxicants, fuel and light, clothing and bedding, refreshments, footwear, toilet, domestic utensils and others have been combined into three indices for the three sectors using the sector specific consumption expenditure on these items as weights. These indices are given in Table 3.5.

Using these indices, the value of consumption expenditure of agriculture, industry and rest of the economy on agricultural and industrial finished products at constant prices have been worked out; these estimates are given in Table 3.6. The percentage of expenditure of the economy on agricultural finished goods to total expenditure on both agricultural and industrial finished goods is also presented in this table.

It should be noted that the NSS data on consumer expenditure on which our estimates, at current prices, of the final demand of the different sectors are based are in retail prices. Hence the most suitable deflators for purposes of reducing the current price data to constant prices

TABLE - 3.5

Price Indices Used for Deflating the Consumption Expenditure on Agricultural and Industrial Finished Products of Agriculture, Industry and Rest of the Economy

1948-49 - 1958-59 Base (1951-52 = 100)

ITEMS (1)	1948-49 (2)	1949-50 (3)	1950-51 (4)	1951-52 (5)	1952-53 (6)	1953-54 (7)	1954-55 (8)	1955-56 (9)	1956-57 (10)	1957-58 (11)	1958-59 (12)
Composite price index used for deflating consumption expenses on :											
Agricultural products of agricultural sector	88.08	93.15	94.77	100.00	96.99	96.21	79.90	77.28	93.70	98.46	106.42
Agricultural products of industrial sector	88.34	93.15	95.22	100.00	96.85	96.43	80.61	78.20	93.98	98.80	107.04
Agricultural products of the rest of the economy	89.10	94.53	96.51	100.00	96.45	87.07	82.69	80.90	84.79	99.81	109.32
Industrial products of agricultural sector	91.24	92.12	93.33	100.00	87.08	90.61	91.13	85.70	92.85	97.09	98.30
Industrial products of industrial sector	91.73	92.62	93.83	100.00	86.43	90.47	93.09	86.36	93.24	97.36	98.70
Industrial products of the rest of the economy	92.53	93.53	94.65	100.00	85.35	92.04	96.38	87.47	93.92	97.83	99.38

TABLE - 3.6

Value of Consumption Expenditure of the Economy on Agricultural and Industrial Products (Net of Imports and Indirect Taxes)

1948-49 - 1958-59 (at constant '51-52 prices) (in Rs. crores)

ITEMS (1)	1948-49 (2)	1949-50 (3)	1950-51 (4)	1951-52 (5)	1952-53 (6)	1953-54 (7)	1954-55 (8)	1955-56 (9)	1956-57 (10)	1957-58 (11)	1958-59 (12)
1. Expenditure on agricultural finished products of :											
• Agriculture	4688.40	4492.60	4521.96	3650.90	3523.15	3413.58	3575.46	4547.18	3943.90	3959.85	3673.81
• Industry	696.21	667.67	672.67	541.50	537.08	527.00	566.75	696.37	614.01	609.90	565.51
• Rest of the economy	1196.11	1149.75	1159.84	924.83	985.10	996.58	1135.40	1282.26	1182.98	1143.20	1052.79
Sub-Total	6580.72	6310.02	6354.47	5117.23	5045.33	4937.16	5277.61	6525.81	5740.89	5712.95	5292.11
2. Expenditure on industrial finished products of :											
• Agriculture	1656.37	1668.74	1698.74	1392.09	1416.93	1119.25	965.06	1293.24	1007.54	1146.48	1193.74
• Industry	294.19	296.99	303.30	231.96	252.69	172.69	167.98	209.36	180.26	182.75	190.75
• Rest of the economy	747.20	757.20	776.05	523.70	639.16	319.55	407.69	442.25	453.19	372.63	391.45
Sub-Total	2697.76	2722.93	2778.09	2147.75	2308.78	1611.49	1540.73	1944.85	1640.99	1701.86	1775.94
3. Grand Total : (1)+(2)	9278.48	9032.95	9132.56	7264.98	7354.11	6548.65	6818.34	8470.66	7381.88	7414.81	7068.05
4. Percentage of economy's expenditure on agricultural products to its total expenditure on agricultural and industrial products	70.9	69.8	69.6	70.4	68.6	75.4	77.4	77.0	77.8	77.0	74.9

should have been a set of retail price indices.[11] However, in view of the fact that there is no systematic collection of information on retail prices of all the individual commodities we are interested in and for the entire period of our study, we had to do with the wholesale price deflators.

Inferences

It is observed that throughout this period, the economy has been spending a higher absolute amount (at current as well as at constant prices) on agricultural consumption goods than on industrial consumption goods. The movement of ratios (at constant prices) of expenditure on agricultural consumption goods to the total expenditure on agricultural and industrial consumption goods would seem to underline one of our hypotheses in Chapter 1 regarding what might happen to this ratio as an underdeveloped country starts on a programme of development. As incomes in the economy have been generally increasing, the expenditure in real terms incurred on agricultural finished consumption goods as a proportion of the total expenses on agricultural and industrial consumption goods has been increasing. Whereas real net output of agriculture as a proportion of total real net outputs of agriculture and industry has declined from 78 to nearly 70% in this period (vide Ch. 2), the ratio of the economy's real consumption expenditure on agricultural finished goods to the total real consumption expenditures has moved from 71 to 77%.

We can observe three phases in the movement of this ratio : a falling tendency during 1948-49 to 1952-53 followed by a steep rise during 1952-53 to 1956-57 and thereafter a downward slope. These three phases generally coincide with those in the movements of the general prices of both agricultural and industrial goods and of the terms of trade of finished consumption goods. During the first phase are found generally rising prices and improving terms of trade for agriculture (vis-a-vis) industry while in the second phase, agriculture faced an unfavourable turn in its terms of trade, when general prices had a tendency to fall. The terms of trade have again improved in the last phase, when general prices have risen. Thus it shows that whenever agricultural prices were rising faster than industrial prices, the percentage of real expenditure on agricultural finished consumption goods to the total consumption expenditure on agricultural and industrial finished goods has tended to fall and conversely whenever agricultural prices have fallen more than industrial prices, this percentage has moved in the opposite direction, i.e., has risen.

We have examined in this chapter the economy's demand for agricultural and industrial consumption products. It is, however, necessary for us to analyse the intersectoral demand not only for consumption products but for all products i.e. both consumption and intermediate products. For this purpose, we need estimates of values (at current and at constant prices) of basic materials that move between agriculture and industry. The succeeding chapter fulfils this estimation.

NOTES & REFERENCES

1. Ojala, E.M., op.cit. p. 9.
2. For example, the 4th round refers to April-September, 1952. We have assumed that the results of the 4th round shall be true of the entire financial year 1951-52. Further, the NSS started its survey in both rural and urban areas only in 1950-51 Since no such survey existed for earlier years, we have assumed that the results of this round hold good for 1948-49, 1949-50 and 1950-51. Similarly in the case of the 13th round, it has been assumed that its results hold good for 1957-58 and 1958-59.
3. There is precedent to such assumptions -- Desai, Padma "A short term planning model for the Indian economy", The Review of Economics & Statistics, Vol. XLIII, May, 1961. Also her unpublished Ph.D. thesis titled "A short term planning model for the Indian Economy" (Thesis submitted to Harvard University).
4. Since the Census reports do not contain information on the rural-urban classification of the areas of Jammu & Kashmir, we have excluded the estimates of population of these areas from those of all-India. Thus the estimates of population used here will be less than the estimates recorded in the Census reports.
5. Census of India Paper No. 1, 1953 - pp. 8, 10 & 13, Sample verification of the 1951 census count.
6. Census of India -- Part II-B, Gen. Population -- Econ. Tables. Table-B. III. The classification of self-supporting persons by the 7th & 8th categories have

not been mentioned here, as they were not immediately relevant for the purpose of the present work.

7. The census gives information regarding the correspondence between the economic classification of self-supporting persons and the classification of general population by different categories. It is stated in the census report that groups 1, 2, 3, 4, and 5 of self-supporting persons broadly correspond to the population category of "Production other than cultivation" and that groups 6 and 8 correspond broadly to "other services" and "miscellaneous" in population tables. This information has been made use of and the ratio of self-supporting persons in 1(a), (b) and (c) to total self-supporting persons in 1, 2, 3, 4, & 5 has been applied to the population in 1951-52 in the category "production other than cultivation" and an estimate of population in the animal husbandry sector etc. has been made. (The implicit assumption is that population is distributed in these occupations in the same ratio as self-supporting persons). This, added to the estimate of population in "agriculture proper" gives us an estimate of population engaged in agriculture. Similarly applying the ratio of self-supporting persons in forestry, fishery and mining to total self-supporting persons in groups 1, 2, 3, 4 & 5, to the population category of "people in production other than cultivation", we get estimates of population engaged in these occupations. On the same lines, applying the ratio of self-supporting persons engaged in construction to the total number of self-supporting persons in economic classification 6 and 8 to the population category "other services and miscellaneous", we get estimates of population engaged in construction activities. Applying the ratio of self-supporting persons in 2, 3, 4 & 5 to total self-supporting persons in 1, 2, 3, 4 & 5, to the population category of "production other than cultivation", we get estimates of people engaged in "small industries" and "factory establishments". Since we are interested in estimates of population in small enterprises and factory establishments separately, we have made use of the ratio of work force in these two sub-sectors in 1951-52 as given in the Revised estimates of workforce ("Proposals", p.7) and split the population into those in small industries and in factory establishments. The population estimates of forestry, fishery, construction and small enterprises together constitute the population in the "unorganised" subsector of industrial sector while those of factory establishments and mining form the 'organised' sub-sector of the industrial sector. The estimates of population of the former category as well as those of the agricultural sector have been assumed to grow at the geometric rate of growth of population of the rural sector and the organised part of the industrial sector at the urban rate.

8. Taxation Enquiry Commission Report, Vol. I, p. 66.

9. A recent (unpublished) study by Khusro shows that the weighted average of the marginal rate of income tax for different income groups has remained practically unchanged during the decade of planning.

10. The rural and urban per capita expenditures on individual items have been given in 4th round which corresponds to 1951-52. From this data, the weights for agricultural and industrial sectors were calculated on lines explained so far. These weights are gross of imports. (This is one reason we look to 1951-52 as base year).

11. Measurement of economic welfare implies the summation of utilities and therefore the prices should correspond as closely as possible to relative marginal utilities. As Hicks states, this means using retail prices after tax or subsidy -- the prices which face the consumer and on the basis of which he spreads his expenditure over the field of available consumption goods.

4

Intersectoral Demand for Products : For Intermediate Use

AS stated in the previous chapter, it is proposed to undertake an estimation of the intersectoral flows of intermediate products. Intermediate products include not only basic materials, but also other factors of production. In this chapter, the intersectoral movements of basic materials alone will be dealt with for the reason that while factors of production are 'intermediate', they are however not 'products'. The intersectoral mobility of other factors of production will be considered in a subsequent chapter.

The main sources of data are (i) Proposals for a revised series of National Income (CSO), (ii) First and Final Reports of National Income Committee (1951) and (1954), (iii) Report of the Census of Manufacturing Industries (Annual) 1948 to 1958, (iv) Report of the Sample Survey of Manufacturing Industries (Annual) 1949 to 1954, (v) Economic Adviser's Series of Index Numbers of Wholesale Prices, (vi) Annual Statement of Foreign Trade of India and (vii) Monthly Statistics of Foreign Trade of India. With data from these sources, we identify and quantify (at current and at constant prices) the intermediate products traded between agriculture and industry.

Agriculture's Demand for Industrial Products for Intermediate Use

The intermediate products agriculture buys from industry are (i) fertilisers and other chemical manures, (ii) machinery and implements, (iii) oilcakes for livestock feed, i.e. for farm animals and other non-farm animals and (iv) medicine, ghee and salt for farm and service animals. In Chapter 2, we had derived the values, at current prices, of the costs of each of these items. The costs of depreciation in agriculture and animal husbandry sectors along with the costs of repairs and maintenance in the agricultural sector may be deemed to be the current expenses on machinery and equipment. These costs include expenses not only on domestically produced items but also those on imports. The estimated value of inputs (net of imports) at current prices bought by agriculture from the domestic industrial sector is shown in Table 4.1.

For working out the estimates of constant prices, the Economic Adviser's Index numbers of wholesale prices of fertilisers, machinery and equipment and oil cakes available from 1950-51 have been used[1] for deflating the current values of the respective inputs. The estimates at constant prices are also given in this table.

Industry's Demand for Agricultural Products for Intermediate Use

As regards the industrial sector, the subsectors forestry, fishery, mining and construction have hardly any significant input relations with agriculture. It is only the factory establishments sector and the small enterprises sector that buy intermediate products from agriculture.

With regard to the factory establishment sector, in consonance with the procedure adopted by us for computing the gross and net outputs of the industries dependent on agriculture for their raw materials, it has been assumed that for these industries, the values of inputs bought from agriculture as per CMI results, after due corrections (vide Chapter 2) should be fairly good estimates. For those industries for which the SSMI figures of value added have been projected and also for the rice-milling industry, it has been assumed that the implicit (agricultural) input -- value added ratio of these industries as per CMI data holds good. Applying these ratios to the projected estimates of value added of these industries,

TABLE - 4.1

Value of Inputs Used by Agriculture and bought from the Domestic Industrial Sector

1948-49 - 1958-59

(In Rs. Crores)

ITEMS (1)	1948-49 (2)	1949-50 (3)	1950-51 (4)	1951-52 (5)	1952-53 (6)	1953-54 (7)	1954-55 (8)	1955-56 (9)	1956-57 (10)	1957-58 (11)	1958-59 (12)
1. At current prices	242.5	250.5	242.4	238.5	245.0	262.7	275.2	270.3	285.1	289.6	320.0
2. At constant (51-52) prices	279.0	284.9	271.7	238.5	239.2	260.5	282.8	281.1	275.1	274.0	291.9

the estimates of inputs bought by them from agriculture have been calculated.

With regard to the tanning and vegetable oils industries, these are also in the small enterprises sector. There is no way of finding out the actual values of the inputs of these industries in the small enterprises sector. Hence we have assumed that the production of hides and skins and oilseeds net of exports is transported to the industrial sector. The vegetable oils industry uses some foodgrains also and the same has been estimated on the basis of the ratio of value of foodgrains to value added of this industry according to CMI data. The global approach of taking the value of output net of exports as representative of the sales to the domestic industrial sector has been used in some other industries -- tobacco[2], tea, coffee and rubber -- for two reasons. Firstly, the CMI does not cover these industries; secondly, these products are bought by the small enterprises sector as well.

Foodgrains are also consumed as intermediate products by the food processing industries in the small enterprises sector. To estimate this, the value added of this industry has been first worked out using the information for the food, drink and tobacco group of small industries

TABLE - 4.2

Value of Inputs Used by Industry and Bought from the Domestic Agriculture

1948-49 - 1958-59

(In Rs. Crores)

ITEMS (1)	1948-49 (2)	1949-50 (3)	1950-51 (4)	1951-52 (5)	1952-53 (6)	1953-54 (7)	1954-55 (8)	1955-56 (9)	1956-57 (10)	1957-58 (11)	1958-59 (12)
1. At Current Prices	780.38	966.81	998.33	1116.37	1007.42	1063.42	1048.76	967.93	1223.31	1298.96	1372.47
2. At Constant (1951-52) Prices	1031.66	1159.42	1046.28	1116.37	1351.24	1215.70	1357.90	1356.61	1403.46	1458.25	1501.78

as in Revised Estimates[3] and the separate estimates of the different industries in this group in the Sample Survey Report of Small Manufacturing Enterprises[4]. The ratio as given in the latter Report, of inputs to value added of the food, drink and tobacco industry was applied to the food processing industry alone. Further it was found from the NSS Report No. 19 on Small Scale Manufacturing Establishments that nearly 85 percent of the inputs in small industries are primary materials. A figure of 90 percent has been derived by Dhar[5] in his study on small industries in Delhi. Using this latter figure, we have derived the value of foodgrains consumed by the food processing industries in the small enterprises sector.

The value at current prices thus derived of inputs bought by various industries from agriculture have been netted of imports[6]. With the help of the price indices of individual inputs, the values of intermediate products demanded by industry from the domestic agricultural sector at constant (51-52) prices have been derived. These values at current and constant prices are given in Table 4.2.

Table 4.3 gives the time-series of the ratio of the value

TABLE - 4.3

Input-Output Coefficients — Agriculture and Industry

1948-49 - 1958-59

[At Constant (51-52) Prices] (In Rs. Crores)

ITEMS (1)	1948-49 (2)	1949-50 (3)	1950-51 (4)	1951-52 (5)	1952-53 (6)	1953-54 (7)	1954-55 (8)	1955-56 (9)	1956-57 (10)	1957-58 (11)	1958-59 (12)
1. Gross output of agriculture	6557	6312	6202	6200	6923	7245	6947	7065	7438	6838	7648
2. Value of industrial inputs consumed by agriculture	279.0	284.9	271.7	238.5	239.2	260.5	282.8	281.1	275.1	274.0	291.9
3. Input (from industry) — output (of agriculture) coefficient	0.0425	0.0451	0.0438	0.0394	0.0346	0.0359	0.0408	0.0398	0.0369	0.0400	0.0382
4. Gross output of industry	3594	3738	3769	4201	4483	4494	4825	5322	5439	5825	6031
5. Value of agricultural inputs consumed by industry	1031.7	1159.4	1046.3	1116.4	1351.2	1215.7	1357.9	1356.6	1403.5	1458.3	1501.8
6. Input (from agriculture) — output (of Industry) coefficient	0.2873	0.3101	0.2776	0.2658	0.3014	0.2705	0.2814	0.2549	0.2580	0.2504	0.2490

of inputs bought by agriculture from industry to agricultural gross output and the ratio of the value of inputs bought by industry from agriculture to industrial gross output (all at constant prices). These may be called input (from industry) — output (of agriculture) coefficients and input (from agriculture) — output (of industry) coefficients respectively.

Retentions of Agriculture and Industry

The difference between the gross value of output of a sector and the total of its net output and its demand for intermediate products produced by a second sector gives us an idea of the first sector's demand for intermediate products which may be produced by itself or by a third sector. Using this as the basis, the estimates of value of demand of each of agriculture and industry, for intermediate products which may be produced by that sector itself or may be coming from the rest of the economy have been calculated. These may be called "retentions/ expenditures on the products of the rest of the economy". From this value, we can separate the value of retentions of that sector. Thus with regard to the agricultural sector, retentions for intermediate use consist of seed, organic manure and cost of feed of farm and non-service animals (other than the cost on oilcakes and medicine and ghee). In order to find the value of the industrial sector's retentions of its own products for intermediate use, we have identified the payments of this sector by way of bank charges and insurance premia as its expenses on the products of the rest of the economy and deducted the same from the value of retentions/expenses on the products of the rest of the economy. Using the general industrial price index, the corresponding values of retentions at constant prices have also been computed. The value of retentions for intermediate use in agriculture and industry at constant prices are presented in Table-4.4.

In the following chapter, we shall use the results obtained so far and examine the movements of intersectoral demand for products in general.

TABLE - 4.4

Value of Retentions for Intermediate Use in Agriculture & Industry

1948-49 - 1958-59

(At constant (51-52) prices)

(In Rs. Crores)

ITEMS (1)	1948-49 (2)	1949-50 (3)	1950-51 (4)	1951-52 (5)	1952-53 (6)	1953-54 (7)	1954-55 (8)	1955-56 (9)	1956-57 (10)	1957-58 (11)	1958-59 (12)
1. Value of retentions in agriculture	1040.30	930.70	786.60	887.00	1072.70	992.20	890.60	987.80	992.30	928.70	972.90
2. Value of retentions in industry	968.76	887.59	923.83	1329.70	1306.93	1257.68	1441.35	1759.69	1732.78	1959.51	2025.37

NOTES & REFERENCES

1. Current values of these inputs had been earlier computed by us (Chapter 2) on lines similar to the estimation of national income, using wholesale prices. Thus the most appropriate indices for deflating them to constant prices are those of wholesale prices.

2. It has been assumed the value of output of tobacco net of exports and net of 20% of the value is available for the next year (Marketing of Tobacco in India, DMI Series 1951).

3. "Proposals", p. 114.

4. National Sample Survey Reports -- 9th & 10th Rounds-Report, No. 43.

5. Dhar P.N. Small Scale Industries in Delhi, Asia Publishing House (1958).

6. This does not apply to industries where the global approach has been adopted.

5

Intersectoral Demand for Products : For All Uses

IN the last two chapters, we had evolved time-series of value of intersectoral demand for consumption goods as well as for inputs. It is intended here to analyse these results. For this, we shall use the results at constant prices only, as they depict 'real' changes.

Demand, Supply and Marketed Surplus

The total demand of the economy for the products of a sector may be conceived of as the sum of the demand for its products for final and intermediate uses; each of these two categories is made up of the demand by the three sectors of the economy, viz., agriculture, industry and rest of the economy. In the case of agricultural products, the demand of the rest of the economy for intermediate use is almost negligible and has therefore been omitted by us from consideration. In the case of industrial products, however, the demand of the rest of the economy for intermediate use may be somewhat larger, but this has not been calculated by us.

The supply of a sector's products is the gross output of that sector at constant prices. We have already derived the estimates of the value of gross output of agriculture and industry in Chapter 2. Further, we require estimates of marketed surplus of the products of agriculture and industry, both total and that part which is exported to industry and agriculture respectively. The total domestic demand for a sector's products less the value of its retentions for intermediate and final uses may be considered to be, in effect, the value of its marketed surplus (i.e. marketed to the rest of the domestic sectors of the economy). Similarly, of the two sectors, agriculture and industry, the value of demand by one sector for the other sector's products, for intermediate and final uses together, may be deemed to be the value marketed by the latter sector to the former.

Keeping in view the above definitions, the annual values (at constant prices) of demand of agriculture, industry and rest of the economy for agricultural products for intermediate and final uses[1] as also those of marketed surplus of agriculture have been given in Table 5.1. Similar estimates for industrial products are provided in Table 5.3. Indices of supply, demand and marketed surplus of agricultural and industrial products are shown in Tables 5.2 and 5.4 respectively. Tables 5.2 and 5.4 also furnish some complex relationships, viz. (i) percentage of gross output of agriculture/industry marketed to the rest of the domestic sectors of the economy[2] (ii) percentage of gross output of agriculture/industry exported to industry/agriculture respectively (iii) percentage of a sector's (agriculture or industry) total consumption expenditure[3] directed towards the finished consumption products produced by the other sector (iv) percentage of a sector's total input expenditure[4] on the inputs produced by the other sector and (v) percentage of expenditure of agriculture/industry on inputs and final products from industry/agriculture to its total expenditure on all products.

Economy's Demand for Agricultural Products

The value of aggregate demand for all agricultural products, whether in intermediate or in final use has fluctuated and has a tendency to fall and has in fact fallen, based on triennium averages in the beginning and end of the decade by 5 percent as against a rise of 15 percent in the gross output of agriculture. The total demand of the economy for agricultural products for final use has moved similar to that for all agricultural products. During 1948-49 — 1958-59, this has decreased by nearly

TABLE - 5.1

Demand and Marketed Surplus - Agricultural Products

1948-49 - 1958-59 (at constant '51-52 prices) (in Rs. crores)

ITEMS (1)	1948-49 (2)	1949-50 (3)	1950-51 (4)	1951-52 (5)	1952-53 (6)	1953-54 (7)	1954-55 (8)	1955-56 (9)	1956-57 (10)	1957-58 (11)	1958-59 (12)
1. Expenditure on agricultural final products by :											
• Agriculture	4688.40	4492.60	4521.96	3650.90	3523.15	3413.58	3575.46	4547.18	3943.90	3959.85	3673.81
• Industry	696.21	667.67	672.67	541.50	537.08	527.00	566.75	696.37	614.01	609.90	565.51
• Rest of the economy	1196.11	1149.75	1159.84	924.83	985.10	996.58	1135.40	1282.26	1182.98	1143.20	1052.79
Sub-Total	6580.72	6310.02	6354.47	5117.23	5045.33	4937.16	5277.61	6525.81	5740.89	5712.95	5292.11
2. Expenditure on agricultural intermediate products by :											
• Agriculture	1040.30	930.70	786.60	887.00	1072.70	992.20	890.60	987.80	992.30	928.70	972.90
• Industry	1031.66	1159.42	1046.28	1116.37	1351.24	1215.70	1357.90	1356.61	1403.46	1458.25	1501.78
Sub-Total	2071.96	2090.12	1832.88	2003.37	2423.94	2207.90	2248.50	2344.41	2395.76	2386.95	2474.68
3. Grand Total : (1)+(2)	8652.68	8400.14	8187.35	7120.60	7469.27	7082.16	7526.11	8870.22	8136.65	8099.91	7766.79
4. Marketed surplus to industry & rest of the economy :	2923.90	2976.80	2878.80	2582.70	2873.40	2739.30	3060.10	3335.20	3200.50	3211.40	3120.10
5. Marketed surplus to industry only :	1727.87	1827.09	1718.95	1657.87	1888.32	1742.70	1924.65	2052.98	2017.47	2068.15	2067.29
6. Percentage of (1) to (3)	76.1	75.1	77.6	71.8	67.5	69.7	71.3	73.6	70.5	70.5	68.1

TABLE - 5.2

Indices of Real Demand, Supply and Marketed Surplus; Some Relationships — Agricultural Products

1948-49 - 1958-59 1951-52 = 100

ITEMS (1)	1948-49 (2)	1949-50 (3)	1950-51 (4)	1951-52 (5)	1952-53 (6)	1953-54 (7)	1954-55 (8)	1955-56 (9)	1956-57 (10)	1957-58 (11)	1958-59 (12)
1. Index of all demand for agricultural products	121.52	117.97	114.98	100.00	104.90	99.46	105.69	124.57	114.27	113.75	109.07
2. Index of supply of agricultural products	105.75	101.80	100.03	100.00	111.65	116.85	112.03	113.95	119.95	110.29	123.35
3. Index of marketed surplus of agriculture to industry and rest of the economy	113.21	115.25	111.46	100.00	111.25	106.06	118.48	129.13	123.92	124.34	120.80
4. Index of marketed surplus of agriculture to industry only	104.22	110.21	103.68	100.00	113.90	105.12	116.09	123.83	121.69	124.75	124.70
5. Percentage of surplus marketed to industry and rest of the economy	44.59	47.16	46.41	41.66	41.51	37.81	44.05	47.21	43.03	46.96	40.80

(Contd....)

TABLE - 5.2 (...Contd.)

Indices of Real Demand, Supply and Marketed Surplus; Some Relationships — Agricultural Products

1948-49 - 1958-59 1951-52 = 100

ITEMS (1)	1948-49 (2)	1949-50 (3)	1950-51 (4)	1951-52 (5)	1952-53 (6)	1953-54 (7)	1954-55 (8)	1955-56 (9)	1956-57 (10)	1957-58 (11)	1958-59 (12)
6. Percentage of supply marketed to industry	26.35	28.96	27.71	26.74	27.28	24.05	27.70	29.05	27.13	30.24	27.03
7. Percentage of Industry's expenditure on agricultural consumption products to its total consumption expenditure	70.10	69.20	68.90	70.00	68.00	75.30	77.10	76.80	77.30	76.90	74.80
8. Percentage of industry's expenditure on inputs produced by agriculture to its total input expenditure	51.50	56.50	53.10	45.60	50.90	49.10	48.50	43.50	44.70	42.70	42.60
9. Percentage of industry's expenditure on agricultural final products and inputs to its total expenditure on all products	57.50	60.60	58.40	51.10	54.80	54.90	54.50	51.00	51.30	49.10	48.30

TABLE - 5.3

Demand and Marketed Surplus — Industrial Products

1948-49 — 1958-59 (at constant '51-52 prices) (in Rs. crores)

ITEMS (1)	1948-49 (2)	1949-50 (3)	1950-51 (4)	1951-52 (5)	1952-53 (6)	1953-54 (7)	1954-55 (8)	1955-56 (9)	1956-57 (10)	1957-58 (11)	1958-59 (12)
1. Expenditure on industrial final products by :											
• Agriculture	1656.37	1668.74	1698.74	1392.09	1416.93	1119.25	965.06	1293.24	1007.54	1146.48	1193.74
• Industry	294.19	296.99	303.30	231.96	252.69	172.69	167.98	209.36	180.26	182.75	190.75
• Rest of the economy	747.20	757.20	776.05	523.70	639.16	319.55	407.69	442.25	453.19	372.63	391.45
Sub-Total	2697.76	2722.93	2778.09	2147.75	2308.78	1611.49	1540.73	1944.85	1640.99	1701.86	1775.94
2. Expenditure on industrial intermediate products by :											
• Agriculture	279.00	284.90	271.70	238.50	239.20	260.50	282.80	281.10	275.10	274.00	291.90
• Industry	968.76	887.59	923.83	1329.70	1306.93	1257.68	1441.35	1759.69	1732.78	1959.51	2025.37
Sub-Total	1247.76	1172.49	1195.53	1568.20	1546.13	1518.18	1724.15	2040.79	2007.88	2233.51	2317.27
3. Grand Total : (1)+(2)	3945.52	3895.42	3973.62	3715.95	3854.91	3129.67	3264.88	3985.64	3648.87	3935.37	4093.21
4. Marketed surplus to agriculture & rest of the economy :	2682.57	2710.84	2746.49	2154.29	2295.29	1699.30	1655.55	2016.59	1735.83	1793.11	1850.09
5. Marketed surplus to agriculture only :	1935.37	1953.64	1970.44	1630.59	1656.13	1379.75	1247.86	1574.34	1282.64	1420.48	1485.64

TABLE - 5.4

Indices of Real Demand, Supply and Marketed Surplus; Some Relationships — Industrial Products

1948-49 - 1958-59 1951-52 = 100

ITEMS (1)	1948-49 (2)	1949-50 (3)	1950-51 (4)	1951-52 (5)	1952-53 (6)	1953-54 (7)	1954-55 (8)	1955-56 (9)	1956-57 (10)	1957-58 (11)	1958-59 (12)
1. Index of all demand for industrial products	106.18	104.83	106.93	100.00	103.74	84.22	87.86	107.26	98.19	105.90	110.15
2. Index of supply of industrial products	85.55	88.98	89.72	100.00	106.70	106.95	114.84	126.68	129.46	138.64	143.55
3. Index of marketed surplus of industry to agriculture and rest of the economy	124.52	125.83	127.49	100.00	106.55	78.88	76.85	93.61	80.58	83.23	85.88
4. Index of marketed surplus of industry to agriculture only	118.69	119.81	120.84	100.00	101.57	84.62	76.53	96.55	78.66	87.11	91.11
5. Percentage of supply marketed to agriculture and rest of the economy	74.64	72.52	72.87	51.28	51.20	37.82	34.31	37.89	31.91	30.79	30.68

(*Contd....*)

TABLE - 5.4 (...Contd.)

Indices of Real Demand, Supply and Marketed Surplus; Some Relationships — Industrial Products

1948-49 - 1958-59 1951-52 = 100

ITEMS (1)	1948-49 (2)	1949-50 (3)	1950-51 (4)	1951-52 (5)	1952-53 (6)	1953-54 (7)	1954-55 (8)	1955-56 (9)	1956-57 (10)	1957-58 (11)	1958-59 (12)
6. Percentage of supply marketed to agriculture	53.85	52.26	52.28	38.81	36.94	30.70	25.86	29.58	23.58	24.37	24.63
7. Percentage of agriculture's total consumption expenditure spent on industrial consumption products	26.10	27.10	27.30	27.10	28.70	24.70	21.30	22.10	20.40	22.50	24.50
8. Percentage of agriculture's total input expenditure spent on inputs produced by industry	21.10	23.40	25.70	21.20	18.20	20.80	24.10	22.10	21.70	22.80	23.10
9. Percentage of agriculture's total expenditure spent on the final products and inputs produced by industry	25.30	26.50	27.10	26.40	26.50	25.10	21.80	22.10	20.60	22.50	24.20

13 percent. However, the economy's demand for agricultural products for intermediate use has increased (21 percent). Besides, the proportion of the economy's expenditure on agricultural products for intermediate use to its total expenditure on these products for intermediate and final uses increased from 23.9% in 1948-49 to 31.9% in 1958-59.

Industry's Demand for Agricultural Products

The demand of the industrial sector for all agricultural products, i.e. the marketed surplus of agricultural products to the industrial sector depicts a slowly rising tendency, i.e. by a linear rate of around 1.7 percent per annum. If we examine the composition of this demand, the industrial demand for agricultural consumption goods shows a falling trend; over the period, the decline is of the order of 12 percent. As against this, the industrial demand for inputs from the agricultural sector has risen by nearly 3 times as much as the decline in its demand for agricultural consumption products.

In this connection, the present work has also studied the movement of the (agricultural) input- (industrial) output coefficients (Chapter 4). On an average, the cost of agricultural inputs used in industry has been 27 percent of the gross output of industry and nearly 50 percent of total inputs used by industry. Diagram 5.1 shows that the input-output coefficient has a declining trend. The coefficient has decreased from 0.29 in 1948-49 to 0.25 in 1958-59. This is because while industrial output had increased at an annual rate of around 6 percent, inputs from agriculture have risen at a much slower rate of around 4 percent.

Further, while the total expenditure of the industrial sector on all products and for all uses has been rising by almost 40 percent over this period, the percentage expended on agricultural products for all uses has declined by 16 percent. This decline has exhibited itself in a 21 percent decline in the percentage of expenditure of this sector on agricultural intermediate products to its total

DIAGRAM - 5.1

(Agricultural) **Input** — (Industrial) **Output Coefficients**

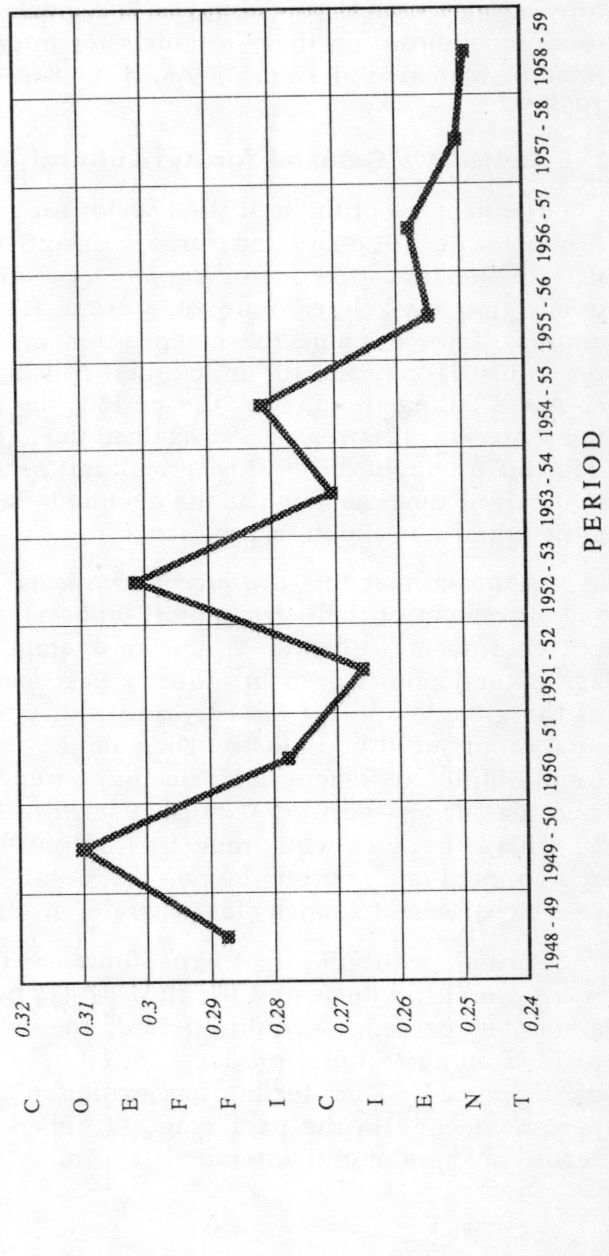

expenses on both agricultural and industrial intermediate products. On the other hand, the industrial sector has been gradually increasing the proportion of its expenditure on agricultural final products to its total expenditure on all final products. This percentage which was 70 in 1948-49 rose to 75 in 1958-59. (Diagram 5.2)

While this gives a picture of the fluctuations in demand by industry for agricultural products, it is also possible to examine how the 'effective supply' of agricultural products has behaved. The effective supply of agricultural products, in general, is the surplus that has been marketed by agriculture to the industrial sector and the rest of the economy. The percentage of marketed surplus as defined by us earlier to total agricultural output has been computed for every year and represented in Diagram 5.3. The percentage of agricultural surplus (marketed to the industrial sector and the rest of the economy) to the total supply of all agricultural products has portrayed a declining tendency, though the order of decline is rather small. On the other hand, the percentage of total agricultural output marketed to the industrial sector alone has shown a marginal rise. During the decade under consideration, the range of the former percentage has been 37 to 47 percent while the latter has fluctuated between 24 and 30 percent. The percentage of gross output of agriculture that is marketed to the other sectors of the economy at its maximum level is 47 percent. It is true that our estimate excludes agricultural exports to foreign countries. It has been observed that agricultural exports have recorded a rise during 1949-50 -- 1956-57[5]. Yet the absolute values of exports at current prices even in the peak year (1955-56) was only 7.6 percent of the current value of agricultural production in that year[6]. The implied fact is that after allowing for exports (abroad) of agricultural products, the order of self consumption in agriculture seems to be rather high. However, the demand of the agricultural sector for its own products for intermediate and final uses, has been declining slowly.

DIAGRAM - 5.2

Industry's Expenditure on Agricultural Products

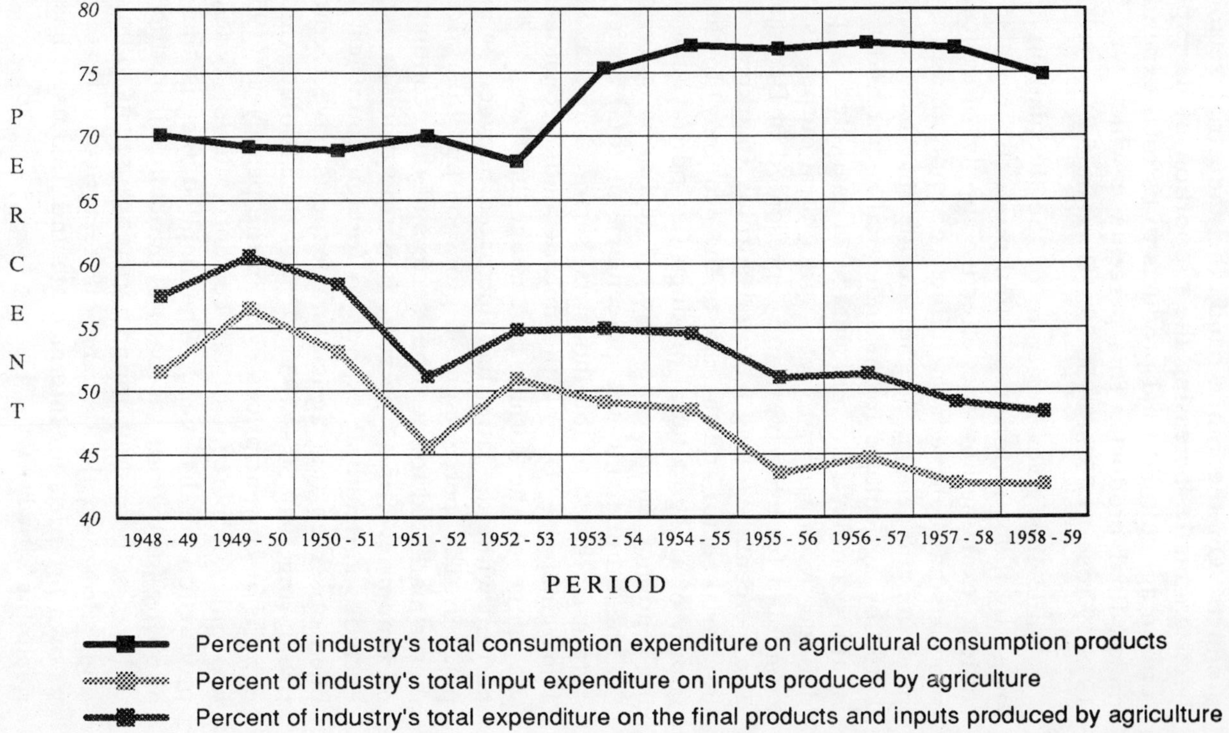

DIAGRAM - 5.3

Percentage of Agricultural Output Marketed

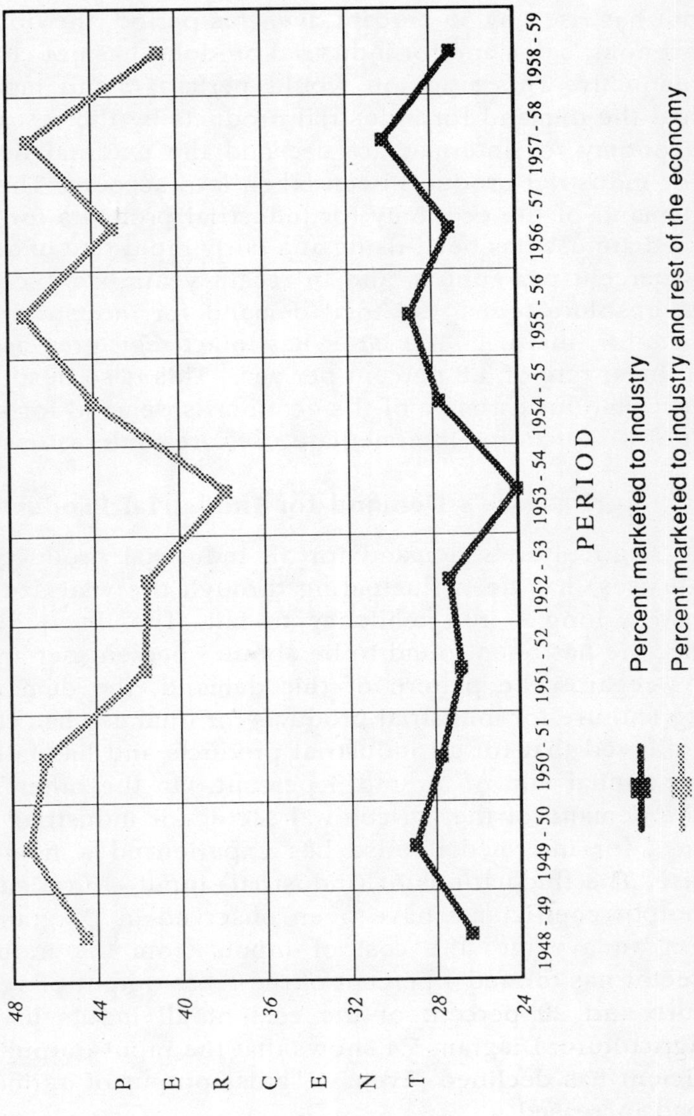

Economy's Demand for Industrial Products

We shall now proceed to study the demand for and supply of industrial products. While industrial gross output has risen by 56 percent over this period, the domestic economy's demand for industrial products has not changed distinctly. This situation would perhaps stand modified had the demand for industrial products by the rest of the economy for intermediate use and the external demand for industrial products been taken into account. The total demand of the economy for industrial products for intermediate use has been rising at a fairly rapid rate of around 8 percent per annum, and in recent years has exceeded, in absolute terms, the total demand for industrial products for final use. The latter has infact registered a fall at a linear rate of 3.8 percent per year. This is so despite the fact that our estimate of the economy's demand for industrial products for intermediate use, are underestimates.

Agriculture's Demand for Industrial Products

Agriculture's demand for all industrial products (for all uses) has been fluctuating through the years and has had a long -- run tendency to fall. The linear rate of decline has been found to be about 3 percent per annum. As regards the pattern of this demand, the demand of agriculture for industrial products for final use has closely followed that for all industrial products and has fallen at an annual rate of around 3 percent. On the other hand, the demand of the agricultural sector for industrial products for intermediate use has experienced a negligible rise. The fluctuations of (industrial) input -- (agricultural output coefficients have been observed in Diagram 5.4. On an average, the cost of inputs from the industrial sector has formed 4 percent of the gross output of agriculture and 20 percent of the cost of all inputs used by agriculture. Diagram 5.4 shows that the input-output coefficient has declined. Even so, gross output of agriculture had increased.

Further, both the absolute expenditures of agriculture on all products (industrial and agricultural) as well as its

DIAGRAM - 5.4

(Industrial) **Input** — (Agricultural) **Output Coefficients**

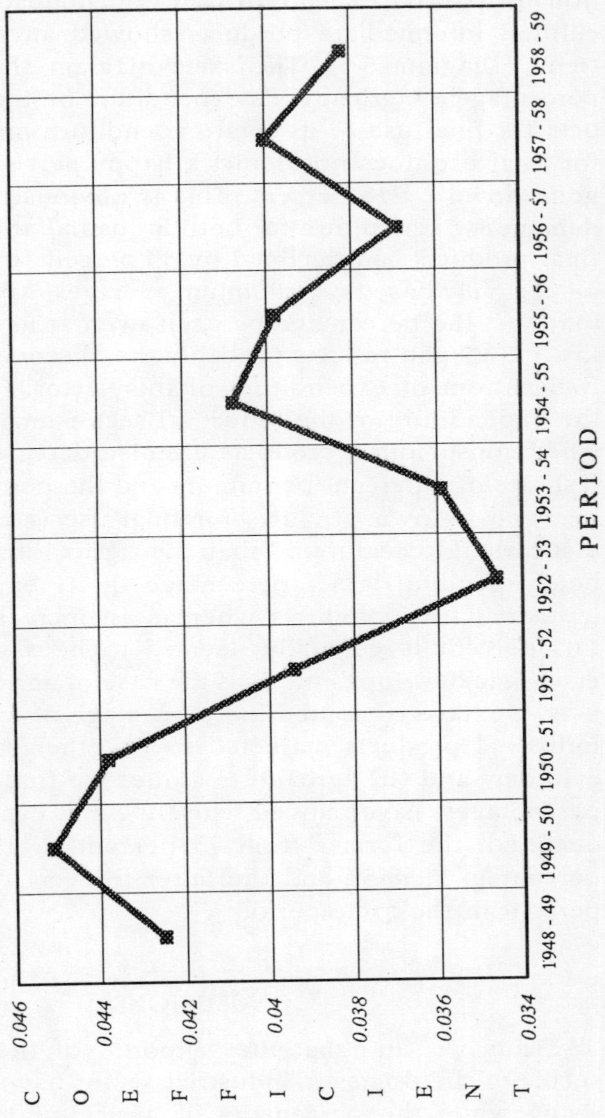

relative expenditure on only industrial products for all uses have fallen during this period. Again, agriculture's expenditure on industrial intermediate products in relation to its total expenditure on both industrial and agricultural intermediate products showed an imperceptible trend (Diagram 5.5). The same diagram shows that the percentage of agriculture's expenditure on industrial products for final use to its total expenditure on all products for final use does not depict a happy movement and has gone down by 16 percent. This is obviously because the demand by agriculture for both industrial and agricultural final products had declined by 33 percent and 16 percent respectively based on triennium averages. Apart from fluctuations, the percentage by itself even at its maximum, is low i.e. 29 and reflects probably the absence of a diversified pattern of expenditure of this sector. It is true that the expenditure of the industrial sector on industrial finished consumption products has also declined at a rather fast rate of 3 percent per annum and the percentage spent by it on its own products for final use is not high. The disheartening feature is that the agricultural sector has been spending lesser percentage of its expenditure on industrial final products whereas an increasing trend in this percent is generally deemed to be associated with economic development. As is the case of agricultural products, we have computed the percentage of total supply of industrial products marketed to (i) other sectors of the economy and (ii) agriculture alone. We find that the two percentages have moved closely with each other and declined, the former from 75 percent in 1948-49 to 31 percent in 1958-59 and the latter from 54 percent to 25 percent in the same period.

CONCLUSIONS

Thus we find that the "exports" of the agricultural sector to the domestic industrial sector have been slowly rising while the percentage of agricultural output marketed to industry has also shown a marginal rise. On the other hand, the imports' of agriculture from the domestic

DIAGRAM - 5.5

Agriculture's Expenditure on Industrial Products

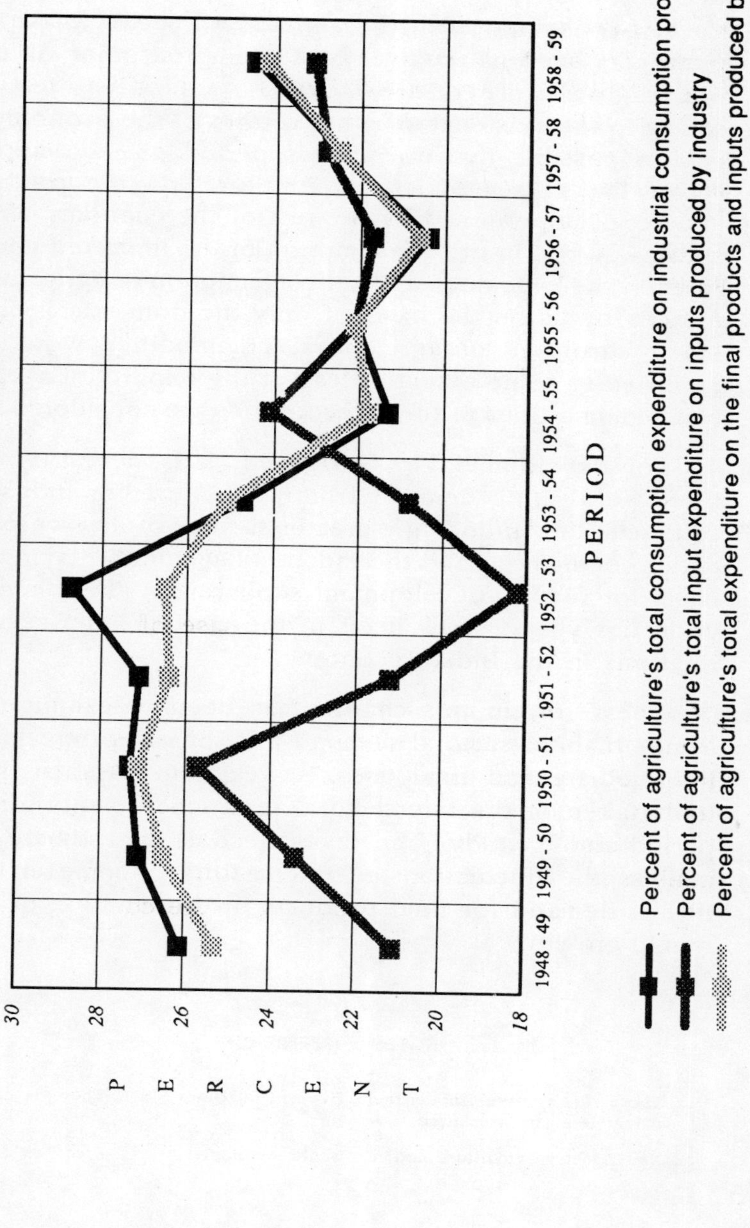

industrial sector have shown a significant decline. Moreover, the percentage of industrial output marketed to agriculture has also declined at a very fast rate. These last mentioned two results, combined with our earlier observation of a fairly high percentage of output being retained for self-consumption in the agricultural sector, make the picture rather unattractive from the stand-point of economic growth. There are, however, some qualifications owing to the existence of other sectors of the economy. It is thus possible that during this period, the agricultural sector had increased its `expenditure' on the products and services produced by the rest of the economy not to speak of a rise in the consumption of the imported goods. Further, the large degree of selfconsumption of agricultured noticed by us on the basis of only the domestically marketed surpluses of agricultural commodities would be modified to some extent at least if the exports of agricultural commodities to foreign countries are considered too.

For development to feed itself, it is necessary that there be a rising demand from agriculture for industrial products, thus inducing a greater surplus of its own products to be marketed to the industrial sector and laying the basis for further development. Apparently, this phenomenon has yet to show itself in the case of inter-sectoral relations in the Indian economy.

The effort in this chapter has been to examine the trends of inter-sectoral demand relations in products, for intermediate and final uses. A treatment has also been undertaken of the intersectoral input-coefficients for the period under study. The task ahead is to estimate and analyse the fluctuations in intersectoral income elasticities of demand for final products, in the context of economic growth.

NOTES & REFERENCES

1. These results have already been given in Chapters 3 & 4. They are consolidated here and presented.
2. i.e. industry/agriculture and rest of the economy.

3. Total consumption expenditure on agricultural consumption products and industrial consumption products.

4. Total expenditure on inputs from agriculture and on inputs from industry.

5. Poduval R.N. : Prices, Trade and Marketing of Agricultural Commodities in India. Table VI p. 63 in Studies in Indian Agricultural Economics (1958) ed. J.P. Bhattacharjee.

6. Ibid p. 63.

6

Income Elasticities of Intersectoral Consumer Demand

IN the previous chapter, we had examined the behaviour over time of the intersectoral real demand for products for final and intermediate uses. We had observed a gradually rising 'export' curve of agricultural products to the domestic industrial sector as against a declining 'import' curve of industrial products into the domestic agricultural sector. Further, the demand of agriculture and industry for agricultural consumption products and industrial consumption products had declined during this period. This has to be explained, at any rate, partly by the impact[1] of the generally rising trend of prices of consumption goods. However, it would be of interest to isolate the 'income' effect from this picture and examine the magnitude of income elasticities of consumer demand of either sector for each of these two categories of goods. This has been attempted in the present chapter.

Income Elasticity of Demand and Expenditure Elasticity of Demand

What we are trying to estimate here is the 'expenditure' elasticity of demand and not the 'income' elasticity of demand. Since our work in this direction is bound to be based on the National Sample Survey Results regarding the pattern of Consumer expenditure in the country and since these survey reports present the pattern of expenditure only by 'expenditure classes', the meaningful relationship that can be evolved out of these data can only be the 'expenditure' elasticities of demand. It is true that the 'income' elasticity of demand for a product can be estimated by adjusting the 'expenditure' elasticity of demand for this product with the income elasticity of total national consumption expenditure. However, in view of the fact that there is no authentic estimate of the latter, it is decided to derive the estimates of only the intersectoral expenditure elasticities of demand. The implication is that the expenditure elasticity of demand can be deemed to be in fact an overestimated 'income' elasticity of demand, in so far as there is some saving done by individuals. With this qualification, we shall be using the term 'income elasticity of demand' as synonymous with 'expenditure elasticity of demand'.

Estimates of income (or expenditure) elasticities of demand which are proposed to be derived in this chapter shall be based not on time-series analysis but on cross-section analysis. The main problem in measuring the income elasticity of demand for a commodity is to isolate the income effect from the effects of all other factors. The family budget data which form the basis for cross-sectional analysis pertain to a point of time when other factors including prices remain constant. Therefore, the variations observed in consumption could be related to the variations in incomes and expenditures of the person. It should be remembered that the income or expenditure function based on cross-sectional data would characterise the behaviour of different expenditure classes at a point of time and cannot be generalised to hold good over a period of time, when incomes or total expenses of the economy may be changing. We may, with these clarifications, proceed to estimate the expenditure elasticities of demand.

Method of Estimation of Expenditure Elasticity of Demand

Firstly, the NSS data (Reports for the 3rd, 4th, 5th, 7th, 10th and 12th rounds) have been made use of. The NSS gives per capita expenditure in rupees by per capita expenditure class-intervals in rural and urban areas separately and by different items of consumption.

The method of classification of these twelve items as agricultural, industrial and service items as in chapter 3 has been observed in the estimation of income elasticities of demand too. However, since it was not possible to separate 'pan' and 'refreshments' in the data by per capita expenditure classes (as we could do in the case of data for all expenditure classes), we had to resort to the procedure of omitting the miscellaneous group completely and including the 'other food items' group wholly with the agricultural finished product groups. The per capita expenditures in Rs. on agricultural and industrial finished products were thus calculated for rural and urban areas.

As far as the agricultural sector is concerned, the rural pattern can be taken to be representative. But in the case of the industrial sector, the rural pattern holds good for the 'unorganised' sub-sector and the urban pattern for the 'organised' subsector. The NSS gives for each round the distribution of estimated number of persons by expenditure classes in rural and urban areas respectively. We have for each year the population estimates of the 'unorganised' and the 'organised' sub-sectors of the industrial sector of the economy (Ch. 3). Assuming that the distribution of population by expenditure classes in rural areas holds good for the unorganised subsector and that in the urban areas for the organised subsector, the population for each year in unorganised and the organised sub-sectors was distributed among the expenditure classes according to the rural and urban patterns respectively. It was possible in this manner to arrive at estimates of population distributed by expenditure classes in unorganised and organised sub-sectors of the industrial sector.

The estimated number of persons in organised and unorganised sub-sectors in each expenditure class were applied as weights respectively to the urban and the rural per head expenditure in each category of goods in that expenditure class. This resulted in a weighted average of per head expenditure representative of that in the industrial sector for each expenditure class and on each

TABLE - 6.1

Per Capita Monthly Expenditure in Rs. on Agricultural & Industrial Final Products in Agriculture and Industry - By Per Capita Expenditure Classes and by the Different Rounds of the National Sample Survey

Per capita expendi-ture class intervals	3rd round		4th round		5th round		7th round		8th round		10th round		12th round	
	Expenses on Agrl. prod.	Expenses on Ind. prod.	Expenses on Agrl. prod.	Expenses on Ind. prod.	Expenses on Agrl. prod.	Expenses on Ind. prod.	Expenses on Agrl. prod.	Expenses on Ind. prod.	Expenses on Agrl. prod.	Expenses on Ind. prod.	Expenses on Agrl. prod.	Expenses on Ind. prod.	Expenses on Agrl. prod.	Expenses on Ind. prod.
(1)	(2)	(3)	(4)	(5)	(6)	(7)	(8)	(9)	(10)	(11)	(12)	(13)	(14)	(15)
							AGRICULTURAL SECTOR							
0-8	4.10	1.29	4.11	1.26	4.05	1.26	4.73	1.03	4.31	1.08	4.61	1.22	4.97	0.98
8-11	6.74	2.02	6.41	1.99	6.37	1.88	6.84	2.05	6.76	1.93	6.64	1.92	7.32	1.59
11-13	8.35	2.37	8.25	2.29	7.84	2.54	8.91	1.89	8.28	2.46	8.59	2.31	8.95	2.20
13-15	9.30	2.98	9.19	2.65	8.94	3.09	9.71	2.87	9.18	3.06	9.62	2.88	10.36	2.42
15-18	11.58	3.24	11.02	3.02	10.87	3.22	10.96	3.33	10.75	3.63	10.90	3.60	11.70	3.18
18-21	13.34	3.91	12.81	3.39	11.86	3.91	12.27	4.32	11.54	4.80	12.48	4.48	13.49	3.92
21-24	14.64	4.63	14.20	4.27	13.78	4.35	13.88	5.44	13.42	5.34	14.16	4.98	15.14	4.51
24.28	15.92	5.03	15.32	4.85	15.41	5.05	14.76	7.00	15.09	7.05	15.38	6.15	15.66	5.99
28-34	19.06	6.23	17.89	5.16	17.02	5.70	16.23	8.10	16.13	7.31	17.44	8.01	18.27	6.86
34-43	21.94	7.26	21.73	6.65	20.10	6.82	18.23	9.21	19.98	9.81	19.29	9.51	21.16	7.55
43-55	26.09	9.36	23.10	8.18	24.42	9.42	24.87	11.32	23.44	14.29	27.14	9.08	24.93	10.88
55 & above	36.12	12.82	32.71	12.80	25.56	10.59	32.58	17.56	22.53	17.66	31.96	21.40	30.77	21.63

(*Contd...*)

TABLE - 6.1 (...Contd.)

Per Capita Monthly Expenditure in Rs. on Agricultural & Industrial Final Products in Agriculture and Industry - By Per Capita Expenditure Classes and by the Different Rounds of the National Sample Survey

Per capita expendi-ture class intervals	3rd round		4th round		5th round		7th round		8th round		10th round		12th round	
	Expenses on Agrl. prod.	Expenses on Ind. prod.	Expenses on Agrl. prod.	Expenses on Ind. prod.	Expenses on Agrl. prod.	Expenses on Ind. prod.	Expenses on Agrl. prod.	Expenses on Ind. prod.	Expenses on Agrl. prod.	Expenses on Ind. prod.	Expenses on Agrl. prod.	Expenses on Ind. prod.	Expenses on Agrl. prod.	Expenses on Ind. prod.
(1)	(2)	(3)	(4)	(5)	(6)	(7)	(8)	(9)	(10)	(11)	(12)	(13)	(14)	(15)
INDUSTRIAL SECTOR														
0-8	4.11	1.32	4.15	1.28	4.06	1.27	4.75	1.00	4.32	1.09	4.61	1.21	4.96	0.98
8-11	6.70	2.04	6.38	2.00	6.28	1.95	6.77	2.00	6.73	1.89	6.62	1.88	7.24	1.60
11-13	8.16	2.47	8.01	2.34	7.76	2.51	8.71	1.96	8.11	2.39	8.44	2.31	8.84	2.16
13-15	9.15	3.02	8.92	2.78	8.85	3.09	9.63	2.86	9.04	3.03	9.45	2.87	10.10	2.49
15-18	11.08	3.37	10.67	3.17	10.58	3.36	10.91	3.20	10.52	3.53	10.66	3.60	11.37	3.24
18-21	12.78	4.09	12.34	3.52	11.43	3.98	12.02	4.04	11.61	4.53	12.14	4.33	13.00	3.87
21-24	14.14	4.77	13.52	4.40	13.31	4.54	13.66	5.28	12.95	5.22	13.71	5.00	14.43	4.57
24-28	15.56	5.21	14.69	4.96	14.91	5.23	14.76	6.48	14.34	6.79	14.99	6.03	15.47	5.74
28-34	18.17	6.36	17.05	5.44	16.37	5.83	16.70	7.63	16.01	7.08	16.98	7.50	18.01	6.42
34-43	21.00	7.61	20.42	7.08	19.41	7.30	18.44	8.74	19.27	8.92	18.92	8.69	20.36	7.70
43-55	24.64	9.51	21.72	8.67	22.99	9.97	23.48	10.92	21.83	12.15	25.42	9.46	24.66	10.12
55 & above	34.20	13.88	31.76	13.68	27.78	12.09	31.76	14.99	27.45	17.37	32.38	18.86	32.74	18.68

category of goods. Thus, the per capita expenditure of agricultural and industrial sectors on agricultural and industrial goods by each expenditure class was obtained. (Table -6.1)

This forms the basis for our calculations of the 'expenditure' elasticity of demand of each sector for its own products as well as that for the products of the other sector. It was observed that a double logarithmic curve provided a very good fit for these data. Further, this particular type of function is convenient in that the parameters can be estimated easily and algebraic manipulation is simpler than with most other forms. Of course, the double logarithmic function implies the assumption of constancy of elasticity for all income or expenditure levels. It would be more realistic to assume a variable elasticity which is lower for higher income groups, higher for lower income groups and which decreases monotonically as income increases. However, the fact of closeness of fit and the convenience and elegance of the function itself led to the choice of the double logarithmic function. The resulting estimates of expenditure-elasticity of demand of each sector for its own products and also for the products of the other sector for each round of Survey and the average estimate for all the rounds are presented in Table-6.2.

Three things are evident from an examination of Table-6.2. In the first place, the income (or expenditure) elasticities of demand of both the agricultural and the industrial sectors for each of the two categories of goods are generally less than unity. Thus, both in the case of agricultural consumption products and industrial consumption products, at every point of time, the marginal propensity to consume is less than the average propensity to consume.

Secondly, the income elasticity of demand of the agricultural sector for agricultural products has been fluctuating between 0.594 and 0.772. On an average, the magnitude has been 0.7. The income elasticity of demand of the industrial sector has not been far different from the above.

The same has been ranging from 0.645 to 0.749 thus yielding an average of 0.694 for all the rounds of survey. As against this, the income elasticity of demand of the agricultural sector for industrial products has moved between 0.777 and 1.060. The average estimate has been 0.914. With a very nearly similar average of 0.906, the income elasticity of demand of the industrial sector for industrial products fluctuated within 0.796 and 1.028. Thus, it can be held that in the case of each of these categories of goods, the income elasticity of demand of the agricultural sector has been similar to that of the industrial sector.

TABLE-6.2

Expenditure Elasticity Coefficients

Rounds	Demand for Agricultural Products Expenditure elasticity	Demand for Industrial Products Expenditure elasticity
	of agricultural sector	of agricultural sector
3rd round	0.772	0.826
4th round	0.744	0.777
5th round	0.747	0.815
7th round	0.657	1.047
8th round	0.594	1.060
10th round	0.710	0.933
12th round	0.673	0.940
Average expenditure elasticity coefficient	0.700	Average expenditure-elasticity coefficient 0.914
	of Industrial Sector	of Industrial Sector
3rd round	0.749	0.830
4th round	0.713	0.796
5th round	0.724	0.837
7th round	0.645	1.028
8th round	0.673	1.009
10th round	0.690	0.924
12th round	0.665	0.918
Average expenditure elasticity coefficient	0.694	Average expenditure elasticity coefficient 0.906

Thirdly, the income elasticity of demand of these sectors has been higher for industrial products than for agricultural products. The implication is that at every point of time, if people of lower expenditure classes moved into higher ones, the tendency was to spend a higher proportion of the additional expenditure (or income) on industrial goods in relation to that spent on agricultural goods.

From these results, one may infer perhaps that even when a poor country with backlogs of unemployment, under-employment, mal-nutrition and low incomes starts to get additional employment and income, the marginal propensity of consumption of the economy in relation to the average propensity of consumption is higher for industrial products than for agricultural products.

Thus, in this and the last two chapters, we have made a study of intersectoral demand for products. However, when we considered the intersectoral demand for products for intermediate use, we had taken into account only the basic materials. We have, therefore, yet to examine the intersectoral mobility of factors of production. The succeeding chapter deals with this problem.

NOTES & REFERENCES

1. It is true that we have eliminated the 'price factor', in that we are examining only the expenditures at constant prices. However, there is still the 'impact of price change' which is contained even in the estimates at constant prices.

7

Intersectoral Flows of Factors of Production

IN the previous chapters, we were concerned with the movements of products between the sectors. The investigation into the problem of factor flows is a more exacting one, especially in view of the structural and institutional barriers to such flows. Quantitative estimation of factor movements on the basis of existing data is a complicated task. Yet an attempt is made here to examine the possibilities of movements of labour from the agricultural to the industrial sector and of capital from the industrial to the agricultural sector. The problem in the case of labour has been analysed from the demand aspect. We have made use of the data in the non-agricultural sector alone to decide the issue of the existence or absence of labour flows from the agricultural sector. As regards capital flows, we have tried to examine the problem with the help of work already done in this field. However, in so far as our study examines the relationships between agriculture and industry which is only a part of the non-agricultural sector, it becomes difficult for us to state conclusively if the migrations of labour, if any, to the industrial sector are from the agricultural sector or from the rest of the economy and similarly if the inflows of capital funds into the agricultural sector are from the industrial sector or from the rest of the economy. Yet this difficulty has been overcome to some extent, in the case of labour, by an examination of the push factors operating on the supply of agricultural labour. As regards the source of the capital funds flowing into the agricultural sector, however, the matter has been left as an open question.

Movements of Labour

The first systematic study of the problem of labour movements between agricultural and non-agricultural sectors of the Indian economy has been undertaken by Khusro in a recent study.[1] His work suggests a useful line of analysis for future research workers in this field. Work in the present chapter has been conducted mainly on these lines and it is, therefore, necessary to state briefly, the methodology of that work as also its conclusions.

Khusro's analysis of the projections of demand for and supply of labour in the non-agricultural sector relates to the period 1951-76. Taking the Planning Commission's projections[2] of national income for these years as the basis, his study estimates the employment potential that will be needed to produce this income. The annual incremental demand for labour in the non-agricultural sector is obtained after taking into account three factors, viz., the projected annual addition to national income, the marginal capital-output ratio, and the marginal capital-labour ratio. Against the estimated annual increments in the demand for labour in the non-agricultural sector, the study places the estimates of annual supplies of labour emerging from within that sector. These annual supplies include (i) the natural growth of the non-agricultural population, (ii) the increase in the participation rate of labour owing to social changes and (iii) the reduction in disguised unemployment among workers in non-agricultural production and elimination of unemployment in urban areas. On this basis, the above study estimates that till 1976, there can be no net absorption of agricultural population in the nonagricultural sector.

Three differences between Khusro's study and our exercise have to be clarified. Firstly, while Khusro examines the possibilities of movements between the agricultural and the non-agricultural sectors, our work is concerned only with the movements between agriculture and industry. Secondly, the study referred to, estimates the annual increments to demand for labour in the non-agricultural sector while we have used the current information on the actual work force in the industrial sector to represent the demand for labour in that sector. Thirdly, while Khusro's analysis runs in terms of a comparison between annual increments to demand for and supply of labour, our argument is carried on the basis of a comparison between total demand for and supply of labour.

Estimates of workforce for each of subsectors of the industrial sector are available in the "Proposals"[3] for the years 1951-52 and 1955-56 to 1958-59. For years prior to 1951, comparable estimates of work force are presented in the Final Report.[4] Information for 1952-53 to 1954-55 has become available from the CSO.[5] On this basis, the annual aggregate estimates of total demand for labour in the entire industrial sector have been computed. The supply of labour in a sector comes from two sources, viz., (i) natural growth of population and (ii) reserves of unemployed and underemployed persons. Khusro has estimated the backlog of employable non-agricultural labour force for 1951.[6] Further, on the basis of a recent study,[7] Khusro assumes an annual rate of diminution of the pool at 2.4% owing to the exit of its members through death, old age etc. We have accepted these estimates of both the size of the 'backlog' and the rate of diminution of the pool. In the previous chapter, we had derived estimates of population in the industrial sector. Not all the population, however, constitutes the labour force. The children, the aged, the sick, and a large proportion of married women who are voluntarily unemployed for physical, social and other reasons, fall outside the job-seeking population. Thus in 1951, out of a non-agricultural population of 107.5 millions, about 42 millions constituted the labour force. Thus the labour participation rate was 39%. We assume that the same rate is true of the industrial sector also. With economic development and social change, it is possible that more and more previously unemployed for certain social and other reasons may begin to desire to work. It has been found in certain studies that this participation rate may tend to increase linearly to 45% by 1975-76[8]. On the basis of this, the values of the increasing participation rate from 1948-49 to 1958-59 have been noted.

Applying this rate to the respective estimates of population in the industrial sector, the annual estimates of the job-seeking population have been computed (Table).

The following procedure has been adopted to estimate the annual excess of supply of labour (including the 'backlog' of employable labour force) over the demand for labour in the industrial sector. We know the size of the 'backlog' of employable labour force as it stood in 1951. We have already calculated the estimates of demand for labour as also the natural supply of labour in this sector for the same year. Thus it is possible for us to find out for 1951, the excess of the total supply of labour over the total demand for labour in this sector. Applying the separation rate of 2.4% to the estimate of the unutilised 'backlog' of 1951, the estimate of 'backlog' of employable labour for 1952 is calculated. This procedure is carried forth for the subsequent years and suitably for years earlier to 1951. The results are presented in Table.

It is of considerable interest to note that the unutilised 'backlog' of employable labour force in the industrial sector has been diminishing at a fairly rapid rate so that in the last year of the period of our study, the 'backlog' has been completely wiped out, thus creating a net demand for labour force in the industrial sector. This conclusion may seem contradictory to Khusro's, for the latter maintains that at least for 25 years from 1951, there can be no net absorption of labour from the agricultural to the non-agricultural sector. This apparently different conclusion of ours becomes significant especially in view of our earlier procedure of equating the entire 'backlog' of employable non-agricultural labour force with the industrial sector. To the extent that such an equality has been assumed, it in fact amounts to an overestimation of the supply of labour available for the industrial sector. Even assuming that the number of persons in this 'backlog' of employable non-agricultural labour force, who belong by origin to the industrial sector, but who wish to seek employment in the 'rest of the economy' (i.e. the non-industrial, non-agricultural sector) is equal to the number of persons in

TABLE

Demand for and Supply of Labour in Industry

1948-49 — 1958-59

(in millions)

ITEMS (1)	1948-49 (2)	1949-50 (3)	1950-51 (4)	1951-52 (5)	1952-53 (6)	1953-54 (7)	1954-55 (8)	1955-56 (9)	1956-57 (10)	1957-58 (11)	1958-59 (12)
1. Population in industrial sector	35.50	36.22	36.96	37.71	38.47	39.25	40.04	40.86	41.68	42.52	43.38
2. Participation rate of labour	38.28	38.52	38.76	39.00	39.24	39.48	39.72	39.96	40.20	40.44	40.68
3. Natural supply of workforce	13.59	13.95	14.33	14.71	15.10	15.50	15.90	16.33	16.76	17.20	17.65
4. 'Backlog' of employable labour-force	20.44	17.79	15.45	13.16	11.14	9.51	8.03	6.49	5.04	3.63	1.67
5. Total supply of labour force in industry	34.03	31.74	29.78	27.87	26.24	25.01	23.93	22.82	21.80	20.83	19.32
6. Total Demand for labour in industry:	15.83	15.92	16.30	16.46	16.50	16.78	17.28	17.66	18.08	19.12	19.76
7. Un-utilised backlog of employable lab. force (5) - (6)	18.20	15.82	13.48	11.41	9.74	8.23	6.65	5.16	3.72	1.71	- 0.44

this backlog who belong by origin to the rest of the economy, but who wish to seek employment in the industrial sector, still our correspondence of the entire backlog of employable non-agricultural labour force to the industrial sector implies an overestimation, to the extent it contains the persons who belong, by origin, to the 'rest of the economy' and who also want to get employed therein. In sofar as this overestimation has been done, we are in fact allowing for a net migration of labour from the 'rest of the economy' to the industrial sector. If despite this overestimation, there arises a net demand for labour in the industrial sector, it probably points to the fact that the demand for labour in the 'rest of the economy' as against the natural supply of labour in that sector is so low as to offset the net demand for labour in the industrial sector, thus leading to a net excess of supply of labour in the entire non-agricultural sector -- which in fact is Khusro's conclusion. But to the extent, a net demand for labour appears to have emerged in the industrial sector in the final year of our study, (and in view of our overestimation of the 'backlog' of employable labour force available for the industrial sector), it is quite possible that while unemployment has been existing in the 'rest of the economy', the industrial sector itself has been drawing labour from the agricultural sector.

Whether this is true or not cannot be maintained conclusively; we can at best list some of the factors which generally point to comparative rigidity in the mobility of labour out of agriculture so that any excess demand for labour in the industrial sector might have been met to some extent by the 'rest of the economy'.

Factors Impeding Outflow of Agricultural Labour

It is true that the outward movement of labour from agriculture depends on the absorptive capacity of industry and the professions. Thus as Bellerby states "The first requirement of healthy agriculture is active and stable industry ... During the process of expansion, industry is in every economic respect, the ally of agriculture. The larger and more rapidly expanding the non-farm sector, the greater, other things being equal, will be the mobility of the farming personnel."[9] But there are many structural and institutional factors which impede the demand-incited movement of labour.

Mention may be made of some of these factors. Foremost among these perhaps is the inherent psychological attachment which the peasant feels towards his land. As is well-known, the ability to continue for long periods on reserves of soil fertility and accumulated stocks, and the assurance of some degree of security, although at a low income level, cause occupational immobility outwards agriculture. Further, wide differences in language, personal education, social customs and cultural values between rural and urban areas hinder a smooth outflow of labour from agriculture. Standards of clothing and personal outlay are less exacting while spare-time occupations may be inexpensive and income-yielding, in the villages. It has been rightly pointed out that underemployment is most extensive at the peripheries of urban-industrial areas of influence and it decreases as the centres of such areas are reached. In fact, the greater distances of industrial factories from the villages check free flow of labour out of agriculture. Again, the farm workers may lack proper training and knowledge needed for industrial jobs. They may not have had the necessary capital to equip themselves with this industrial training, not to speak of the lack of funds for making a move out of the village. The Recruiting Officers in the factories are more inclined to recruit persons who are working off the farms, since it is felt that such persons do not require as much training for industrial work and do not have as much of an adjustment problem as the agricultural labourers. Thus it seems that a net outflow of labour from agriculture is rather a remote possibility so that any inflow of labour into the industrial sector may have taken place only or very largely from the 'rest of the economy'.

Movements of Capital

It is by no means easy to estimate gross or net capital movements between the agricultural and the industrial sectors. No comprehensive empirical work has been undertaken so far on this issue but mention can be made of a few studies[10] on savings and investments in the different sectors of the Indian economy, which have some relevance to the problem. We shall here examine the question of capital flows between the sectors on the basis of these studies.

As has been already observed in Chapter 2, the inherent seasonal character of agriculture in general and the peculiarities of Indian agriculture in particular have resulted in a per head income in agriculture which is depressed both absolutely and relatively to industry. The subsistence nature of Indian farming, the price insensitiveness of the farmer, the structural disabilities under which he works, the looming phenomenon of increasing pressure of population on land -- all have contributed to such low levels productivity of agriculture that the possibility of the emergence of savings from within agriculture has been greatly reduced. Even if savings do emerge, there is a "serious misdirection of funds"[11] into non-farm investments. Apart from this, there has been a strong tendency for the saving class in the agricultural sector, namely, the landowning or the rentier class, to fritter away the "surpluses" in luxurious and wasteful consumption. These factors act as a drain on what little savings are available for investment within agriculture.

The RBI study[12] on savings and investment in the Indian economy, has provided tentative estimates of savings in the agricultural sector, for two years 1951-52 and 1956-67. These estimates have been formed on the basis of the Reports of the Rural Credit Survey.[13] The study shows that savings of the agricultural sector were negative in 1951-52 to the extent of Rs. 67 crores. The position however had improved in 1956-57 when the agricultural sector had positive savings of the order of Rs. 131 crores. The question of the exactness of these magnitudes need not detain us. What can be discerned is the fact that through the years the agricultural sector has emerged from a dis-saving to a saving sector. While this absolute improvement is very likely, it is nevertheless not possible to state categorically if this change also implies a favourable change in the credit position of the agricultural sector viz-a-vis the industrial or the non-agricultural sector. In this connection, it is necessary to distinguish between two things i.e. the supply of savings arising from within the agricultural sector and the supply of savings available for the agricultural sector. It may be reasonably assumed in an ex-post sense that the investment that had taken place in agriculture in a particular year is the entire supply of savings available for agriculture in that year; so that the estimate of net or new investment in agriculture can be deemed to be the increment to the supply of savings for agriculture in that year.

With this clarification, it is possible to examine the relative availabilities of savings to the agricultural and the non-agricultural sectors during the period of our study. According to the R.B.I. study, during 1951-52 and 1956-57, the supply of savings from within agriculture had increased from a negative figure of Rs. 67 crores to a positive one of Rs. 131 crores, thereby implying an increment of Rs. 198 crores. As against this, the net investment (at current prices) has been earlier estimated by us for the years 1951-52 to 1956-57 (Chapter 2). The total of net investments works out to around Rs. 2000 crores. Thus there has been substantial increment to the actual supply of saving which was available for agriculture. Whether these funds have been coming from the industrial sector or from the rest of the economy is, however, a difficult problem to settle. But the fact of capital inflows into agriculture stands out.

The fact of capital inflows has also been confirmed by the Report of the Rural Credit Survey.[14] The report observes that "... whether on current account or on capital account, even in the post-war period, the country-side is seen to be requiring a large flow of funds from the urban areas". On the basis of various calculations made in this report, regarding the balance of payments position of the rural sector vis-a-vis the urban sector in the Indian economy, the report concludes that "roughly one-half to two-thirds of the total funds lent within the rural area were probably derived from the urban areas, so that only from about a third to a half of such funds might have been rural in origin."[15] It should be noted that this excludes the importation of investment capital by owners of rural property or business residing in urban areas. On the other hand, there is capital investment including lending of funds by rural residents to persons or businesses in the urban areas which, however, the report holds, might be considered to be negligible. All in all, it seems that "in terms of the present distribution of incomes in society, and the shares of that income going to different classes determined by such factors as socio-economic structure and the terms of trade between rural and urban areas and occupations, the above appears to be the general picture. This means that in the existing situation, for continued sustenance or for development finance, agriculturists and rural residents must continue to draw funds year after year to a substantial extent from the urban areas."[16]

NOTES & REFERENCES

1. Khusro, A.M.: Economic Development with No Population Transfers, A Study in Demand for and Supply of Labour in the Non-Agricultural Sector of the Indian Economy -- Occasional Papers, Institute of Economic Growth, Delhi.
2. Government of India, Planning Commission, Second Five Year Plan, New Delhi, 1956.
3. "Proposals" p.7, Tables 1.2 and 1.4.
4. Final Report of National Income Committee (1954) p. 23.
5. My thanks are due to the CSO for allowing me to use this information.
6. Khusro Op. cit., p. 31.

"Backlog" (or "Pool") of Employable Non-Agricultural Labour Force: 1951

(In millions)

1. Urban unemployed	3.415
2. Rural Non-Agricultural Underemployed	2.400
3. Petty Traders	0.649
4. Casual Workers	1.090
5. Domestic Servants	0.434
6. Women of Working age:	
(a) Rural Non-Agricultural	1.726
(b) Urban Non-Agricultural	3.444
	13.158

7. Tilak, V.R.K.: "Population Growth and Employment Requirements, 1951-66", Employment News, Vol. III, No. 8, April, 1958. Quoted by Khusro: "Economic Development With No Population Transfers", p. 31.

8. Datar, B.N.: The Second Five Year Plan: Employment Approach: Papers relating to the formulation of the Second Five Year Plan, 1956. Quoted by Khusro: p. 27.

9. Bellerby, J.R.: Agriculture-Industry Relative Incomes, p. 322.

10. a) Reserve Bank of India Bulletin, March 1960: "Estimates of Saving in the Indian Economy" Division of Development and Planning of the Economics Department b) Reserve Bank of India Bulletin, August 1961: "Savings and Investment in the Indian Economy" V.V. Bhatt. c) National Income Statistics -- "Estimates of Gross Capital Formation in India", C.S.O. d) "Savings in India" -- National Council of Applied Economic Research, India. e) Report of the All-India Rural Credit Survey (1951-52) Vol. I, Survey Report, Part-I -- Rural Families. f) Report of the All-India Rural Credit Follow-up Survey (1956-57).

11. John, P.V.: Some Aspects of the Structure of Indian Agricultural Economy, 1947-48--1957-58, Ph.D. thesis for Delhi University, p. 139.

12. RBI, March 1960, op.cit.

13. All India Report of Rural Credit Survey (1951-52), Survey Report p. 1052.

14. Ibid.

8

Intersectoral Terms of Exchange

HAVING examined the intersectoral flows of products and factors of production, it is now necessary to study the terms at which these have been traded between agriculture and industry. The level of living of a country or of a sector of a country, or of any economic unit would depend, among other things, upon the relative prices obtained by that country or sector or unit. In other words, the level of living will depend upon the quantity of the things that can be acquired in return for a unit of the things sold. Thus "the less self-sufficient the community is, the more important are its terms of trade in determining, along with its productiveness, how good a living it gets."[1]

The concept of 'terms of trade' is one of the most useful analytical tools of international trade. It has been applied extensively in the long term analysis of the benefits derived by the national economies from international trade. It is thus "a short-hand index of certain complex forces operating on the balance of payments and real wages as well as a way of isolating an important factor determining real income changes between the two nations."[2] The applicability of the concept of 'terms of trade' to international trade lies in the fact of rigidities and immobilities of the factors of production between different countries. It is because of these structural disabilities in the dynamic allocation of factors of production that fluctuations in benefits derived from international trade are directly reflected in changes in the terms of trade.

The application of this concept to inter-sectoral analysis requires the same assumption of rigidities in the mobility of resources between the sectors. Of course, it is not possible to maintain that there is absolute factor immobility between the two sectors. But still, the relative fixity of land, the occupational, personal and social factors which impede the outward mobility of agricultural labour accompanied by the lack of adequate openings in the non-agricultural sector for the absorption of under-employed agricultural labour, impose rigidities on inter-sectoral movement of resources. It can, therefore, be assumed that the terms of trade analysis of inter-sectoral exchange of goods and services will be useful in explaining or indicating the changes in the relative well-being of the sectors.

There have been several interpretations of the concept of "Terms of Trade". These have been listed below:

(i) Commodity or net barter terms of trade,
(ii) Gross barter terms of trade,
(iii) Single factoral terms of trade,
(iv) Double factoral terms of trade,
(v) Real cost terms of trade,
(vi) Utility terms of trade, and
(vii) Income terms of trade.

The commodity or the net barter terms of trade have been called the most 'natural'[3] interpretation. It is represented by the ratio $\frac{eP_1}{eP_0} \Big/ \frac{iP_1}{iP_0}$

where eP_1 = Price index of exported commodities in the period '1'

eP_0 = Price index of these commodities in the base year '0'

iP_1 = Price index of imported commodities in the period '1'

iP_0 = Price index of these commodities in the base year '0'

A rise in this ratio would mean a movement 'favourable' to the exporting sector. However, this type of terms of trade does not take into account, the 'invisible' items in the balance of payments. Thus in order to correct the commodity or "net barter" terms of trade for unilateral transactions, or for exports or imports which are surrendered without counter-payment such as tributes and immigrants' remittances etc., Taussig introduced the concept of "gross barter terms of trade". This is measured as the ratio of the physical quantity of imports to the physical quantity of exports. The higher this ratio, the more favourable are the terms of trade.

But the fortunes of a country or a sector depend not only on the prices received in relation to the prices paid and not only on the quantities of goods that have to be given up in relation to the quantity of goods received, but also upon relative productivities. As Ricardo observed "We shall sell our goods at a high money price, and buy foreign ones at a low money price but it may well be doubted whether this advantage will not be purchased at many times its value, for to obtain it, we must be content with a diminished production of home commodities; with a high price of labour and a low rate of profits."[4] Moreover, for inter-sectoral analysis (as in the case of agriculture and industry), such high prices of agricultural products would lead to high costs of living and high costs of production in the industrial sector which would further bring about a contraction in production plans. Thus in real terms both the sectors would suffer.

Though numerically the commodity terms of trade (net or gross) may show the favourableness or unfavourableness of the terms of exchange to a country or a sector, it does not reveal the position completely. There is need for a terms of trade index which would take into account both relative prices and relative productivities. A first approximation to this is the Single Factoral Terms of Trade. If it were possible to construct an index of the cost of production in terms of the average technical coefficients of production of the export commodities, and if the commodity terms of trade index was multiplied by the reciprocal of the export commodity technical coefficients index, the result would be the single factoral terms of trade index. It is given by the ratio

$$\frac{\dfrac{e^{P}_{1}}{e^{P}_{0}}}{\dfrac{i^{P}_{1}}{i^{P}_{0}}} \times \frac{e^{F}_{0}}{e^{F}_{1}}$$

where e^{F}_{0}/e^{F}_{1} represents the reciprocal of the index of the cost in terms of the quantity of factors of production used per unit of export. It represents the index of physical amounts of the foreign goods which can be obtained per unit of cost in terms of quantity of factors of production.

An improvement over the Single Factoral Terms of Trade Index is the Double Factoral Terms of Trade Index which represents the number of units of the productive services of the foreign country whose product exchanged for the product of one unit of the productive services of the domestic country. It is given by

$$\frac{\dfrac{e^{P}_{1}}{e^{P}_{0}}}{\dfrac{i^{P}_{1}}{i^{P}_{0}}} \cdot \times \frac{\dfrac{i^{F}_{1}}{i^{F}_{0}}}{\dfrac{e^{F}_{1}}{e^{F}_{0}}}$$

The double factoral terms of trade or the 'true'[5] terms of trade are in fact most relevant for discussions of relative national standards of living or "equilibrium" rates of exchange. Still closer approaches to reality have been achieved by the evolution of the real cost terms of trade index and the utility terms of trade index. In the case of the former, the commodity terms of trade index is corrected not only for changes in the cost of production of the export industries, but also for changes in "disutilities" in the production of the export goods. This index is given by

$$\frac{\dfrac{e^{P}_{1}}{e^{P}_{0}}}{\dfrac{i^{P}_{1}}{i^{P}_{0}}} \times \frac{e^{F}_{0}}{e^{F}_{1}} \times \frac{e^{R}_{0}}{e^{R}_{1}}$$

where e^{R_0}/e^{R_1} = reciprocal of the index of disutility coefficients. However, the amount of gain from trade depends not only on the amount of foreign goods that can be obtained per unit of real cost involved in the production of the export commodities, but also on the relative desirability of the imported goods in relation to those which could have been produced for domestic consumption with the help of the factors of production which are now utilised for export production. To allow for this, an index of the relative average utility per unit of imported commodities and of domestic goods whose internal consumption is precluded by allocation of resources to production for export, should be included. Such an index may be given by $\dfrac{i^{U_1}}{a^{U_1}} \Big/ \dfrac{i^{U_0}}{a^{U_0}}$

where i = imported goods

a = domestic goods whose consumption has been precluded;

so that the utility terms of trade index is given by

$$\frac{\dfrac{e^{P_1}}{e^{P_0}}}{\dfrac{i^{P_1}}{i^{P_0}}} \times \frac{e^{F_0}}{e^{F_1}} \times \frac{e^{R_0}}{e^{R_1}} \times \frac{\dfrac{e^{U_1}}{a^{U_1}}}{\dfrac{i^{U_0}}{a^{U_0}}}$$

The dissatisfaction with the commodity terms of trade analysis stems both from the tendency to treat the changes in the terms of trade as if they represented changes in the "gains from trade" and from the belief that a simple ratio of export-import prices was not a reliable guide to changes in the terms of trade. An attempt to overcome these objections has resulted in the income terms of trade. This corrects the commodity terms of trade for changes in the volume of exports. It is given by the formula :

$$\frac{\dfrac{e^{P_1}}{e^{P_0}}}{\dfrac{i^{P_1}}{i^{P_0}}} \times \frac{e^{Q_1}}{e^{Q_0}}$$

where eQ_1/eQ_0 represents changes in the volume of exports. It reflects for the country concerned, changes in the volume of imports obtainable from its export income. It is obvious from this formula that a deterioration in the commodity terms of trade need not always reduce a country's capacity to import, if only the quantity of exports increases more than the unfavourable movement in the terms of trade.

Of the several types of terms of trade indices discussed so far, the real cost terms of trade index and the utility terms of trade index, though of high technical perfection, cannot be translated into satisfactory quantitative form. As regards the single and the double factoral terms of trade, their theoretical superiority is recognised; but as Haberler has rightly pointed out"...the factoral terms of trade, either single or double, cannot be calculated in practice, for the concept of a 'unit of a productive factor' and thus that of a productivity index is almost impossible to define operationally."[6] It should be emphasised that these difficulties of quantification place even greater constraints on a study for a country like India and specially an inter-sectoral study where one of the sectors happens to be agriculture.

Hence it seems that one has to be content with the less refined measures of the terms of trade viz., commodity terms of trade and income terms of trade. Even here, since we have no information on 'invisible' items of trade and unilateral payments between the sectors, the "gross" barter terms of trade cannot be computed. In fact it has been said that "Both these measures (viz. gross barter terms of trade and income terms of trade) are inferior to and a less reliable guide than the simple commodity terms of trade, because each of them mixes heterogeneous cases which have to be judged differently even if other things remained the same. For example, the income terms of trade show an improvement when, *ceteris paribus*, the quantity of exports increases as well as when import prices fall relatively to export prices. Obviously these cases have opposite welfare significance. The ordinary commodity terms of trade do not give rise to this anamoly. Other things being equal, an improvement in the commodity terms of trade does imply an increase in real national income."[7]

Moreover, it may be maintained that despite the several criticisms that are levelled against the net barter terms of trade, an index of this still forms a significant measure of 'gains from trade' in the short-run. The assumption of constant returns to scale, which is possible during the short run, permits the use of the double factoral terms of trade. Thus in so far as our study here relates to a decade which is not a long enough period for substantial changes in productivity to have taken place, the net barter terms of trade should be a good indicator of the "real" benefits from intersectoral trade.

We shall therefore present for the two sectors agriculture and industry (i) the net barter terms of trade and (ii) the income terms of trade of (a) inputs (b) final outputs[8] and (c) all products. We have already calculated the time-series of composite price indices of (i) agricultural products used by the industrial sector as inputs (ii) agricultural products used by the industrial sector for final consumption (iii) industrial products used by the agricultural sector as inputs and (iv) industrial products used by the agricultural sector as final consumption products. We shall now combine (i) and (ii) to arrive at the index of prices of all products bought by industry from agriculture and similarly (iii) and (iv) have been combined to derive the index of prices of all products purchased by agriculture from industry. These results are consolidated and given in Table-8.1. In this table are also given for reference the general price indices of (i) all agricultural products (ii) all industrial products and (iii) all commodities of the economy.

These composite indices do not include the prices of factors of production, like labour exchanged between the sectors, due to non-availability of systematic and comparable information on the same. To this extent, therefore, our indices are not comprehensive. Keeping this limita-

TABLE - 8.1

Composite Price Indices

1948-49 — 1958-59 (1951-52 = 100)

ITEMS (1)	1948-49 (2)	1949-50 (3)	1950-51 (4)	1951-52 (5)	1952-53 (6)	1953-54 (7)	1954-55 (8)	1955-56 (9)	1956-57 (10)	1957-58 (11)	1958-59 (12)
Price indices of											
1. Agricultural inputs used in industry	77.46	83.61	95.71	100.00	77.54	86.85	78.17	72.74	87.21	89.02	90.89
2. Industrial inputs used in agriculture	87.46	88.31	89.46	100.00	102.57	101.24	98.57	96.96	102.31	106.35	110.27
3. Agricultural finished products used by industry for consumption	88.34	93.51	95.22	100.00	96.85	96.43	80.61	78.20	93.98	98.80	107.04
4. Industrial finished products used by agriculture for consumption	91.24	92.12	93.33	100.00	87.08	90.61	91.13	85.70	92.85	97.09	98.30
5. All products bought by industry from agriculture	80.81	36.66	95.56	100.00	83.48	89.80	78.92	74.42	89.29	92.03	95.86
6. All products bought by agriculture from industry	90.73	91.61	92.81	100.00	89.15	92.03	92.12	87.20	94.11	98.33	99.89
7. All agricultural products	81.62	87.46	94.52	100.00	85.38	89.54	80.56	75.64	88.25	91.26	96.23
8. All industrial products	91.24	88.78	92.56	100.00	83.96	87.55	84.99	81.77	90.45	92.61	95.00
9. All products (agricultural or industrial)	85.90	88.00	94.10	100.00	82.20	85.90	80.10	77.40	86.50	89.10	93.20

tion in view, we have used the above results and presented the net barter terms of trade of (a) inputs (b) final outputs and (c) all products in Table-8.2.

In chapter 4, we had derived the time-series of estimates of values at constant prices of (i) the agricultural products which are bought and used by the industrial sector as inputs and (ii) the agricultural products which are bought and used by the industrial sector as consumption products. These estimates have been made use of, for computing the time-series of income terms of trade between agriculture and industry, viz.

$$\frac{\dfrac{e^{P_1}}{e^{P_0}}}{\dfrac{i^{P_1}}{i^{P_0}}} \times \frac{e^{Q_1}}{e^{Q_0}}$$

for each of (a) inputs (b) final outputs and (c) all products traded. Table-8.3 presents these results.

An analysis can now be undertaken of the fluctuations of agricultural prices vis-a-vis industrial prices not only in general but also in their components. The comparative study of fluctuations will take into account separately as well as jointly the prices of each of the three groups, viz., (a) inputs (b) final outputs and (c) all products traded between agriculture and industry. Subsequently we shall consider the movements of the terms of trade -- both net barter terms and income terms -- between these two sectors. Finally, the impact of the differential changes in the agricultural and industrial prices leading to changes in the terms of trade will be discussed in relation to some important variables.

Comparative Study of Price Fluctuations : Agricultural Prices and Industrial Prices

In Diagram 8.1 are presented the fluctuations of the price indices of (i) all agricultural products (ii) all industrial products and (iii) all products of the economy. A careful scrutiny of the relative movements of these prices brings to light three phases during this period. The first

TABLE - 8.2

Indices of Net Barter Terms of Trade Between Agriculture and Industry

1948-49 — 1958-59

(1951-52 = 100)

ITEMS (1)	1948-49 (2)	1949-50 (3)	1950-51 (4)	1951-52 (5)	1952-53 (6)	1953-54 (7)	1954-55 (8)	1955-56 (9)	1956-57 (10)	1957-58 (11)	1958-59 (12)
1. Terms of Trade of Inputs	88.57	94.68	106.97	100.00	75.60	85.79	79.30	75.02	85.24	83.70	82.42
2. Terms of Trade of Output	96.82	101.51	102.03	100.00	111.22	106.42	88.46	91.25	101.22	101.76	108.89
3. Terms of Trade of Inputs and Outputs	89.07	94.60	102.96	100.00	93.64	97.58	85.67	85.34	94.88	93.59	95.97

TABLE - 8.3

Indices of Income Terms of Trade Between Agriculture and Industry

1948-49 — 1958-59

(1951-52 = 100)

ITEMS (1)	1948-49 (2)	1949-50 (3)	1950-51 (4)	1951-52 (5)	1952-53 (6)	1953-54 (7)	1954-55 (8)	1955-56 (9)	1956-57 (10)	1957-58 (11)	1958-59 (12)
1. Terms of Trade of Inputs	81.83	98.39	100.23	100.00	91.48	93.42	96.42	91.15	107.15	109.31	110.85
2. Terms of Trade of Output	124.51	125.16	126.72	100.00	110.33	103.55	92.62	117.35	114.78	114.58	113.68
3. Terms of Trade of Inputs and Outputs	92.81	104.25	106.77	100.00	106.66	102.56	99.46	105.65	115.47	116.71	119.67

DIAGRAM - 8.1

Indices of Prices of (i) Agricultural Products (ii) Industrial Products (iii) All Products

(1951-52 = 100)

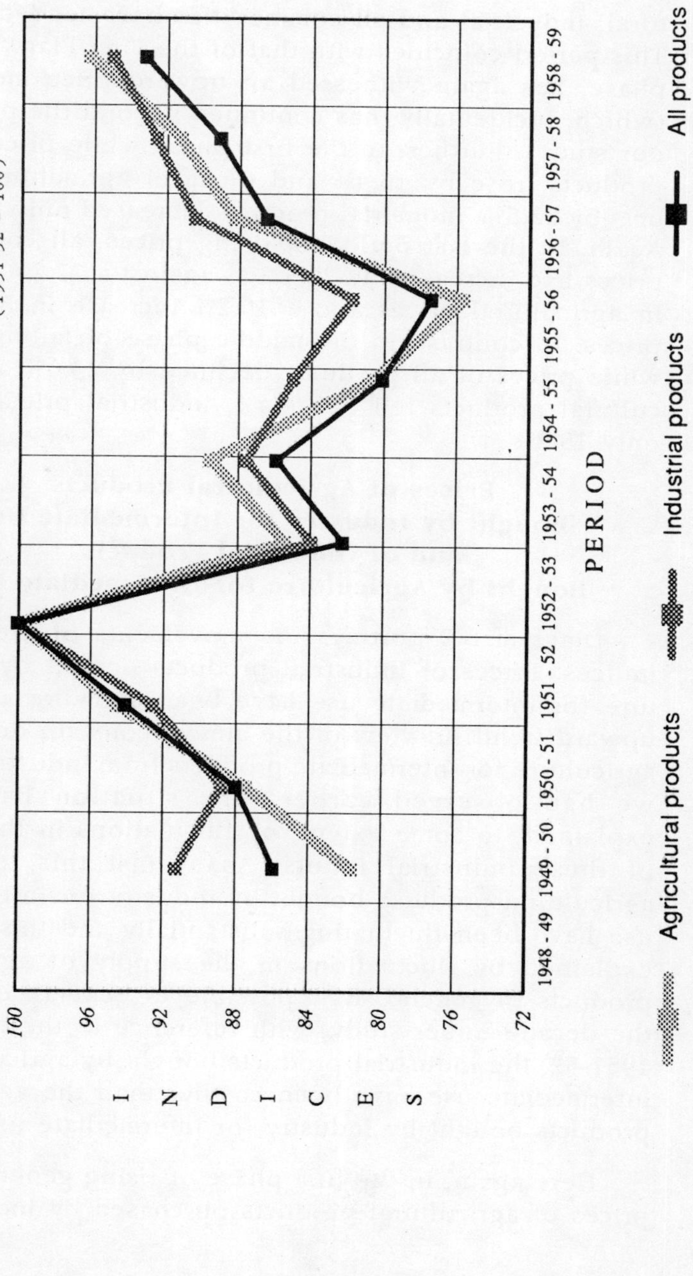

phase from 1948-49 to 1951-52 is characterised by a rising tendency in all the three groups of prices. This is followed by a period of five years, when prices of agricultural, industrial and all commodities have tended to fall. This period coincides with that of the First Plan. The last phase, has again witnessed an upward price movement (which, incidentally, has continued beyond the period of our study). Further, in the first phase while prices of all products, rose by 16.4% and those of agricultural products by 22.5%, industrial products increased only by 9.6%. Again, in the last period of rising prices, all commodity prices had increased by 20.4% as against a 27.2% increase in agricultural prices and a 16.2% increase in industrial prices. In contrast, in the middle phase of falling prices, while prices of all products declined by 23.6% and agricultural products fell by 24.4%, industrial prices fell by only 18.2%.

Prices of Agricultural Products Bought by Industry for Intermediate Use and of Industrial Products Bought by Agriculture for Intermediate Use

Diagram 8.2 portrays the movements of these price indices. Prices of industrial products bought by agriculture for intermediate use have been showing a definite upward trend. In view of the almost constant demand of agriculture for intermediate products from industry, which we had observed earlier, this situation has to be explained, to some extent, by fluctuations in the supply of these industrial inputs. As against this, prices of agricultural products bought by industry for intermediate use have been fluctuating substantially and this is again explained by fluctuations in the supply of agricultural products in general. It is possible to generalise that for the decade under study, with reference to the base year 1951-52, the industrial products bought by agriculture for intermediate use have been costlier than the agricultural products bought by industry for intermediate use.

Here again, in the first phase of rising general prices, prices of agricultural products purchased by industry for

DIAGRAM - 8.2

Indices of Prices of
(i) Inputs Bought by Agriculture from Industry
(ii) Inputs Bought by Industry from Agriculture
(1951-52 = 100)

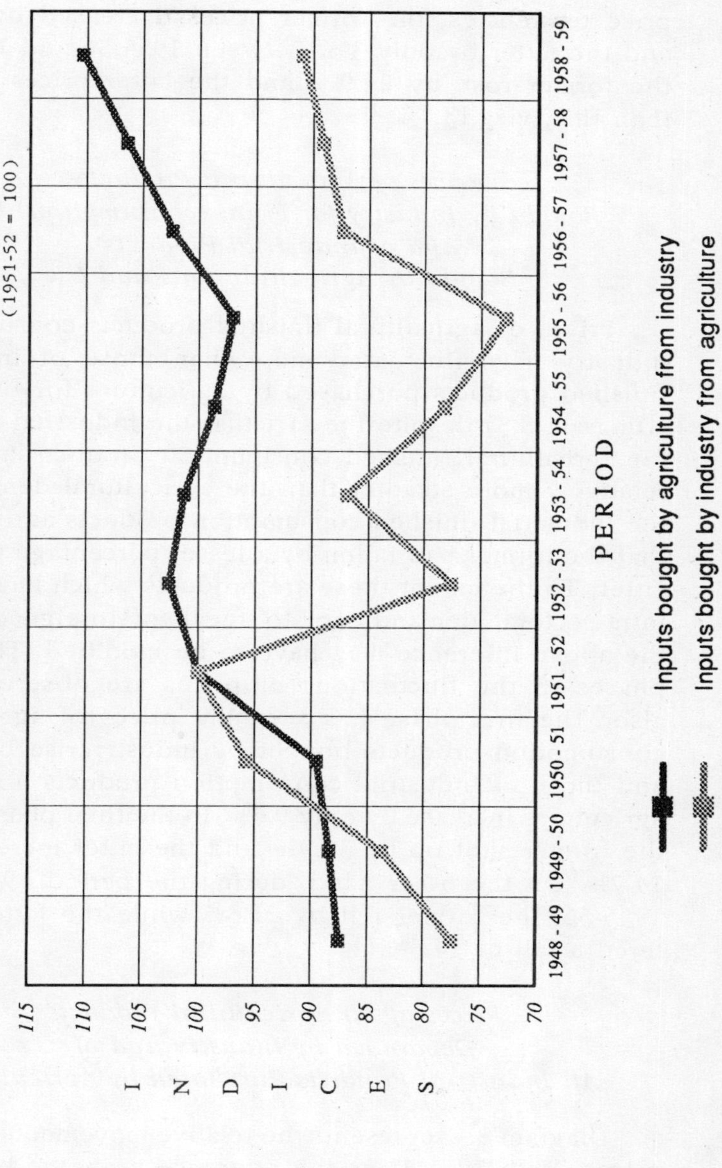

intermediate use rose by 29.1% as against a 14.3% rise in the prices of industrial products purchased by agriculture for intermediate use. In the second phase of declining price tendencies, the former prices decreased by 27.3% and the latter by only 3%. Between 1955-56 and 1958-59, the former rose by 24.9%, and the latter prices by less than this, viz. 13.7%.

Prices of Agricultural Products Bought by Industry for Final (consumption) Use and of Industrial Products Bought by Agriculture for Final Use

Prices of agricultural finished products consumed by industry have fluctuated more than those of industrial finished products purchased by agriculture for final use, (Diagram 8.3) despite the fact that the industrial demand for agricultural finished consumption products has been relatively more steadier than the agricultural demand for the industrial finished consumption products and the fact that the former had fallen by a lesser percentage than the latter. To the extent these are products which might have intra-sectoral demand, not to speak of foreign demand, the above inference may have to be modified. The three phases in the fluctuations of prices are observed here also. The first phase has seen the prices of agricultural consumption products bought by industry rise by 13.0% and those of industrial consumption products bought by agriculture increase by only 9.6%. In the final phase again, the former shot up by 36.9%, and the latter increased by 14.7%. On the other hand, during the period 1951-52 to 1955-56, the former fell by 21.8% while the latter registered a fall of 14.3%.

Prices of All Agricultural Products Demanded by Industry and of All Industrial Products Purchased by Agriculture

Diagram 8.4 represents the relative movements of these prices. With 1951-52 as the reference year, the basket of industrial products demanded by agriculture has been

DIAGRAM - 8.3

Indices of Prices of

(i) Agricultural Consumption Products Bought by Industry

(ii) Industrial Consumption Products Bought by Agriculture

(1951-52 = 100)

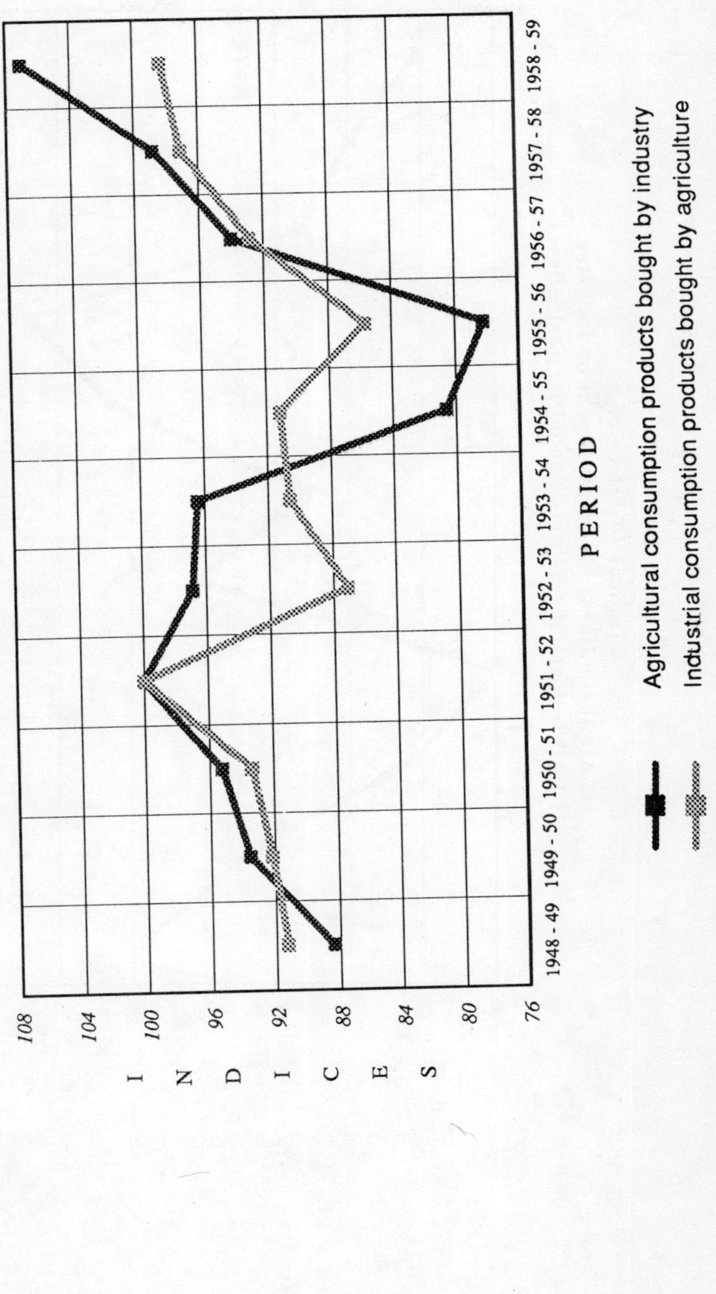

DIAGRAM - 8.4

Indices of Prices of

(i) All Agricultural Products Bought by Industry

(ii) All Industrial Products Bought by Agriculture

(1951-52 = 100)

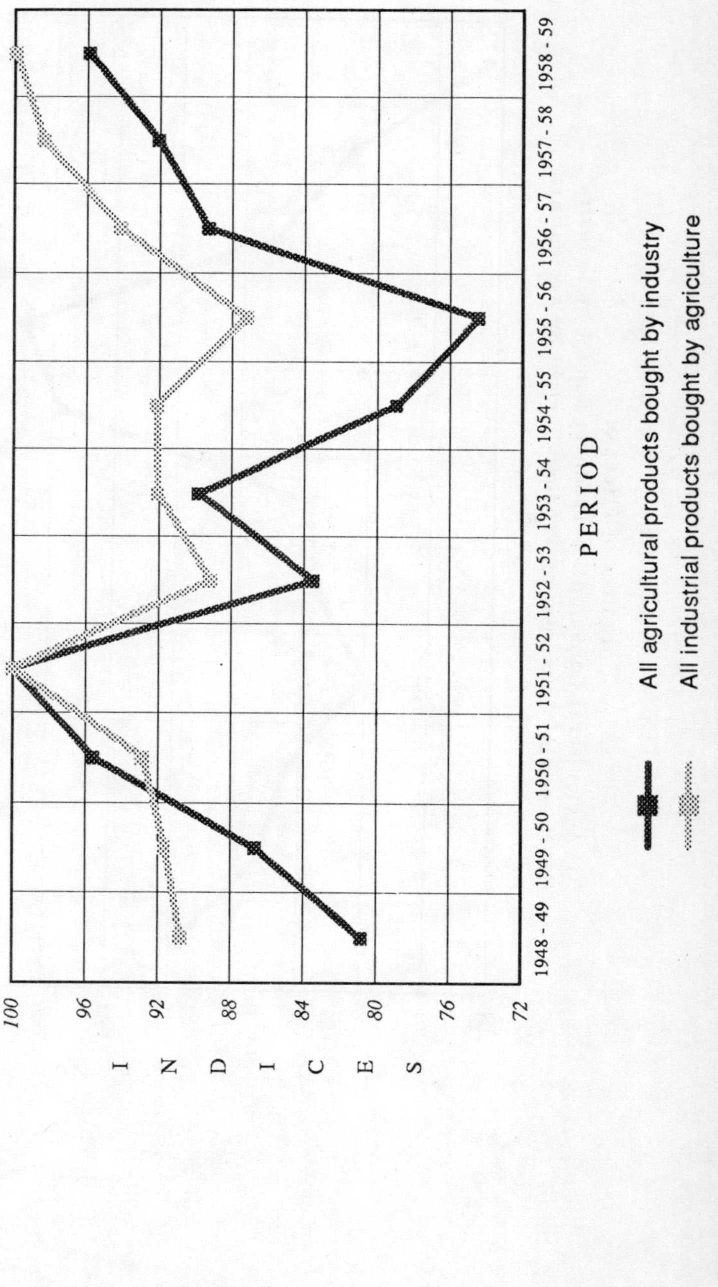

generally costlier than the package of agricultural products demanded by industry. Since we derived a similar conclusion in the case of inputs traded between the two sectors, and since no such categorical inference emerged in the case of final consumption products exchanged between them, the afore-mentioned results perhaps point to the fact that the ratio of agricultural products bought by industry for intermediate use to those bought for final use is higher than the corresponding ratio in the case of the industrial products bought by agriculture. In other words, the proportion of agricultural products bought by industry for intermediate use to the total agricultural products purchased by it for intermediate and for final uses, has been generally higher than the relevant ratio in regard to the industrial products purchased by agriculture during this period. The three phases noted in the case of components of these prices are to be found in the movements of these prices themselves. While in the first phase, prices of all agricultural products bought by industry rose by 23.7%, those of all industrial products bought by agriculture increased only by 10.2%. The following phase of declining prices saw a drop of 25.6% in the former prices and 12.8% in the latter. Subsequently, the former rose by 28.8% as against a rise of 14.6% only in the latter.

Inferences from the relative movements of prices:

(i) Both agricultural and industrial prices have the same direction of change, so that when there is inflation, both sets of prices rise and during deflation, both tend to decline.

(ii) The amplitude of change in agricultural prices is larger than that in industrial prices.

Our results may be taken to testify further to the well-known generalisation that during inflation, agricultural prices rise faster than industrial prices, and that conversely during deflation, the former fall faster than industrial prices.

(iii) Yet another generalisation is possible about the relative changes of agricultural and industrial prices.

> It is held that there is a lag (ranging between a few months and one or two years) between the changes in agricultural prices and those in industrial prices, the former leading and the latter lagging behind. This has not been tested in the present thesis for the obvious reason that a ten-year period, with only two upward phases and one downward phase, is too short a span of time for determining the nature and the dimension of this lag.

Why are there differential changes in agricultural and industrial prices ? Broadly speaking, inflation or deflation can be described respectively in terms of a relative increase or decrease in demand in relation to the supply. Abstracting from the possibilities of relative changes in the demand for agricultural and industrial goods, it may be generalised that when incomes change, demand for all goods change in the same direction. But "changes in the demand for and production of finished goods and services tend to give rise to much greater changes in the demand for and the production of those producers' goods which are used in their production. Slight changes in the demand for final goods may be converted into violent changes in the demand for goods of a more primary order and as the process tends to work through all stages of production, it is quite natural that fluctuations should be violent in those stages which are farthest removed from the sphere of consumption."[9]

As against this, on the supply side, both agricultural and industrial production take time to adjust to changes in demand, and agricultural supply takes a longer time. Agricultural output is both inelastic and inflexible. The seasonal and random variations in agricultural supply are well-known. Supplies of agricultural products come with sudden outbursts within brief ranges of time. And unless organisational machinery in the country is geared (through the provision of storage and ware-housing facilities etc.) for cushioning the impact of these seasonal outbursts, agricultural prices are bound to show violent fluctuations.

The final result of all this is that "... agriculture shares in the cyclical movement of trade in an exaggerated degree."[10]

The relative movements of agricultural and industrial prices having been examined, it is time to analyse the movements of the relationships between these prices or of the terms of trade between agriculture and industry.

Behaviour of Agricultural-Industrial Terms of Trade

At the outset, we should distinguish between the "favourableness or unfavourableness of terms of trade" and the "improvement or deterioration of terms of trade" of a sector or of any economic unit. When the export prices of a sector are higher than its import prices, then the terms of trade are said to be favourable for that sector. Conversely, if the export prices are lower than the import prices, then the exporting sector may be said to be faced with unfavourable terms of trade. On the other hand, the improvement or deterioration in the terms of trade is a concept referring to the 'change' in the terms of trade, which itself may be favourable or unfavourable. Thus even in the case of the terms of trade of a sector which are favourable to it, to start with, the export prices may fall faster than the import prices, so that after this change in the prices of exports and imports, the terms of trade would have worsened or deteriorated, though they may continue to be favourable to that sector. Again, an unfavourable terms of trade may improve because the export prices rise faster than the import prices but still be unfavourable even after this 'improvement'. Thus it should be borne in mind that an improving terms of trade need not necessarily be favourable too; nor a worsening terms of trade need also be unfavourable.

We have earlier derived the time series of (i) net barter terms of trade and (ii) income terms of trade of (a) inputs (b) final outputs (i.e. outputs for final consumption) and (c) all products, traded between agriculture and industry. In the following discussion, we shall be arguing from the point of view of the agricultural sector as the exporting sector.

The net barter terms of trade of all these three types of products shows similar movements. (Diagram 8.5) However, generally, the terms at which outputs for final consumption are traded between agriculture and industry are more favourable to agriculture, while the terms of trade in inputs have been invariably against agriculture. Corresponding to the three phases of rising and falling prices during this decade, the terms of trade in each of (a) inputs (b) final outputs and (c) all products, have also generally experienced similar ups and downs.

The income terms of trade as already explained, measure the volume of imports that can be got with the actual value of exports. Obviously, the problem of unfavourableness or favourableness of this type of terms of trade is out of question. For, the income terms of trade in fact show the volume of imports that can be purchased with the present value of exports. In other words, they indicate the changes in the capacity to import of the sector. However, it is possible to say if the income terms of trade in a particular set of goods have deteriorated or improved, with reference to a base year. Further it may also be inferred whether the income terms of trade in one set of goods are more or less favourable than that in another set.

During the decade under review, the income terms of trade at which all products are exchanged between the sectors have shown a rising trend and, therefore, have been gradually improving in favour of agriculture. In other words, the capacity of agriculture to import the products of industrial sector has been increasing during this period. As against this, the capacity to import of the agricultural sector, outputs for final use from industry does not present a bright picture; i.e. has tended to fall. But agriculture's capacity to import the inputs from industry has behaved better. Despite the fact that the capacity to import final outputs has been deteriorating in the face of an improving capacity to import inputs, the income

DIAGRAM - 8.5

Indices of Net Barter Terms of Trade

(Agriculture — Industry)

(1951-52 = 100)

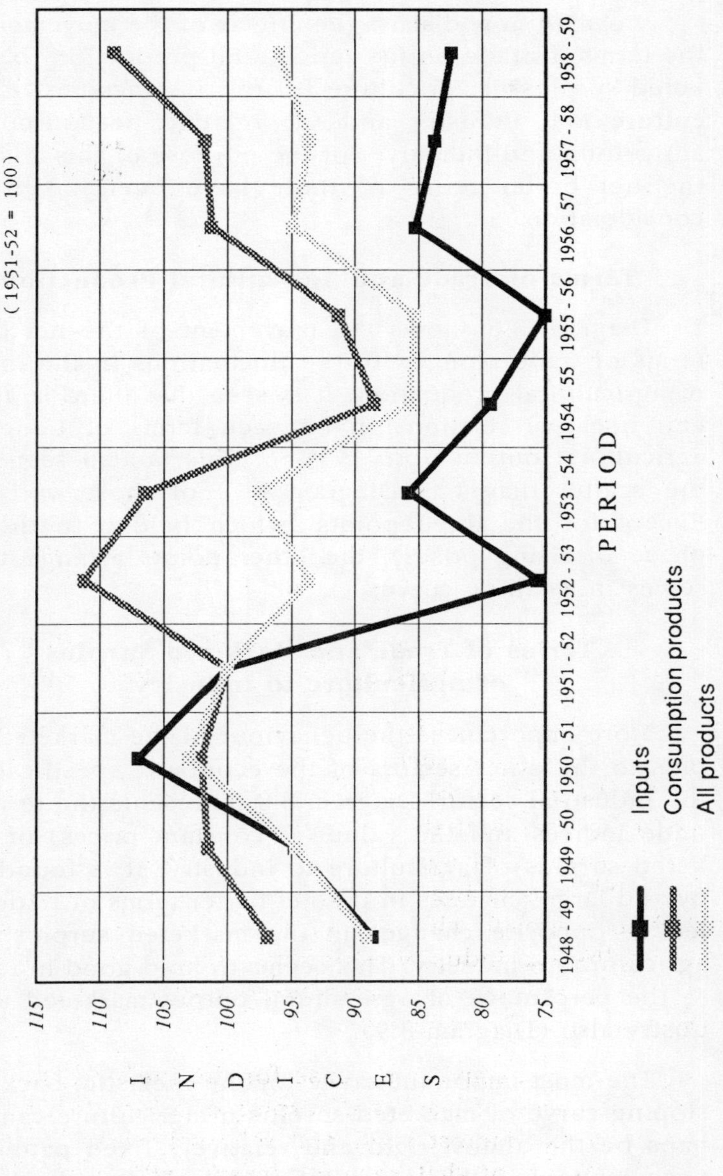

terms of trade in final outputs have been more favourable to agriculture than those in inputs, with reference to 1951-52.

We shall now discuss the effects of the movements of the terms of trade on (a) agricultural production (b) marketed surplus of agriculture (c) relative incomes of agriculture and industry and (d) relative net outputs of agriculture and industry. For the purpose of this analysis, the net barter terms of trade have been taken into consideration.

Terms of Trade and Agricultural Production

Diagram 8.6 shows the movement of the net barter terms of trade along with the fluctuations in the indices of agricultural production. It is seen that there is a general negative relationship between terms of trade and agricultural output upto 1955-56. This is also seen from the scatter diagram (Diagram 8.7) of these variables. Except for the three points (which belong to the last phase of rising prises), the other points arrange themselves in a falling curve.

Terms of Trade and Marketed Surplus of Agriculture to Industry

More important is the behaviour of the marketed surplus to the other sectors of the economy, specifically to the industrial sector. Diagram 8.8 represents the terms of trade indices and the value (at constant prices) of marketed surplus of agriculture to industry. It is found that by and large, changes in the net barter terms of trade had led to opposite changes in the marketed surplus from agriculture to industry. This seems to hold good in regard to the percentage of agricultural output marketed to industry also (Diagram 8.9).

The most important cause for the inelastic, backward sloping curve of marketed surplus of agriculture can perhaps be the almost rigid and relatively fixed pattern of consumption of that sector. Already, we found that the

DIAGRAM - 8.6

Indices of Terms of Trade and of Gross Output of Agriculture

(1951-52 = 100)

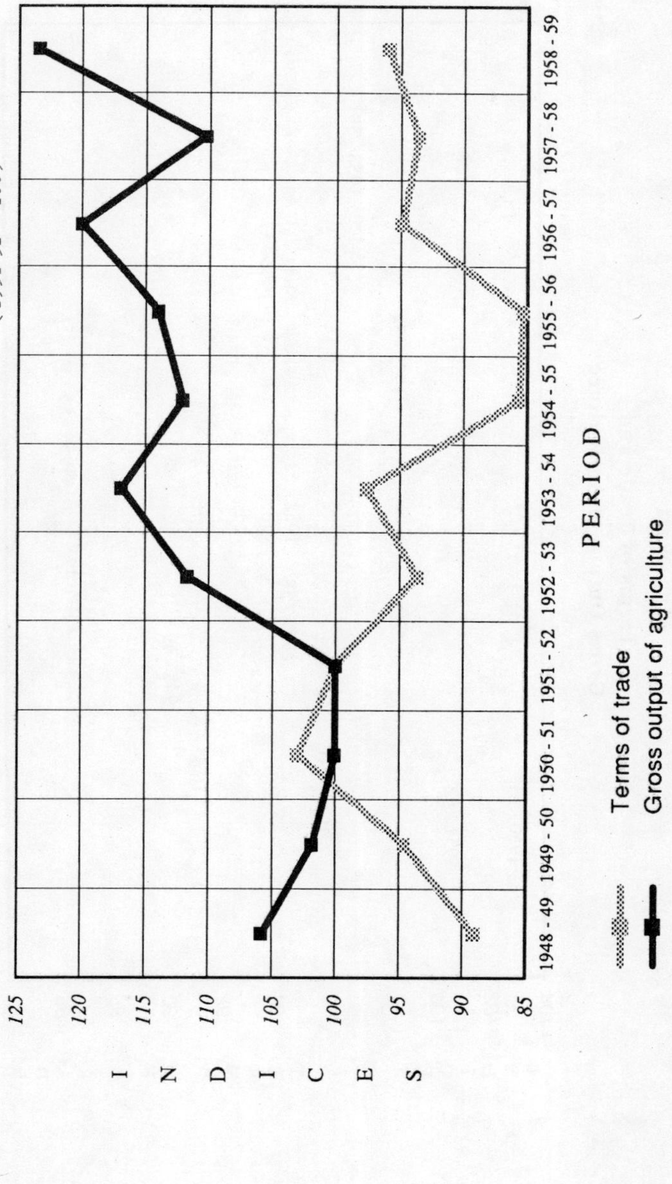

DIAGRAM - 8.7

Terms of Trade and Gross Output of Agriculture

(Scatter)

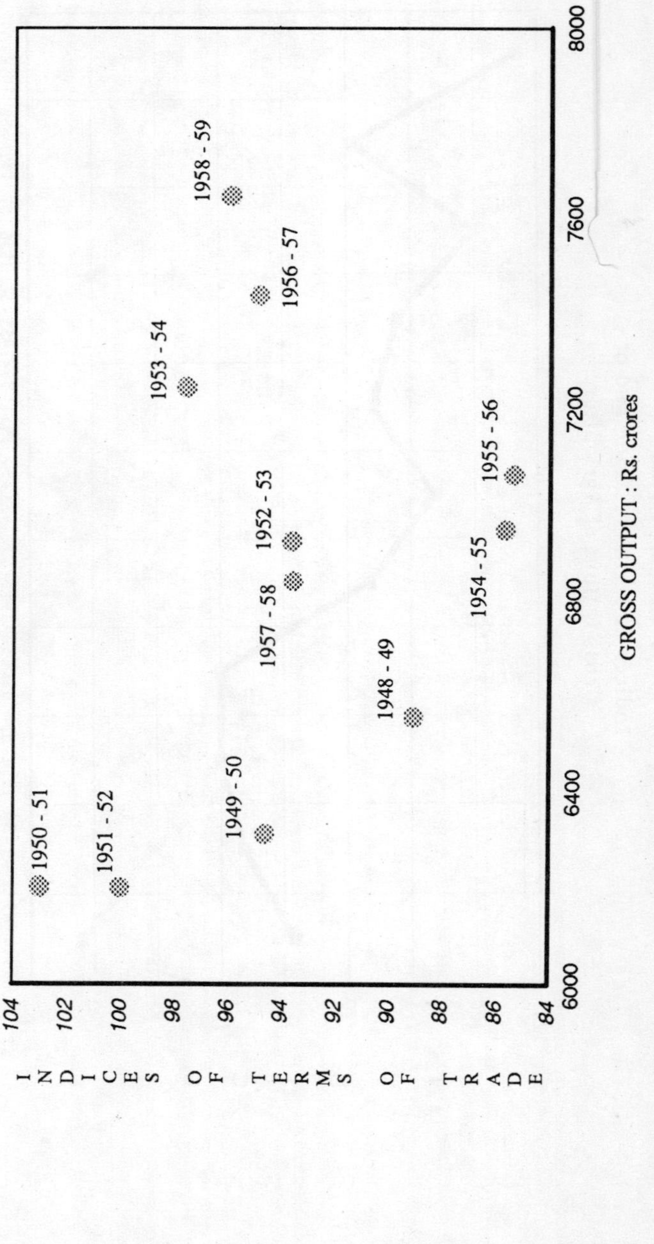

DIAGRAM - 8.8

Indices of Terms of Trade and of Marketed Surplus of Agriculture to Industry

(1951-52 = 100)

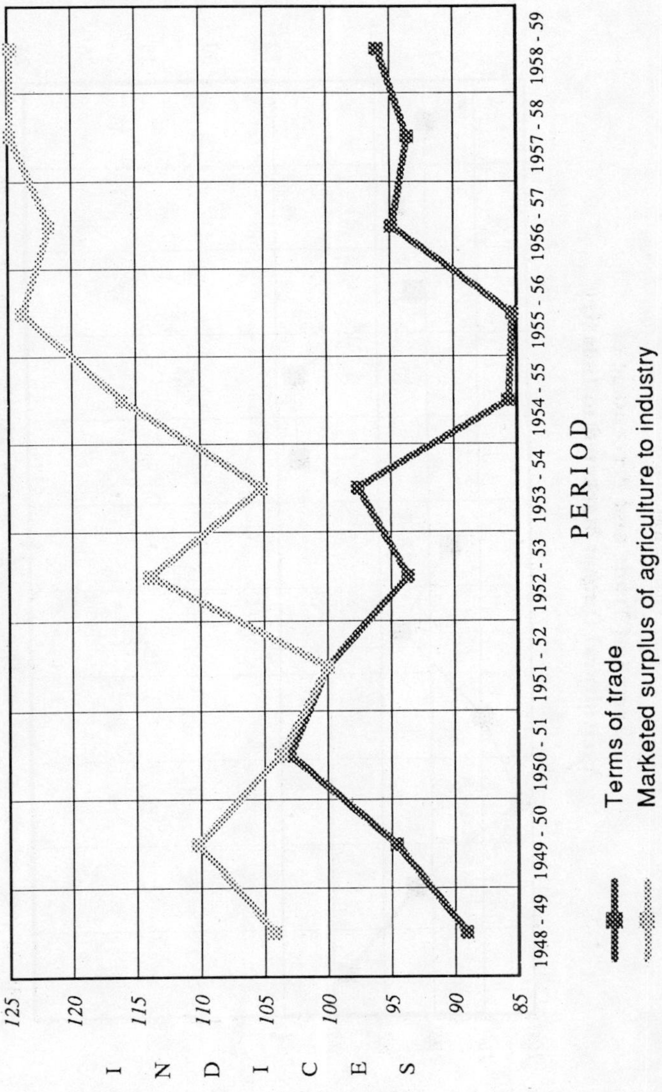

DIAGRAM - 8.9

Terms of Trade and Percentage of Agricultural Output Marketed to Industry

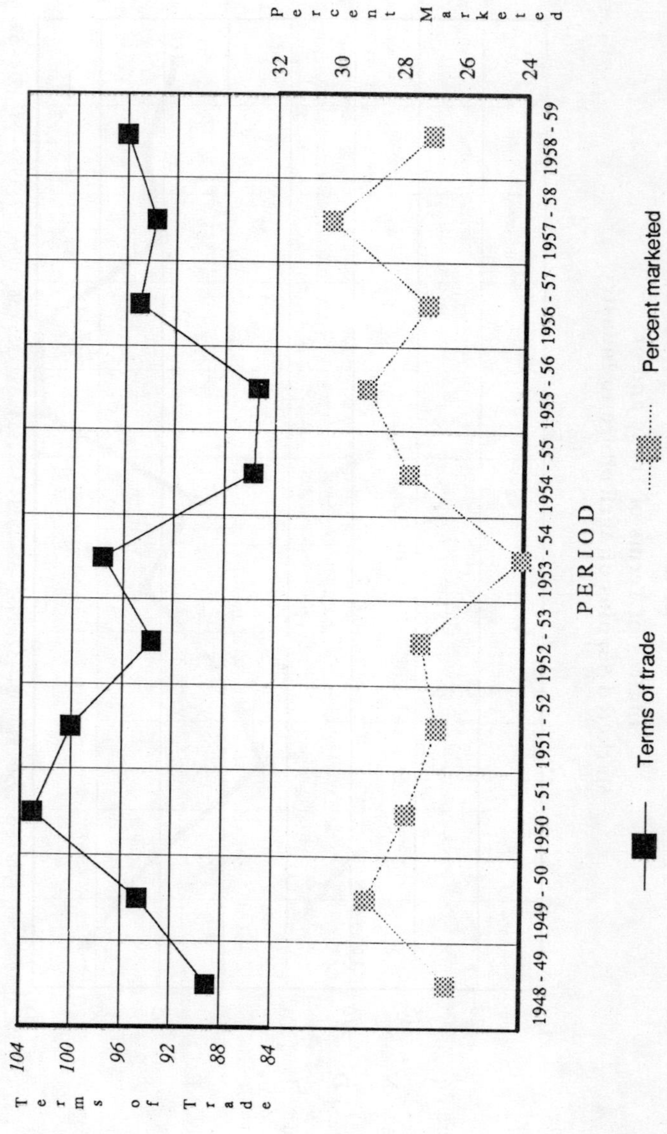

demand of the agricultural sector for industrial products for final use had decreased during this decade. This is accentuated by the prevalence of a high order of self-consumption, the existence of subsistence farming and the low degree of monetisation in the agricultural sector. The final result of all these is reflected in the fixed nature of the cash requirements of the average agriculturist. His object is, therefore, to obtain command of this fixed cash only. It is natural that when agricultural prices rise faster than industrial prices, he can market a smaller proportion of his produce, because "with a smaller volume of sales, the acquires the same command over cash as before and can buy the same basket of non-agricultural goods as before."[12] A redeeming feature, however is the gradually rising trend of marketed surplus of agriculture to industry, in this period.

Terms of Trade and Distribution of Net Incomes and Net Outputs

Diagram 8.10 which shows the movements of the net barter terms of trade and relative money incomes of the two sectors brings out that whenever agriculture's terms of trade were improving, the distribution of money incomes was also improving in favour of the agricultural sector. However, for almost the entire decade the movements of relative money incomes have been unfavourable to the agricultural sector. In contrast, the relative real products have generally (for the first 6 years of the period) run counter to the movement of the net barter terms of trade (Diagram 8.11). The fact that despite these contrary movements of terms of trade and relative real products, fluctuations of relative money incomes have been similar to those of terms of trade, brings to light the following. During inflation and improving terms of trade of agriculture, though the relative real outputs have a tendency to move against agriculture, yet this deterioration has not been of a degree which offsets the improvement in the terms of trade; so that in effect, the relative money incomes move in favour of agriculture. Similarly, when there is deflation and deteriorating terms of trade,

DIAGRAM - 8.10

Indices of Terms of Trade and of Relative Money Incomes

(Agriculture — Industry)

(1951-52 = 100)

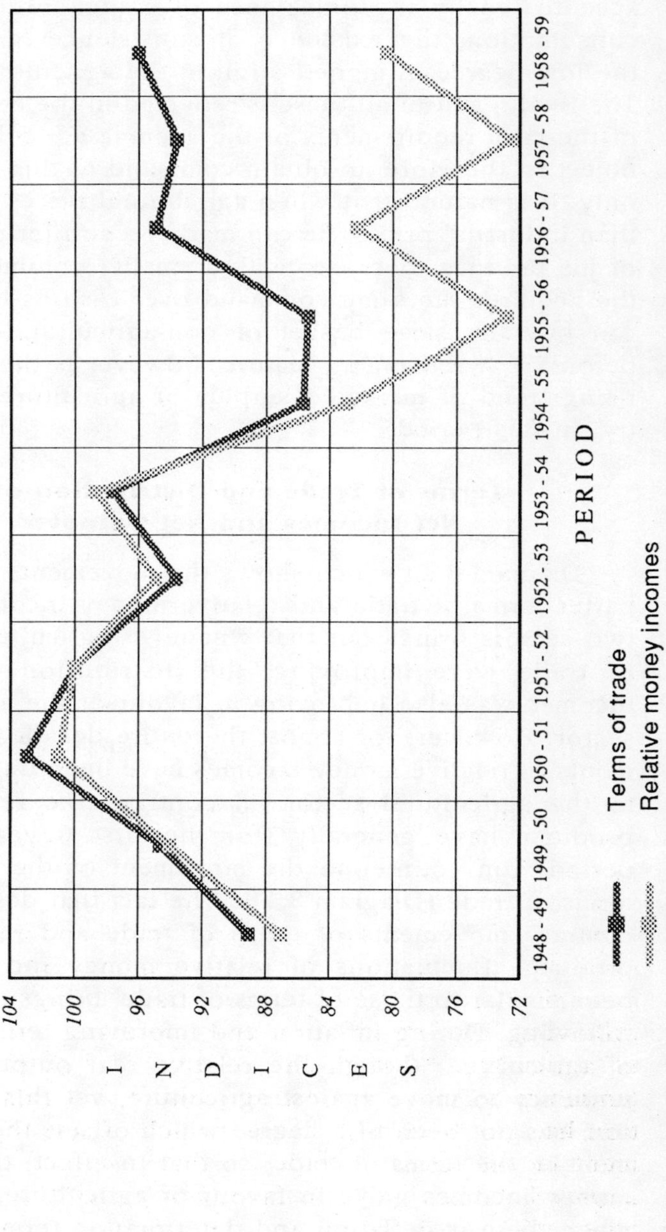

DIAGRAM - 8.11

Indices of Terms of Trade and of Relative Net Outputs

(Agriculture — Industry)

(1951-52 = 100)

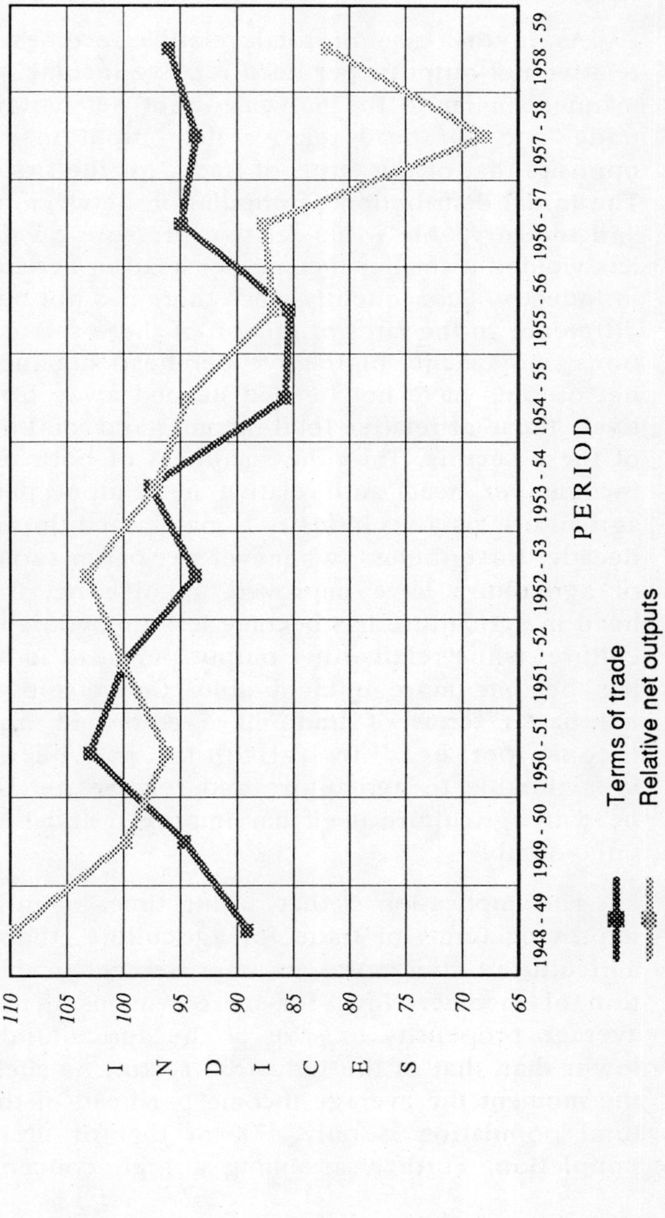

relative real outputs have moved in favour of agriculture; but again, this improvement has not been intense enough to neutralise the deterioration in terms of trade, so that the relative money incomes of agriculture deteriorate.

As in the case of total relative incomes and total relative net outputs, per head relative income moves in a manner similar to the movements of net barter terms of trade; and per head relative net output in a direction opposite that of the terms of trade, for the first six years. The initial distribution of population between agriculture and industry, due to its relative pressure on the former, has yielded a smaller income per head in agriculture than in industry. Subsequently since there has not been a wide difference in the rates of growth of these sectoral populations, movements of relative per head net incomes and net outputs have not been disturbed away from respectively those of relative total incomes and total net outputs of these sectors. Thus the smallness of both relative net income per head and relative net output per head in agriculture vis-a-vis industry is maintained throughout the decade. Nevertheless, whenever net barter terms of trade of agriculture have improved, relative net income per head in agriculture has become less unfavourable to agriculture, while relative net output per head in agriculture has become more unfavourable. Conversely, whenever net barter terms of trade have worsened, relative net income per head in agriculture has become more unfavourable to agriculture and relative net output per head in agriculture itself has improved and become less unfavourable.

The implication is that during times of inflation and improving terms of trade for agriculture, there is, from agriculture's view point, an improvement in the distribution of income. Now, for more reasons than one, the average propensity to save of the agricultural sector is lower than that of the industrial sector. As such, even at the moment the average income per head of the agricultural population is only 47% of that of the industrial population. Further, assuming a high concentration of income among the rentier classes in the agricultural sector, and that the benefits of improving terms of trade are realised largely by large landowners and rentiers, one is bound to be sceptical regarding the 'reinvestment' possibilities of the surplus thus generated. For as Lewis points out, "Eighteenth century British economists took it for granted that the landlord class is given to prodigal consumption rather than to productive investment and this is certainly true of landlords in underdeveloped countries. Hence, given two countries of equal incomes, in which distribution is more unequal in one than in the other, savings may be greater where distribution is more equal, if profits are higher relatively to rents. It is the inequality which goes with profits that favours capital formation, and not the inequality which goes with rents."[13] Again, institutional arrangements for the mobilisation of savings are better both in coverage and effectiveness in the non-agricultural) sector rather than in agriculture. Improving terms of trade for agriculture means higher relative prices of food as also of raw materials for the industrial sector, and would put up costs of living and costs of production for the industrial sector and lead to a 'profit squeeze' and a 'pruning of production plans'. As a result of inflation of food and raw material prices, "the sector which is the main saver (the industrial sector) is obliged to save less while the sector which habitually cannot save very much (the agricultural sector) gets more income and does not save very much."[14] It is probably due to such consequences of rising prices and improving terms of trade for agriculture that the third and fourth years of the Second Plan had a hard time in finding the necessary domestic savings for the Plan.

On the other hand when there are deteriorating terms for agriculture, there is generally an improvement in the relative product of agriculture vis-a-vis industry, which improvement, however, is at a slower pace than the deterioration in the terms of trade. In other words, the relative prices of agriculture (in relation to those of industry) have fallen at a faster rate than the rate at which relative products of agriculture have improved. This is a favourable atmosphere for self-sustained growth. For in this circumstance, not only relative agricultural product is increasing, but it is being made available at a lesser relative price so that the benefits of increased agricultural production are passed on the the industrial sector to be fruitfully ploughed back into the stream of development. Improved agricultural terms of trade are thus of the nature of a constraint or an obstacle to the development of the industrial sector; but all the same, improved agricultural terms of trade seem to be a necessary accompaniment of agricultural growth which in turn is essential condition for industrial and general growth. In other words, the somewhat restraining direct effects on industry of improved agricultural terms of trade are more than offset ultimately by the indirect effects which emerge from agricultural growth which, in turn, is complimentary to industrial development.

It is on the basis of this, that arguments are usually extended for the mobilisation of the surpluses -- physical as well as monetary -- in the agricultural sector, through higher taxation of this sector and a deliberate worsening of the terms of trade against this sector, not to speak of the positive proposals for pushing up agricultural production.

In this chapter, it has been possible for us to examine the relative movements of prices of agriculture and industry as also the fluctuations in terms of trade between these sectors and derive some inferences regarding the impact of these fluctuations on certain variables which seem important from the standpoint of economic development.

NOTES & REFERENCES

1. Brown, A.J.: An Introduction to the World Economy, p. 78.
2. Rostow, W.W.: Process of Economic Growth, Ch. 8, p. 169.
3. Robertson, D.H. "Utility and all that", p.175.
4. Ricardo D, Notes on Malthus p. 76.

5. Robertson, D.H. Utility and all that, p. 175.

6. Haberler, G. Survey of International Trade Theory -- The Terms of Trade -- p. 26.

7. Ibid, p. 27.

8. By 'final outputs' we mean the products used for final consumption.

9. Haberler, G. Prosperity and Depression, p. 86.

10. Kirk, John H. Agriculture and the Trade Cycle, p. 3.

11. The volume of exports referred to here is the marketed surplus of agriculture to industry alone. The value of marketed surplus of agriculture to industry at constant (51-52) prices has already been calculated in an earlier chapter (vide Table 1 Ch. 5)

12. Khusro, A.M.: "General and Sectoral Price Stability", Working Paper, Institute of Economic Growth, Delhi.

13. Lewis, W. Arthur: "Economic Development With Unlimited Supplies of Labour", The Manchester School, May 1954, Reprinted in "Economics of under development", Singh & Agarwala, pp. 419-20.

14. Khusro, A.M., op cit.

9

A Summary of Behaviour Pattern Among the Crucial Variables

IN the beginning of this work, we had developed sets of hypotheses amounting to a theoretical framework of intersectoral relations separately for a developing and a developed economy. Thereafter, the magnitude and behaviour of some important variables pertaining to agriculture-industry relationships during 1948-49 – 1958-59 were studied. This final chapter aims at giving a resume of the framework of intersectoral relations and highlighting the main results.

In an underdeveloped economy which has launched a conscious programme of development, investments are undertaken in agriculture and industry. These lead to a primary increase in the money incomes in these sectors. But in the initial stages, a very high proportion of increment to incomes may be spent on food and other consumption products. Further, the rising demand for industrial products would generate an increased derived demand for agricultural raw materials used in industry. Hence the demand for all agricultural products would rise faster than that for industrial products. As against this, supplies of both groups of products take time to adjust; due to structural rigidities and seasonal and random influences, agricultural supply takes a longer time. The inelasticity of agricultural supply curve is also partly due to the elastic or 'unlimited' supplies of labour in agriculture. Industrial production may not rise at a fast enough rate to clear off the backlogs of unemployment and underemployment. As a result, inflationary tendencies would exhibit themselves in agricultural prices rising faster than industrial prices and improving terms of trade for agriculture with industry. Rising agricultural prices neither dampen the demand (due to price inelasticity of demand) nor induce more supply or marketed surplus of agriculture (due to positive but inelastic or negative slope of this curve). Despite improving terms of trade, the relatively higher pressure of population in agriculture yields a per head income and net output in agriculture much lower than in industry. The per head relative net output in agriculture may also be expected to fall. But if the improvement in terms of trade is proportionately larger than this fall, the final outcome would be an improving per head relative income in agriculture.

We had estimated and analysed the variables which make up the aforesaid framework. We may now enumerate the basic variables which have been quantified on a time-series basis, for the period 1948-49 - 1958-59.

Table of Basic Variables Estimated on a Time-Series Basis

1948-49 — 1958-59

S.No.		Variables	Prices	
1.	a)	Net Investments in Agriculture	Current and	Constant
	b)	Net Investments in Non-Agriculture	"	"
2.	a)	Gross Output in Agriculture	"	"
	b)	Gross Output in Industry	"	"
3.	a)	Costs of Production in Agriculture	"	"
	b)	Costs of Production in Industry	"	"
4.	a)	Net Output in Agriculture	"	"
	b)	Net Output in Industry	"	"
5.	a)	Agriculture's demand for consumption goods produced by Agriculture	"	"
	b)	Agriculture's demand for consumption goods produced by Industry	"	"
6.	a)	Industry's demand for consumption goods produced by Industry	"	"
	b)	Industry's demand for consumption goods produced by Agriculture	"	"

(Contd...)

(...*Contd*....)

S.No.	Variables	Prices
7. a)	Rest of the economy's demand for consumption goods produced by Agriculture	Current and Constant
b)	Rest of the economy's demand for consumption goods produced by Industry	" "
8. a)	Agriculture's demand for intermediate products produced by Agriculture	" "
b)	Agriculture's demand for intermediate products produced by Industry	" "
9. a)	Industry's demand for intermediate products produced by Industry	" "
b)	Industry's demand for intermediate products produced by Agriculture	" "
10. a)	Agriculture's demand for all products produced by Agriculture (ie. self consumption in Agriculture)	" "
b)	Agriculture's demand for all products produced by Industry (i.e. marketed surplus of Industry to Agriculture)	" "
11. a)	Industry's demand for all products produced by Industry (i.e. self-consumption in Industry)	" "
b)	Industry's demand for all products produced by Agriculture (i.e. marketed surplus of Agriculture to Industry)	" "
12 a)	Income elasticity of demand of Agriculture for consumption goods produced by Agriculture	
b)	Income elasticity of demand of Agriculture for consumption goods produced by Industry	
c)	Income elasticity of demand of Industry for consumption goods produced by Industry	
d)	Income elasticity of demand of Industry for consumption goods produced by Agriculture.	
13. a)	Input (from Industry) - output (of agriculture) coefficients	
b)	Input (from Agriculture) - output (of Industry)	" "
14. a)	Demand of Industry for Labour	
b)	Supply of Labour from within the Industrial sector	" "
15.	Supply of capital from within the Agricultural sector Current Prices	
	Composite price indices of	
16. a)	i. all agricultural products	
	ii. all industrial products	
	iii. all products.	

(*Contd*...)

(...*Contd*....)

S.No.	Variables	Prices
	b) i. all agricultural products purchased by industry for intermediate use.	
	ii. all industrial products purchased by agriculture for intermediate use.	
	c) i. all agricultural products purchased by industry for final use	
	ii. all industrial products purchased by agriculture for final use.	
	d) i. all agricultural products purchased by industry for intermediate or final uses.	
	ii. all industrial products purchased by agriculture for intermediate or final uses.	
17.	Net barter terms of trade in products	
	a) for intermediate use	
	b) for final use	
	c) for all uses	
18.	Income terms of trade in products	
	a) for intermediate use	
	b) for final use	
	c) for all uses.	

RESULTS

Investments, Outputs, Incomes and Demand

During the decade under consideration, net investments have been rising in the agricultural and the non-agricultural sectors. Increasing investments have led to rising gross and net outputs in agriculture and in industry, both at current and at constant prices. However, these increases have been at differential rates. The relative performance of the industrial sector in terms of output generation has been far better than that of agriculture. Relative agricultural net incomes as well as net outputs exhibited a declining trend and there has been a deterioration in the share of income going to agriculture. The showing of per head income or output in agriculture vis-a-vis that in industry is not different.

While total incomes and outputs have generally been increasing in both industry and agriculture, the total expenditures of the economy on agricultural consumption goods and on industrial consumption goods have each depicted a falling trend. However, the total expenditure on agricultural consumption goods had fallen at a slower rate than that on industrial consumption goods so that the expenditure of the economy on agricultural finished goods in relation to industrial finished goods had in fact increased. This decreasing trend in the economy's expenditure on final products of agriculture or of industry would be modified had our estimates taken into consideration the demand for imports too, which have been increasing. It is also possible that this declining tendency has been the result of generally rising price levels in the economy. The increasing trend of national income and this decreasing trend of consumption of agricultural and industrial products point to the fact that the demand of the economy for the products of the rest of the economy has been increasing. Speaking of balance of occupations in a developing economy. Brown observes that "the occupations which absorb marked higher proportions of the working force as income increases are, naturally those for whose products demand increases sharply with income, provided the efficiency of labour in them is not too markedly superior in the more advanced economies and provided, too, that if their products are dear in relation to other things in richer countries, this does not choke demand off too much. Generally, these conditions seem to be fulfilled by the group of occupations connected with wholesale and retail distribution; and also various professional services."[1] As against this, the economy's demand for intermediate products, whether from the agricultural sector or from the industrial sector has been rising. We now proceed to observe the behaviour of intersectoral demand for products for intermediate use, final use and all uses.

Intersectoral Demand

Industrial demand for all agricultural products has been a slowly rising curve. Of this, the industrial demand for agricultural products for final use declined while that for intermediate products from the agricultural sector increased at a fairly rapid rate. The percentage spent by this sector on all agricultural products whether for final or for intermediate use, to its total expenditure on all products, irrespective of their origin or of their use, declined. Since gross industrial output had increased at a faster rate than its demand for intermediate products produced by agriculture, the input (from agriculture) -- output (of industry) ratio decreased. This probably shows a more intensive and efficient use of agricultural inputs in industry.

Agriculture's demand for all products produced by industry, had shown a tendency to decline. Agricultural demand for industrial products for final use also fell as against a negligible rise in that for industrial products for intermediate use. The percentage of agriculture's expenses on all industrial products whether for final or for intermediate use to its total expenses on all products declined. The input (from industry) -- output (of agriculture) coefficient has registered a fall due to the faster rate of growth of agricultural gross output.

This analysis of intersectoral product movements leads to the conclusion that while the intersectoral demand for inputs had generally risen, that for products for final use, however, declined. This latter phenomenon of falling consumer expenditures when incomes where rising was considered to be due to the 'price effect'. To isolate the 'income effect', the income (or expenditure) elasticities of demand of each of the sectors for agricultural consumption goods and industrial consumption goods were calculated on the basis of cross-section data. The main inference that emerged was that, generally, both these sectors had a higher income elasticity of demand for industrial goods than for agricultural goods, thus showing their high relative marginal intensity of demand for the former vis-a-vis the latter.

Supplies and Marketed Surpluses of Agricultural and Industrial Products

Agricultural supply although rising has been fluctuating quite a bit, thus certifying to the characteristic instability of agricultural output. But more important than the total supply is the "effective" supply or the "marketed surplus" of agriculture to other sectors of the economy, and particularly to industry. The absolute amount of marketed surplus as also the percentage of total supply marketed to industry alone has increased, only slightly. However, while the absolute amount of marketed surplus by agriculture to all other sectors had somewhat increased, the percentage of agricultural output marketed to these sectors declined.

Trends apart, the percentage of total agricultural supply marketed to all other sectors of the economy has been ranging between 37 to 47%, the corresponding range being 24 to 30% in respect of industry. This gives an average estimate of nearly 57% of agricultural produce being retained for self consumption. This indicates the subsistence nature of agriculture, and may be deemed to be the result of the organisational nature of an underdeveloped economy. In an industrialised economy where the community consists of a small number of employers and a large number of employees, production for market is the rule. But in an underdeveloped economy, where household enterprises dominate and where there is no strict distinction between farm accounts and family accounts, production is carried on not for exchange but for self-consumption. Such a state of affairs is not conducive to economic growth, in so far as the mechanics of development consists in generating surpluses and reinvesting these surpluses for further advancement.

Industrial production has recorded a fairly good rate of growth. But more important is the surplus marketed to agriculture, for that is likely to indicate the extent of participation of the agricultural sector in economic growth. It is found that the absolute amounts marketed to agriculture by industry have been declining while the percentage of this to total industrial output had also declined even faster. This is not very encouraging and points to the lack of a diversified pattern of consumer expenditure in the agricultural sector.

Terms of Trade Between Agriculture and Industry

Our analysis has revealed that with reference to the base year 1951-52, industrial products bought by agriculture for intermediate use were costlier than agricultural products purchased by industry for intermediate use and also that the basket of industrial products bought by agriculture for all uses has been costlier than that of agricultural products bought by industry for all uses.

Taking the decade as a whole, the general trend of all prices agricultural as well as industrial, has been a rising one. Our investigation into the relative movements of prices of agricultural products and industrial products, whether for intermediate or for final uses, was carried out during the three phases when rise and fall in prices were alternating. When general prices were rising, agricultural prices rose more than industrial prices; and conversely when general prices fell, agricultural prices fell more sharply than industrial prices. When there was inflation, agriculture generally enjoyed improving terms of trade while during deflation, its terms of trade worsened relative to industry. We have earlier made a clear distinction between improvement and deterioration of terms of trade and favourableness and unfavourableness of terms of trade. The former has to do with relative rates of change of prices, while the latter is a matter of relative levels of prices. Taking the period as a whole, agriculture continued to have unfavourable terms of trade with industry, though they were less unfavourable during inflation and more unfavourable during deflation.

It was noted that net barter terms of trade and agricultural gross output were generally negatively related. Further, it was found that by and large, when the net barter terms of trade improved, the amount of agricultural products marketed to industry fell and the converse was true too in times of deterioration. Also, net barter terms of trade and income terms of trade have been behaving similarly; and this would seem to be an indication of the inelasticity of the amount marketed by agriculture to industry, in relation to the movements of terms of trade. It appears that the marketed surplus curve of agriculture is inelastic and negative sloping. The negative relationship was true of the percentage of agricultural output marketed to industry as also to all the sectors of the economy. Net barter terms of trade and relative incomes in agriculture were both behaving similarly; at least for the first 6 years of our study, the relative net outputs in agriculture showed movements opposite to those in the terms of trade. Whenever terms of trade improved, there was an improvement in the distribution of income in favour of the agricultural sector, thereby creating a tendency for locking up the surpluses generated due to development in a sector which lacks an inherent "propensity to invest".

While these were the results regarding product flows between the sectors and terms of trade, our enquiry into the problem of factor flows suggested that for almost the entire period of our study, there might have been no net labour flows from agriculture to industry. It was found that the unutilised "backlog" of employable labour force in the industrial sector has been diminishing at a fairly rapid rate so that in the last year of the period of our study, the "backlog" was completely absorbed. The result however pertains only to the industrial sector and has nothing to do with a near full-employment position in the non-agricultural sector (including the industrial sector) as a whole as our study does not take into account the demand for and supply of labour in the rest of the economy. The situation would then appear to be that while unemployment has been existing and perhaps growing in the rest of the economy, the industrial sector itself has been close to the point of drawing labour from agriculture. The prevalence of under-employment within the non-agricultural sector as a whole would seem to make it difficult for any net transfer of labour from agricultural sector to nonagricultural sector. In actual fact, however, agricultural working population, unaware of the limited opportunities in nonagriculture, keeps on shifting to nonagriculture, causing in part the phenomenon of urbanisation (though at a reduced rate in the 1950's compared to the 1940's.) Some of those who shift, succeed in getting jobs, and probably displacing some already employed in non-agriculture; others do not get jobs and return to the agricultural sector and yet others get partly employed and perhaps create partial unemployment among those who otherwise would be more fully absorbed in work. Again for the whole period of our study, there were capital inflows into agriculture from non-agriculture though they were less in some years and more in others. Owing to many reasons, e.g. low output per head, the savings propensity of the agricultural sector is much too small so that agricultural investment has to be financed substantially from the non-agricultural or industrial sectors. The co-operative banking mechanism is one of the main instruments of transfer of urban-industrial funds to the agricultural sector.

Thus, during these ten years, the relative share of agriculture (vis-a-vis industry) in (i) total investments undertaken in the economy, (ii) total incomes, (iii) total net outputs as also (iv) total of expenditures of the economy on agricultural and industrial products, has declined. Further, the relatively higher pressure of population dependent on agriculture had depressed the per head income and the per head net output in agriculture far below the respective magnitudes in industry. Again the rates of growth of population in agriculture and industry being not very different from each other, the faster rate of growth of industrial net output vis-a-vis agricultural net output, has reflected itself in a deteriorating tendency in the ratio of per head income and net output of agriculture to that of industry. However, industrial supply has not grown at a fast enough rate to induce labour outflows from agriculture while at the same time, despite large capital inflows into agriculture, agricultural supply neither has grown as fast as industrial supply nor has it become adequate to meet the demand.

The characteristic disinclination of agriculture to participate in development activity was revealed in the negative relationship of (i) prices and agricultural supply (ii) prices and marketed surplus of agriculture to industry (iii) prices and percentage of agricultural supply marketed to industry and (iv) prices and relative net outputs in agriculture vis-a-vis industry. In addition to these was also observed a high order of self-consumption in agriculture, coupled with a falling import curve overtime of industrial products into agriculture, both of which testify to the somewhat rigid pattern of consumer demand in agriculture. The only redeeming phenomenon in this rather gloomy side of agricultural supply seems to be that the export curve overtime of agricultural products to industry and also to the rest of the economy has registered a gradual (though imperceptible) rise.

We have particularly resisted in this work the temptation to policy suggestions and recommendations with a view to bringing about a structural reorganisation of the Indian economy, in particular the agricultural economy, which still seems to be fraught with supply rigidities, inelasticities and market imperfections. The reason for this restraint obviously is that for the correction of each rigidity or imperfection, a whole host of alternative policy prescriptions are conceivable and each of these has different implications from the economic as well as the social standpoints. In that case, unless one has decided to sort out all these implications, it is best to refrain from recommendation and prescription.

It is possible to maintain that a ten-year period is too short a span of time for any significant trends to be detected in the movements of the relevant variables of the study and in their interrelationships. Nevertheless, the endeavour in this work has been to develop some logical hypotheses about the possible inter-sectoral behaviour of a few variables crucial from the standpoint of inter-sectoral relations and then proceed to discover the magnitudes of these variables and the direction of change in them absolutely as well as relative to each other, in the early phase of a country's development. To the extent that this work has managed to estimate, however imperfectly, some magnitudes which were hitherto unestimated, and studied the behaviour of some strategic and crucial variables in relation to time as also in relation to each other, it has cause for some satisfaction.

NOTES & REFERENCES

1. Brown, A.J. An Introduction to the World Economy, pp. 120-121.

Appendix

Problems in Official Estimates of Income

The source material[1] which is used for calculating the official estimates of net output from agriculture is out of date and not very adequate. A concrete instance can be given. Prior to 1953-54, official estimates were mostly based on conventional methods of crop estimation which suffered from various limitations such as subjective errors of over/under estimates of crop condition and yield. The CSO following the practice of the National Income Committee, had made use of some advance information on the results of random crop-cutting surveys conducted by the I.C.A.R. for some principal foodcrops regardless of the fact that some of these results had not been accepted by the Ministry of Agriculture, for their crop estimates. Although the coverage of such experiments went on increasing year after year in respect of crops as well as States, the production estimates were based partly on the results of crop-cutting surveys and partly on conventional methods, and therefore, could not provide a comparable series for national income estimation. From 1953-54 onwards, however, official estimates were used exclusively, regardless of the fact that these were not wholly based on crop-cutting experiments. Thus outturn estimates used in national income estimates[2] suffered from lack of year to year comparability. Again, data used for cost items of agricultural sector is "extremely scanty,"[3]; it relates to local enquiries for widely different purposes and is of extreme doubtful generality even for these local areas, being based on a few case studies rather than on any scientific survey.

Official estimates of net output of animal husbandry sector are mainly based on Marketing Reports on Livestock products. Here again, the criticism of the antiqueness of data crops up. These estimates are based on ad hoc surveys on milk yield rates etc. conducted by the Directorate of Marketing and Inspection in 1941. With regard to the forestry sector, no allowance is made for the unrecorded production of timber and firewood in official estimates of net output. The value of this unrecorded production forms nearly 33% of the value of the corresponding recorded production during 1955-56 -- 1959-60.[4] Further, the value of the minor products was adopted in the official estimates without any modification from the Indian Forest Statistics. But, as in the case major products, these are also very likely to suffer from under-reporting or non-reporting or both. For official series, use was made of the Census of Manufacturing Industries' input prices of timber and fuelwood. But these prices contain trade and transport margins and are not representative of a large bulk of timber. The manufacturing industries viz., match, plywood, paper, tea-chest etc., use only soft wood which forms a small percentage of total timber. The softwood prices are low compared to hard wood (timber and round wood) prices. Similarly, the source material used in the official estimates of net output of fishery sector does not appear to be either fully reliable or sufficiently detailed. In the case of mining sector, the deduction of 5% (of value of coal output) on account of mining expense and approximately another 5% on account of coal consumed in collieries, hitherto being made for purposes of official estimates, has been shown[5] to be a considerable underestimate of the cost involved.

The procedure of estimation of official series of net output of small enterprises involves some questionable assumptions. This sector is particularly characterised by a dearth of data. The income method, which alone can be used for this sector, requires the estimation of work force in the first instance. For this purpose, exclusive dependence has been placed in official estimates on the 1941-51 census data. Also the derivation of gainful employment in small enterprises as a residual by subtracting the factory counterpart from the total employment in enterprises results in some negative correlation between employment in small enterprises and that in factory establishments which in all probability is not true. Further, as industry-wise employment in factories according to the SSMI was not available since 1953, estimates for later years have been obtained by projecting the 1953 SSMI employment data for each of the 63 industries with the help of employment relatives worked out from the series of employment in factories, brought out by the Labour Bureau. This method may not be considered satisfactory because of the lack of strict comparability between the SSMI and the Labour Bureau classification and also owing to the difference in their scope and coverage. In the case of construction sector also, reliance is placed on the 1941-51 censuses for projecting the work force engaged in construction activity.

There is, therefore, considerable scope for improvement of the official estimates of national income.

Methods of Projection

The salient aspects of the methods of projection we have adopted in estimating the comparable (comparable with Revised Estimates) magnitudes of gross output, costs of inputs and net output of agriculture proper, animal husbandry, forestry, fishery, mining and quarrying, small enterprises and construction for the years 1948-49 to 1954-55 have been given below.

Agriculture

Estimation of Gross Value of Output

For the crops rice, wheat, jowar, bajra, barley, maize, ragi, gram, arhar, linseed, sesamum, groundnut, rape and mustard, sugarcane, jute, coffee, tobacco, dry chillies, black pepper, potatoes, and other pulses, their physical production in 1955-56 (as in the "Proposals") has been projected back upto 1948-49, with the index number of agricultural production[6] for the respective crops. However, for cotton, trade estimates of cotton lint have been used. Tea leaf production has been estimated by relating the base 1955 figure to output of processed tea while for arecanut and cashewnut, the base figure has been adjusted for changes in acreage[7] in the earlier years and also for improved reporting. Adjustment for improved reporting has been done also in the case of banana, sweet potatoes and coconuts. Estimates of mango production for earlier years has been prepared on the basis of 'Report on Marketing of Mangoes in India, 1958.'[8]

In the "Proposals", production of various crops has been evaluated at average wholesale prices over the marketing period. In the case of all the above crops, the physical production thus estimated for earlier years has been evaluated at prices derived by projecting backwards the prices implicit in the value and production figures for 1955-56 with the Economic Adviser's Revised Index Numbers of Wholesale Prices (EA's index) (1952 = 100) of the relevant crops. Information from the `Final Report' on implicit prices for years prior to the period of coverage of the EA's revised index numbers, and in some cases, the old series of EA's index numbers with 1939=100 as base have been used. For wheat, bajra, gram, sugarcane, rapeseed, linseed, groundnut, jute, tobacco and potatoes, the relevant indices were averaged over their harvest periods[9] for purposes of projection. For other crops, the annual index numbers have been used as such.

As for bye-products, (i) the value of straw in 1955-56 has been adjusted simultaneously for changes in acreage under cereals and pulses and in the CMI input prices and also for differences in area reporting (ii) the base year value of fodder crop has been moved backwards with the area under these crops (corrected for differences in reporting) and EA's index of prices of cereals (iii) the benchmark value of rice husk was projected backwards with production of rice and of bran with the value of rice output (iv) Cotton seed production was extended in the ratio of official to trade estimates of cotton (v) value of grass for earlier years was derived by adjusting the base year value for changes in CMI input prices of grass (vi) value of sugarcane tufts for earlier years has been moved with area under sugarcane corrected for differences in reporting (vii) procedure in 'Proposals for each of the other bye products' has been followed in detail (viii) for many unspecified products other than bye-products, the per acre values in base year were related to the movement in per acre values of other specified crops (ix) value added by organised rice milling industry has been taken from the Final Report for 1948-49 to 1950-51 after making a nominal mark up on account of factories employing 10-19 workers and using power, and for 1951-52 to 1953-54, SSMI estimates have been used; for 1954, CMI results after adjustment to make them comparable with SSMI coverage of workers, were used.

Cost of Production of Agriculture

(i) For seed, the same proportions as in 'Proposals' have been taken (ii) market charges were derived in accordance with changes in value of agricultural output in these years (iii) benchmark value of depreciation and organic manure in 1955-56 was moved backwards with changes in gross area sown adjusted for differences in acreage reporting (iv) estimates of current repairs and maintenance for earlier years were got by adjusting the base figure for changes in earnings of rural skilled workers and in the total gross area sown (corrected for differences in reporting) (v) data on irrigation charges have been obtained from CSO (vi) data on chemical fertilisers have been taken from "Fertiliser Statistics", 'Final Report' and the CSO. As in the 'Proposals', an adjustment has been made of 2% of net output of agriculture for non-reporting areas.[10] The costs we had estimated consistent with the original net output can no longer be consistent with the adjusted net output. Hence, the value of the cost items (except for fertilisers and irrigation charges which being based on current data would be unaffected by this adjustment to net output) have been inflated to the same extent of 2%.

Animal Husbandry

For deriving comparable figures for earlier years, the 1945, 1951 and 1956 All India Livestock Censuses have been used to interpolate linearly the number of each of the different categories of livestock and poultry. Production of each of milk and its products has been moved backwards with the estimated number of total female breeding population of cows and buffaloes and the EA's index of prices applied to the implicit price of these products in base year. Beef, buffalo, sheep, goat and pork meats, hides and skins, poultry eggs, wool etc. have been estimated with the help of estimated number of respective animals and EA's price indices. Value of increment to stocks has been taken from CSO's recent publication on gross capital formation in India.

Costs of animal husbandry have been derived for earlier years using the same method as in 'Proposals' and relevant indicators. For distributing the costs between service and non-service animals, the total working population of cows and buffaloes and the entire population of horses, ponies, donkeys, mules and camels have been regarded as kept for services. Of these, the male and female working cattle and buffaloes in rural areas have been assumed to be kept for services on farms and rural carting. For this purpose, the rural-urban livestock ratio available only in the 1956 livestock census has been assumed to hold good for all the earlier years. The estimated number of service -- agricultural and others -- and non service animals have been converted to cattle equivalents using the equivalence scale given in the 'Proposals'. The cost of feed of non-service animals is attributed to the animal husbandry sector. Other costs (for materials and depreciation) have been allowed for on the same lines as in "Proposals."

Forestry

Besides using data on major products from the Indian Forest Statistics, unrecorded production and value of minor produce was estimated on similar lines as in 'Proposals'.

Fishery

For valuation of production estimates of fish (marine fish and inland fish) given in 'Proposals', the respective implicit prices in 1955-56 were moved backwards with EA's price indices for fish. Value added for salting curing has been estimated using the combined factors, of production and prices of fish. The value of subsistence fishing has been estimated on the basis of the value in 1955-56, production of inland fish and the average price of the marketable surplus of inland and marine fish taken together.

Mining and Quarrying

The gross output for years prior to 1955-56 have been derived by first estimating the gross and net output figures for these years as per conventional estimates, and applying thereafter to these estimates the average ratio of the revised gross output estimates to conventional estimates for 1955-56 to 1958-59.

Small Enterprises

The estimates of net output in each of seven groups of small enterprises were estimated by moving back the bench mark value with appropriate production and price indicators and for changes in work force. In this projection, use was made of (i) value added in cotton, jute and woollen textiles for the textiles group (ii) combined production relatives of raw hides and skins (estimated by us while calculating the output of animal husbandry sector), tanned hides (SSMI) and leather footwear in the factory sector for leather and leather products and (iii) estimated net availability of oilseeds for the small sector, net availability of tobacco and production of foodgrains for subgroups of fats and oils, pan, tobacco and bidi and food items for getting the estimates for food, drink and tobacco enterprises. For other industries, the combined index of production of the textiles and tailoring, leather products and food, drink and tobacco and agricultural production were used. Using the average ratio of gross output to value added estimates from the NSS Report on

Small Scale Industries (No. 43) 1955-56, estimates of gross output for these industries were obtained.

Construction

The value of net output of Construction was derived by adjusting the 1955-56 figure with the combined movement of the indices of rural skilled earnings and work force in 'Construction'

NOTES & REFERENCES

1. We shall not go in detail, into the various gaps in the statistical basis of the official series. The same has been dealt with in exhaustive details, in the "Proposals". We shall also not refer to the weaknesses of the official estimates for the factory establishments sector; for we are not using either the official estimates or the 'Revised Estimates' for this sector.
2. "Proposals", C.S.O. pp. 21-22.
3. Final Report of the National Income Committee (1954) p. 37.
4. "Proposals", C.S.O. p. 76.
5. Analysis of Balance Sheets of Joint Stock Companies, August and November 1959 – Reserve Bank of India Bulletin – Quoted in the "Proposals", pp. 93-94.
6. This index of agricultural production is being published by the Ministry of Food & Agriculture. It is a fixed base quantity index of the Laspeyre's type. It seeks to link up the production of each year with that of 1949-50 through pairs of comparable figures for each two successive years which are available under the Ministry's system of crop estimation. These indices of agricultural production as published from year to year in the monthly journal of "Agricultural Situation in India" indicate correctly the real trend in the production of any agricultural commodity. "In any study of the trends of agricultural production, the correct procedure would be to compare the figures given in a particular crop estimate for the current and the previous year and to use the index numbers for comparisons over any longer period." "Area and Production of Principal Crops in India – Prewar Average to 1960-61." Summary Tables, Ministry of Food & Agriculture, Government of India.
7. Acreage figures have been taken from the Indian Agricultural Statistics. Since, however, crop reporting in agricultural statistics has been improving, there is an element of slight non-comparability over time. We, have, therefore, inflated the acreage data in each case by the extent of increased reporting in 1955-56 as compared to that in the particular year under consideration.
8. Report on Marketing of Mangoes in India (1958), Directorate of Marketing and Inspection, Ministry of Food and Agriculture. For the years 1948-49, 1949-50 and 1950-51, since no figure is available, the outturn figure of 1950-51 has been repeated by us.
9. Indian Crop Calendar, Government of India, Directorate of Economics and Statistics, Ministry of Food and Agriculture.
10. This adjustment for principal crops which is to ensure complete coverage for each of the years is different from the adjustment that we have made to the area or production figures of non-principal crops (as published by the DES Ag) for differences in reporting as between different years.

Bibliography

Agarwala, A.N. and S.P. Singh, ed : *Economics of Underdevelopment*, Oxford University Press, 1958.

Bellerby, J.R. : *Agriculture and Industry - Relative Income*, London; Macmillan and Co. Ltd., 1956.

Bhattacharjee, J.P., ed : *Studies in Indian Agricultural Economics*, Bombay; Indian Society of Agricultural Economists, 1958.

Brown A.J.: *An Introduction to the World Economy*, London; George Allen & Unwin Ltd., 1960.

Clark, Colin : *The Conditions of Economic Progress*, London; Macmillan & Co. Ltd., 1951.

Desai, Padma : *A Short Term Planning Model for the Indian Economy* — Ph.D. Thesis — submitted to the Harvard University, 1959.

Cochrane, W : *Farm Prices, Myth and Reality*.

Dhar, P.N. : *Small Scale Industries in Delhi — A study in Investment, Output and Employment Aspects*, Asia Publishing House, 1953.

Dobb, Maurice: *Soviet Economic Development Since 1917*, London; Routledge and Kegan Paul Ltd., 1957.

Haberler, Gottfried Von : *Prosperity and Depression*, London; George Allen & Unwin Ltd., 1958.

Haberler, Gottfried Von : *Survey of International Trade Theory*, 1955.

John P.V. : *Some Aspects of the Structure of Indian Agricultural Economy — 1947-48 - 1957-59*, Ph.D. Thesis submitted to the University of Delhi, 1962.

Khusro, A.M. : *Economic Development with no Population Transfers — Study in Demand for and Supply of Labour in the Non-agricultural Sector of the Indian Economy*, Asia Publishing House, 1962.

Kindelberger, Charles, P : *Terms of Trade, A European Case Study*, New York; Wiley & Sons, 1956.

Kirk, John : *Agriculture and Trade Cycle.*

Kuznets, Simon : *Six Lectures on Economic Growth*, New York; The Free Press of Glancoe, 1959.

Leontief, Wassily W : *Structure of the American Economy 1919-1939*, Oxford University Press, 1951.

Mundle, Sudipto : *Surplus Flows and Growth Balance : The Intersectoral Flow of Real Resources in India, 1951-71*, New Delhi; Allied Publishers.

Mungekar, B.L. : *The Political Economy of Terms of Trade*, Himalaya Publishing House, Bombay, 1992.

National Council of Applied Economic Research, India, *Long Term Projections of Demand for and Supply of Selected Agricultural Commodities, 1960-61 to 1975-76*, 1962.

Ojala, E.M. : *Agriculture and Economic Progress*, Oxford University Press, 1952.

Raj Krishna : *Farm Supply Response in the Punjab (India - Pakistan) A Case Study of Cotton*, Ph.D. Thesis submitted to the University of Chicago.

Robertson, D.H. : *Utility and All That and Other Essays*, London; George Allen and Unwin Ltd., 1962.

Rostow, W.W. : *The Process of Economic Growth*, London; Clarendon Press, 1960.

Schultz, Theodore, W. : *Economic Organisation of Agriculture*; New Delhi, Mcgraw Hill, 1953.

Youngson, A.J. : *Possibilities of Economic Progress*, Cambridge University Press, 1959.

GOVERNMENT OF INDIA

Central Statistical Organisation :

- Census of Manufacturing Industries.
- Estimates of Gross Capital Formation in India for 1948-49 to 1960-61, 1961.
- National Accounts Statistics, Different Issues.
- Proposals for a Revised Series of National Income Estimates for 1955-56 to 1959-60, 1961.
- Brochure on Revised Series on National Product, 1961.
- National Accounts Statistics, Sources and Methods, April 1980.

- Input-Output Transactions Table: 1983-84, 1990.

Labour Bureau

- Indian Labour Year Book (Annual).

Ministry of Commerce & Industry (Now Ministry of Commerce), Department of Commercial Intelligence

- Annual Statement of Air and Sea-borne Trade of India.
- Annual Statement of the Foreign Trade of India.
- Monthly Statistics of Foreign Trade of India.
- Foreign Trade Statistics in India.
- Ministry of Industry.

Office of the Economic Adviser

- Index Number of Wholesale Prices — Old Series and Revised Series (Weekly).

Ministry of Food and Agriculture (Now Ministry of Agriculture), Directorate of Economics and Statistics

- Indian Forest Statistics.
- Indian Livestock Statistics.
- Agricultural Statistics in India at a glance, May 1992.

Ministry of Finance, Department of Economic Affairs

- First Report of the National Income Committee, 1951.
- Final Report of the National Income Committee, 1954.
- Report of the Taxation Enquiry Commission, 1953-54, vol. I.

National Sample Survey

- Sample Survey of pattern of Consumer Expenditure — Reports of the various rounds of survey.
- Sample Survey of Manufacturing Industries, Reports of the various rounds.
- Sample Survey of small scale Manufacturing Enterprises: Reports of the various rounds.
- Sample Survey of Employment and Unemployment - Various Rounds.

Ministry of Home Affairs, Office of the Registrar General

- Census of India Reports: 1951, 1961, 1971, 1981 and 1991.

Planning Commission

- Five Year Plan Documents (From First Plan onwards)
- Report of the Study group on Parameters on Consumption Sub-Model, March, 1991.

Reserve Bank of India

- Rural Credit Survey, 1951.
- Rural Credit Follow-up Survey, 1956.
- All India Debt and Investment Survey 1981-82.

Others

- Papers read at the Tenth International Conference of Agricultural Economists, Mysore, March 1958.

ARTICLES

Bansil, P.C. : "Problems of Marketable Surplus in Indian Agriculture", *Indian Journal of Economics*, January-March 1961 (Conference Number).

Bhatt, V.V. : "Estimates of savings in the Indian Economy", *Reserve Bank of India Bulletin*, March 1960.

Dantwala, M.L. : "Incentives and Disincentives in Indian Agriculture" *Indian Journal of Agricultural Economics*, vol. 22, No. 21.

Desai, Padma : "A Short Term Planning Model for the Indian Economy", *The Review of Economics & Statistics*, Vol. XLIII, May 1961.

Dorrance, G.S. : "The Income Terms of Trade" *Review of Economic Studies*, 1948-49.

Dharm Narain : "Impact of Price Movements on Areas Under Crops in India : Cotton — A Case Study", *Indian Economic Review*, August 1960.

Fox, Karl A. : "The Study of Interactions Between Agriculture and the non-farm Economy, Local, Regional and National" *Journal of Farm Economics*, Vol. XLIV, No. 1, February 1962.

Gulati, Ashok and Pradeep K. Sharma, "Prices, Procurement and Production: An analysis of Wheat and Rice" *Economic and Political Weekly*, March 31, 1990.

Jose, A.V. : "Agricultural Wages in India" *Economic and Political Weekly, Review of Agriculture*, June 25, 1988.

Jose, A.V. : "Paper on Agricultural Wages in India" for Government of India: National Rural Labour Commission.

Kahlon, A.S. and Tyagi D.S. : Intersectoral Terms of Trade" *Economic and Political Weekly, Review of Agriculture*, December 27, 1980.

Khusro, A.M. "General and Sectoral Price Instability", *Working Paper*, Institute cf Economic Growth, Delhi.

Thamarajakshi R. : Agriculture - Industry Relationships in India, 1948-49 - 1958-59, Doctoral Thesis submitted to University of Delhi, 1963.

————. "Intersectoral Terms of Trade and Marketed Surplus of Agricultural Produce, 1951-52 - 1965-66", *Economic and Political Weekly,* Vol. IX, No. 26, Review of Agriculture, June 28, 1969.

————. "Role of Price Incentives in Stimulating Agricultural Production in a Developing Economy" in Ensminger, Doughlas (Ed), Food Enough or Starvation for millions, Tata-Mcgraw Hill, 1977.

————. "Interrelation between Agriculture and Industry in India" 68th Conference Volume of Indian Economic Association, 1985.

————. "Intersectoral Terms of Trade Revisited" *Economic and Political Weekly,* March 31, 1990.

————. "Food Policy and Rural Poverty Alleviation in India" *Asia-Pacific Journal of Rural Development,* Dhaka Vol. I, July, 1991, No.1.

Tyagi, D.S. : "Domestic Terms of Trade and their effect on Supply and Demand of agricultural Sector" *Economic and Political Weekly,* March 18, 1987.

Vittal, Nalini : "Intesectoral Terms of Trade in India. A study of Concept and Method" *Economic and Political Weekly, Review of Agriculture,* December 1986.

————. "Intersectoral Terms of Trade in India : Reality and the Hype" *Economic and Political Weekly, Review of Agriculture,* September 24, 1988.

Index